Immortal Engines

IMMORTAL ENGINES

Life Extension and Immortality

in Science Fiction and Fantasy

Edited by George Slusser, Gary Westfahl,

and Eric S. Rabkin

The University of Georgia Press   Athens and London

© 1996 by the University of Georgia Press
Athens, Georgia 30602
All rights reserved
Designed by Louise OFarrell
Set in Sabon by Books International
Printed and bound by Braun-Brumfield, Inc.
The paper in this book meets the guidelines for
permanence and durability of the Committee on
Production Guidelines for Book Longevity of the
Council on Library Resources.

Printed in the United States of America

00   99   98   97   96   C   5   4   3   2   1
00   99   98   97   96   P   5   4   3   2   1

Library of Congress Cataloging in Publication Data

Immortal engines : life extension and immortality in science
fiction and fantasy / edited by George Slusser, Gary Westfahl,
and Eric S. Rabkin.
      p.   cm.
Essays originally presented at the 14th annual Eaton
Conference on Science Fiction and Fantasy, University of
California at Riverside, April 1992.
Includes bibliographical references and index.
ISBN 0-8203-1732-2 (alk. paper).
ISBN 0-8203-1733-0 (pbk.: alk. paper)
1. Science fiction—History and criticism—Congresses.
2. Fantastic fiction—History and criticism—Congresses.
3. Longevity in literature—Congresses.   4. Immortalism in
literature—Congresses.   I. Slusser, George Edgar.
II. Westfahl, Gary.   III. Rabkin, Eric S.   IV. Eaton
Conference on Science Fiction and Fantasy Literature
(14th : 1992 : University of California, Riverside)
PN3433.2.I56   1996
809.3'876—dc20   96-10462

British Library Cataloging in Publication Data available

Contents

Prefatory Remarks

Since the beginnings of history, human beings have often expressed a desire for immortality, or at least a longer span of life. It is not surprising, then, that these longings have repeatedly emerged in literature, from ancient myths to modern science fiction and fantasy. After a century of imposed "realist" limits, these genres have revived these desires. The theme of immortality in science fiction was addressed in an earlier anthology of critical essays, Carl D. Yoke and Donald M. Hassler's *Death and the Serpent* (1985). Scientific developments since then, however, have cast a radically different light on the subject of immortality and life extension. Today, many people have their bodies frozen at the time of death, in hopes that later generations will revive them and restore them to health. Physicians have learned how to bring back to life people who have been declared dead, and researchers are examining the genetic and physiological factors that trigger human aging so that they may halt or reverse that process. And as computer scientists advance toward the creation of an artificial—and immortal—machine intelligence, some also speculate about techniques for transferring human personalities into theoretically deathless computers.

In short, while immortality has always been a dream, it now seems a realistic and realizable achievement, perhaps in the very near future. The need has emerged, therefore, to recontexualize the subject of immortality, continuing to examine its influence as an ancient human aspiration while at the same time considering new scientific advances and their impact on life and literature. This volume of essays seeks to fulfill that twofold agenda. It brings together literary critics, philosophers, gerontologists, computer experts, physicists, science fiction writers and biologists to discuss the urgent modern question of whether we can, or should, become immortal.

These essays are original and were first presented at the Fourteenth Annual J. Lloyd Eaton Conference on Science Fiction and Fantasy, held at the University of California at Riverside in April 1992. We thank all the individuals who worked to make the conference a success, especially Gladys Murphy and Daryl Mallett. The conference was sponsored by: The

University Library, The College of Humanities and Social Sciences, the Center for Bibliographic Studies and Research, and the Associated Students of UCR. The editors wish to thank Henry Snyder of the Center for Bibliographic Studies, and Dean Carlos Vélez-Ibañez for financial assistance in preparing this manuscript. Special thanks go to Karen Bellinfante for invaluable help in editing.

Introduction
Immortality: The *Self*-Defeating Fantasy

Eric S. Rabkin

In our oldest tale, *The Epic of Gilgamesh*, from the third millennium B.C.E., the hero learns "a secret thing . . . a mystery of the gods. . . . There is a plant that grows under the water, it has a prickle like a thorn, like a rose; it will wound your hands, but if you succeed in taking it, then your hands will hold that which restores his lost youth to a man."[1] To retrieve immortality, Gilgamesh weights himself with stones and plunges into the life-offering, death-threatening water. But

> deep in the pool there was lying a serpent, and the serpent sensed the sweetness of the flower. It rose out of the water and snatched it away, and immediately it sloughed its skin and returned to the well. Then Gilgamesh sat down and wept, the tears ran down his face . . . "I found a sign and now I have lost it." (117)

Italo Calvino has written that "the ultimate meaning to which all stories refer has two faces: the continuity of life, the inevitability of death."[2] We see both in this founding tragedy, for nature in the form of the snake returns to the pool, able to escape its corporeality and renew it, while humanity in the form of Gilgamesh can only return to the dusty city of Uruk, well built it is true, but ultimately a feeble defense against death. Nonetheless, many still hope for immortality, feeling, like Dostoyevski, that "if you were to destroy in mankind the belief in immortality, not only love but every living force maintaining the life of the world would at once be dried up."[3] Yet our fictions often tell us that immortality is best only as a hope and never as an actuality, for, despite its venerable, obvious, and intimate appeal, the fantasy of immortality masks a terrible reality.

The clearest warnings against immortality, some might suggest, are really warnings against hubris, foolishness, disobedience. The Cumaean Sybil, adored by Apollo, is granted a thousand years of life, but because she spurns the love of the god, he withholds eternal youth and she suffers on and on. Tithonus, beloved of Eos, the Goddess of Dawn, is granted immortality but forgets to ask for eternal youth, so he ages forever in what Tennyson has him call "cruel immortality." Prometheus is by nature an immortal, but because he steals fire for humanity his immortality becomes an eternity of suffering. One could say that immortality in these cases is no worse in itself than gold is in the story of Midas: a fine thing in its proper place, but ironic, indeed tragic, when corrupted. The apotheoses of Greek heros and Hebrew prophets would seem to corroborate this positive view of immortality, as would the irony of so fine a state leading not to happiness but to horror. The question arises, however, can we find an immortality that does not suffer such fatal defects?

It is often said that the central promise of Christianity is immortality: "I am the resurrection, and the life: he that believeth in me, though he were dead, yet shall he live: And whosoever liveth and believeth in me shall never die" (John 11:25–26). History shows that this promise has much appeal, but, curiously, we have very few glimpses of what it would mean to live this perfect immortality. In *Man and Superman*, George Bernard Shaw clearly prefers hell, "the home of the unreal and of the seekers for happiness" to "heaven . . . the home of the masters of reality, and [earth] . . . the home of the slaves of reality."[4] This matter of masters and slaves brings us back to the issue of disobedience. John Milton wrote in the opening lines of *Paradise Lost*

> Of Man's First Disobedience, and the Fruit
> Of that Forbidden Tree, whose mortal taste
> Brought Death into the World, and all our woe. . . .[5]

If Jesus is the New Adam, then his redemption of us is a return to Edenic obedience, for, as Milton clearly says, Death and Disobedience stand against Life and, one presumes, Obedience. Yet a heaven of perfect obedience, when concretely realized, hardly seems human happiness, so dependent is our happiness on notions of individual freedom and of desire. Adam, like Gilgamesh, lost immortality through the intervention of a serpent. One supposes that in heaven there are no serpents, nor any dangers, nor even the sexuality that such serpents in part represent. Shaw's heaven, like St. John's, suffers from what Arthur C. Clarke calls "the supreme enemy of all Utopias—boredom."[6]

The paradigmatic benevolence of Christianity, the compensation as it were for Original Sin and the Flood, is God the Father projecting himself into the mortal reality of Jesus. For believing Christians, of course, this is a unique and pivotal event in human history. But in fiction, the willingness to accept mortality is by no means rare and, where there is no promise of life-everlasting, as there is not, say, for Sidney Carton when he takes Charles Darnay's place at the guillotine at the end of Charles Dickens's *A Tale of Two Cities*,[7] such mortality is the measure of human, not divine, heroism. Jesus can promise the robbers that they will be that day with him in paradise (Luke 23:43), but Sidney Carton can achieve his immortality only in art. However, most of us, I believe, would agree with Woody Allen who said, "I don't want to achieve immortality through my work, I want to achieve it through not dying."[8] Unfortunately, the available images of "not dying" are typically either sketchy, as with the Christian, or grotesque.

In "The Facts in the Case of M. Valdemar" Edgar Allan Poe presents a man mesmerized "*in articulo mortis*."[9] The narrator/hypnotist can calculate the hour of expected death because Valdemar suffers from a progressive wasting disease, but in some sense Valdemar in his inevitable mortality is like us all for, as the inhabitants of Samuel Butler's Erewhon say, "'To be born . . . is a felony—it is a capital crime, for which sentence may be executed at any moment after the commission of the offence.'"[10] Poe's story, readable first as a bizarre science fiction and second as a flagrant satire, has the time from the narrator's "conception" of the mesmerizing project to its end equal nine months, the last seven spent with Valdemar somehow suspended by mesmeric intervention. At a key moment in entrancing Valdemar, the narrator says, "[I] proceeded without hesitation—exchanging, however, the lateral passes for downward ones, and directing my gaze entirely into the right eye of the sufferer" (273). This ostentatiously objective rhetoric of science, on second glance, conceals a satire of extreme unction. Indeed, on a subsequent visit, the narrator elicits vibrations from the tongue of the unbreathing, cold Valdemar, and they say, "'*I am dead*'" (277). Finally the narrator decides to try awakening his subject. The story ends with this paragraph:

> As I rapidly made the mesmeric passes, amid ejaculations of "dead! dead!" absolutely *bursting* from the tongue and not from the lips of the sufferer, his

whole frame at once—within the space of a single minute, or even less, shrunk—crumbled—absolutely *rotted* away beneath my hands. Upon the bed, before that whole company, there lay a nearly liquid mass of loathsome—of detestable putridity. (280)

At the most obvious level, this ending suggests that "there are some things that man was not meant to know," that primal disobedience, such as seeking immortality, may appear to work for a pregnant while but ultimately the divinely ordained human dissolution will have its way. But at a deeper level, this is a grotesque, dirty joke. The ejaculations of the tongue parody the ejaculations of a penis and the quick, spasmodic shrinking "beneath my hands" equates unnatural science with masturbation. Instead of describing fertile seed, the story reveals its narrator's own anxieties by ending with "a nearly liquid mass of loathsome . . . putridity." In Genesis, the very instant Adam and Eve ate the apple "they knew that they were naked" (Genesis 3:7). With mortality comes sexuality; those who seek immortality, the power of the gods, seek, perhaps unknowingly, to exchange procreation for creation. Mary Shelley's Frankenstein can restore dead flesh to what may well be permanent life, but the monster, more human than his creator, seeks only a bride,[11] while Victor, like Poe's masturbatory narrator, holds off death with his own hands alone. In *Interview with the Vampire*, Anne Rice's youthful auditor, when he hears the vampire's first description of drinking away someone else's life, says, "'It sounds as if it was like being in love.' The vampire's eyes gleamed. 'That's correct. It is like love,' he smiled."[12] But, of course, it is a love without procreation. Immortality, for the angels, for the devils, and for the creatures of modern science, is a childless state, and to that extent a denial of human potential and of human happiness.

Freud, in *Beyond the Pleasure Principle*, suggested that "we have adopted . . . the hypothesis that all living substance is bound to die from internal causes . . . because there is some comfort in it,"[13] meaning that all our own failures and our own ultimate demise seem less terrible if seen as either comparatively small or as inevitable. He goes on to assert that "The notion of 'natural death' is quite foreign to primitive races; they attribute every death that occurs among them to the influence of an enemy or of an evil spirit." Freud does not seem to recognize that our seeking of fatal causes—heart failure, cancer, gunshot—reflects no different motive. Instead, in the spirit of Victor Frankenstein, Freud expresses admiration at the writings of August Weismann who introduced the division of living substance into mortal and immortal parts. The mortal part is the body in the narrower sense—the 'soma'—which alone is subject to natural death. The germ-cells, on the other hand, are potentially immortal, in so far as they are able, under certain favourable conditions, to develop into a new individual, or, in other words, to surround themselves with a new soma. (616–17)

This is an amazing statement. First, Freud's utter silence here about earlier divisions of the living substance into body and soul reveals a powerful scholarly blindness which can be motivated, one supposes, only by a desperate need to believe that some progress is being made in the eternal human confrontation with death. Second, the focus on the germ-cells, "on the other hand," is as isolated and masturbatory in its own way as Poe's focus on mesmerism, another trick of the mind, like Freud's notion of the death wish, to hold back the ultimate terror. And third, this notion of immortality for the germ-cell reduces the human being as we would normally view it to a mere convenience. While this may be the view of modern sociobiology observing what Richard Dawkins has called "the selfish gene,"[14] it has little to do with the aspirations of individuals.

But surely we are not our mere bodies. If one lost a finger, the self would not change. But what if one lost an arm? Or the ability to procreate? It is clear that we are not much like our younger selves at the age of, say, three, when we were all prepubic, utterly dependent, and largely ignorant—indeed, there may be few atoms in our living bodies that have not been replaced over the years—yet we like to think of ourselves as continuous. This is in part an example of the famous philosophical conundrum of the farmer's axe:

> "Have you had that axe a long time?"
> "Oh, yes. Twenty years. I've replaced the handle three times and the head twice."

The persistence of the individual is a fantasy, clearly, yet a productive fantasy without which we would have no sense of self, and hence without which the very notion of immortality would be reduced to mere persistence, a state not unlike that of a rock.

Modern science fiction has, of course, imagined selves concretized if not in rocks then in silicon. In Clarke's *The City and the Stars*, citizens of Diaspor live so mind-numbingly long that they eventually voluntarily walk back into the Hall of Creation where machines "analyze and store the information that would define any specific human being"[15] and then they give themselves back up to silence—one should not call it death—until recalled by the Central Computer at some random future time to live with a newly randomized mix of ten million of Diaspor's billion potential citizens. Yet in this immortal utopia, where merely to speak the name of desire is to have it materialize, our hero Alvin is not just another revenant but "'in literal truth . . . the first child to be born on Earth for at least ten million years'" (17). It is he who brings fecundity and progress back to a stagnant world. There is no real human life without mortality, without the risk of death. From among all the traits that characterize us, we choose to call ourselves "mortals." This is the wisdom of Pinocchio.

In William Gibson's *Neuromancer*, one character is a so-called "construct," a computer chip containing the knowledge and personality of a famous denizen of "cyberspace," the virtual reality of the infosphere. He is activated by some "meat" characters who need his help, and he agrees to aid them but with one proviso: at the end of the adventure, "'I want to be erased.'"[16] Apparently disembodied immortality is as much a trap for Dixie Flatline as aging, embodied mortality is for Tithonus. We understand why, I think, when Case, the protagonist, tells Dixie that "'Sometimes you repeat yourself, man.'" "'It's my nature,'" Dixie punningly replies (132). Given enough time, and no body to respond to a changing environment, we would all repeat ourselves, living out patterns, no matter how grand, that lead ultimately to the merest repetition, and hence the destruction of any sense of individuality. Thus it is that the sentient computer HAL, in Clarke's *2001: A Space Odyssey*, ceases to be a character—an individual— but continues to function as a computer when his "higher function" boards are removed and he is reduced to repeating the calculations and self-identifying serial numbers first programmed into him.[17] It is for the same reason that Olaf Stapledon in *Star Maker* praises not swarming "hive minds" that obliterate the individual but the "intricate symbiosis" represented by a perfect marriage, by that "prized atom of community"[18] in which two may depend upon each other—and procreate—but in which each maintains essential individuality, and risks individual death.

Against this view, we have *Blood Music*, in which Greg Bear lets loose a plague of "intelligent leukocytes" on the world, and the world is transformed, all of us ultimately parts of a planetary hive mind. The protagonist says, "'if I die here, now, there's hundreds of others tuned in to me, ready to *become* me, and I don't die at all. I just lose this particular me. . . . it becomes impossible to die.'"[19] Bear's protagonist may believe that, but identical twins do not: no matter the duplication of information in another copy, the death of the individual as contemplated *by that individual* is death indeed. And the capacity to die is a great, self-defining freedom, the ultimate existential freedom according to Sartre and Camus, and the very ground of conflict between the individual and the state, as seen in the hospitalized, limbless combat victim in Dalton Trumbo's *Johnny Got His Gun*,[20] in Brian Clark's tube-fed paraplegic in *Whose Life Is It Anyway?*,[21] and in D-503, the protagonist of Eugene Zamiatin's *We*, after the "splinter [of imagination] has been taken out of [his] head" and he is reduced to a permanent, idiot grin, for "Reason must prevail."[22] This happy state of inevitable obedience is the ultimate Eden, and the splinter removed from D-503 is the "thorn" of the plant Gilgamesh sought, its prickle reminding us that we are alive as individuals only when we are subject to death.

It is said that when Michelangelo completed the idealized Medici tombs ordered by Pope Clement VII someone remarked on an absence of realism. "Who will care," the great sculptor replied, "in a thousand years' time, whether these are their features or not?"[23] Indeed. On the day jazz great Duke Ellington died, John Chancellor began his nightly television newscast by saying that "Edward Kennedy 'Duke' Ellington died this morning of cancer of the lungs and pneumonia. Later in the program we'll hear him play for us."[24] Idealized in stone or vinyl, the great achieve immortality not in themselves but only in their leavings, an immortality that supplants, and hence defeats, the self.

St. Paul promises us that here on Earth "we see through a glass, darkly; but then [after Judgment Day] face to face: now I know in part; but then shall I know even as I am known" (1 Corinthians 13:12). This notion of ideal knowledge in eternity is not limited to the Western world. The voice in *Brihadaranyaka Upanishad*, pleads

> Lead me from the unreal to the real!
> Lead me from darkness to light!
> Lead me from death to immortality![25]

But who is this *me*? Who is this *I*? When Moses asks on Mt. Sinai to see God face to face, God, who favors Moses, withholds this favor "for there shall no man see me, and live" (Genesis 34:20). St. Paul understood this, too. Speaking of the resurrection after Judgment Day, he says "Behold, I shew you a mystery; We shall not all sleep, but we shall all be changed, / In a moment, in the twinkling of an eye, at the last trump: for the trumpet shall sound, and the dead shall be raised incorruptible, and we shall be changed. / For this corruptible must put on incorruption, and this mortal *must* put on immortality" (1 Corinthians 15:51–53). When we put on incorruption, we are all changed: we are changed into ideals, into endless repetitions, into sterile vampires, childless angels, works of art, computer chips. We are changed into objects for the contemplation of others but in the process we lose our very selves. Immortality is a self-defeating fantasy, a desperate defense against death. Finally, who would choose such a neutered eternity? Not Tennyson's Tithonus.

> . . . Let me go; take back thy gift.
> Why should a man desire in any way
> To vary from the kindly race of men,
> Or pass beyond the goal of ordinance
> Where all should pause, as is most meet for all?
> . . .
> Release me, and restore me to the ground.[26]

Notes

1. Anonymous, *The Epic of Gilgamesh*, trans. N. K. Sandars (Harmondsworth, England: Penguin, 1960), 116.

2. Italo Calvino, *If on a Winter's Night a Traveler*, trans. William Weaver (New York: Harcourt, 1979), 259.

3. John Bartlett, *Familiar Quotations*, 15th ed. (Boston: Little, Brown, 1980), 581:19.

4. George Bernard Shaw, *Man and Superman* (1903; Baltimore: Penguin, 1969), 139.

5. John Milton, *Paradise Lost* (1667; New York: Odyssey, 1962).

6. Arthur C. Clarke, *Childhood's End* (1953; New York: Ballantine, 1972), 75.

7. Charles Dickens, *A Tale of Two Cities* (Philadelphia: T. B. Peterson, 1859).

8. Laurence J. Peter, *Peter's Quotations: Ideas for Our Time* (New York: Bantam, 1977), 260.

9. Edgar Allan Poe, "The Facts in the Case of M. Valdemar," in *The Portable Poe*, ed. Philip Van Doren Stern (New York: Viking, 1973), 269.

10. Samuel Butler, *Erewhon* (1872; New York: New American Library, 1960), 145.

11. Mary Shelley, *Frankenstein* (1818; New York: Oxford University Press, 1969).

12. Anne Rice, *Interview with the Vampire* (New York: Ballantine, 1976), 31.

13. Sigmund Freud, "Beyond the Pleasure Principle," in *The Freud Reader*, ed. Peter Gay (New York: Norton, 1989).

14. Richard Dawkins, *The Selfish Gene* (New York: Oxford University Press, 1976).

15. Arthur C. Clarke, *The City and the Stars* (New York: Harbrace, 1956), 15.

16. William Gibson, *Neuromancer* (New York: Ace, 1984), 206.

17. Arthur C. Clarke, *2001: A Space Odyssey* (New York: New American Library, 1968), 156–57.

18. Olaf Stapledon, "Star Maker," in *Last and First Men and Star Maker* (New York: Dover, n.d.), 255, 257.

19. Greg Bear, *Blood Music* (New York: Ace, 1985), 197.

20. Dalton Trumbo, *Johnny Got His Gun* (1939; New York: Bantam, 1970).

21. Brian Clark, *Whose Life Is It Anyway?* (New York: Dodd, Mead, 1978).

22. Eugene Zamiatin, *We* (1920; New York: Dutton, 1952), 217–18.

23. Clifton Fadiman, ed., *The Little, Brown Book of Anecdotes* (Boston: Little, Brown, 1985), 399.

24. Eric S. Rabkin, *The Fantastic in Literature* (Princeton: Princeton University Press, 1976), 76.

25. Bartlett, *Familiar Quotations*, 56:20.

26. Alfred Tennyson, "Tithonus," in *Selected Poetry*, ed. Herbert Marshall McLuhan (New York: Holt, 1956).

Part I

Approaches to Immortality

Philosophical Models of Immortality in Science Fiction

John Martin Fischer and Ruth Curl

Science fiction is often described as a literary genre well suited to philosophical speculation. SF and philosophy share a common interest in the question of immortality, and comparisons and contrasts can be made regarding their respective treatments of the theme. We propose here a sketchy taxonomy of different models or pictures of immortality offered by philosophers and SF writers. After noting important differences in these models, we shall suggest that some problems and concerns expressed by philosophers and SF writers alike are the result of conflating different models. It is our hope that these comparisons will provide a preliminary sense of the way SF can be said to function as philosophical discourse.

Our discussion will use as its base the analytical framework presented in Bernard Williams's influential discussion of immortality, *The Makropulos Case: Reflections on the Tedium of Immortality*.[1] This simple and natural framework involves two criteria to make immortality truly appealing: first, there must be a future in which an individual can recognize himself or herself—someone genuinely *identical* to the individual, not just qualitatively similar or with several identical properties. Second, the future life of the individual must be *appealing* (in some way) to that individual; it cannot involve constant torture, hard labor, tedium, or the like. These conditions can be dubbed the *identity condition* and the *attractiveness condition*. With these, we can construct a taxonomy of different models of immortality (see table 1).

Although our focus will be the immortality of sentient creatures or constructs, another treatment of immortality in science fiction is also

3

Table I   A Taxonomy of Immortality

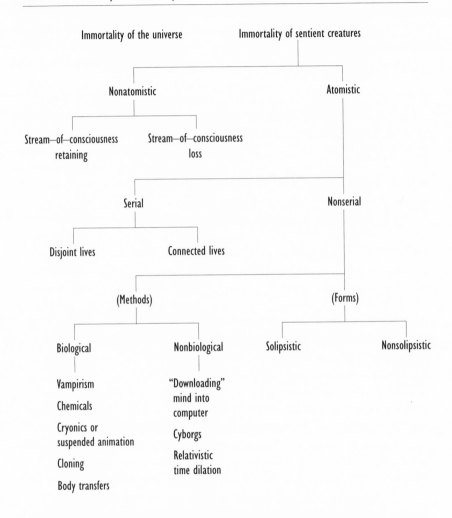

Immortality of the universe   Immortality of sentient creatures

Nonatomistic   Atomistic

Stream—of—consciousness   Stream—of—consciousness
retaining   loss

Serial   Nonserial

Disjoint lives   Connected lives

(Methods)   (Forms)

Biological   Nonbiological   Solipsistic   Nonsolipsistic

Vampirism   "Downloading"
                    mind into
Chemicals   computer

Cryonics or   Cyborgs
suspended animation
                    Relativistic
Cloning   time dilation

Body transfers

possible: universe immortality, in which there is an attempt to overcome laws of entropy to create an immortal world, forever self-perpetuating. The center of attention here is not the immortality of sentient creatures but rather the immortality of the physical universe.[2] Only science fiction seems to deal with universe immortality; and while it is not our focus, this vision of immortality merits attention because it has no corollary in other fields of literature or philosophy.

We turn now to depictions of immortality pertaining to sentient entities, beginning with a distinction between *nonatomistic* and *atomistic* concepts of immortality. The former involves a kind of *fusion* of different individuals into a type of immortal entity; the latter involves the immortality of individuals. The nonatomistic model usually involves the merging of various individuals into some sort of superorganism. The individual's stream of consciousness may either be retained, as in Greg Bear's *Blood Music*, or lost, as in Arthur C. Clarke's *Childhood's End* and one episode of Robert A. Heinlein's *Methuselah's Children*.[3]

In *Blood Music*, a brilliant researcher, after losing his job, injects himself with lymphocytes he has genetically manipulated so that he can smuggle them out of the lab and continue his research. The altered lymphocytes then invade the biosphere and trigger the mutation of humanity into a new organism composed of individually intelligent cells. Eventually the cells unite to form a superintelligent being. Each cell can either function separately or compartmentalize with other cells, which can then isolate themselves to work on various problems. Bear's vision of the mutation and transformation of humanity is best expressed in the novel's last lines: "Nothing is lost. Nothing is forgotten. It was in the blood, the flesh. And now it is forever" (*BM* 247).

In *Childhood's End*, children and adolescents transform beyond the comprehension of the rest of humanity. Clarke's vision clearly shows a complete but unintentional and uncontrollable break with human characteristics, memories, and emotions. In *Methuselah's Children*, members of the Howard Families (immortals in a mortal world) fleeing persecution on Earth and searching for a hospitable planet encounter the Little People, who "in an utterly basic sense . . . differed from humans in kind. They were not individuals. No single body of a native housed a discrete individual. Their individuals were multi-bodied, they had group 'souls.' The basic unit of their society was a telepathic rapport group of many parts. The number of bodies and brains housing one individual ran as high as ninety or more and was never less than thirty-odd" (*MC* 134–35).

Clearly, there can be different versions of both nonatomistic concepts, including differences in the nature of the transition from individuals to composites, which can be a genetic mutation (as in *Blood Music*, ignoring for the moment the manipulation by Vergil) or a nonmutational evolutionary transformation (as in *Childhood's End*). And there can be differences in the nature of the composites: for example, there may be one or many composites, and the existence of the composites might be relatively desirable or undesirable.

But any sort of nonatomistic immortality—even one in which the nature of the composite's existence is relatively attractive—appears to run afoul of

Williams's first criterion: the identity criterion. Arguably, the types of fusion envisaged in nonatomistic models (even ones that somehow preserve individual streams of consciousness) do not allow individuals to look forward to *their own* future existence. As such, these nonatomistic models are not very appealing models of immortality.

Is it then appropriate to eliminate nonatomistic models? When we look to the future we seem to care about the welfare of our communities and friends, the planet and its nations. We might care about the continued development of the arts, the preservation of natural beauty, and the attainment of human rights and distributive justice; but we care *especially* about how *we ourselves* will fare—we especially look forward to future pleasurable states of ourselves and particularly reject prospective unpleasant future states of ourselves. So, for example, if we are told that some future individuals will be tortured horribly for days, we can genuinely regret this; however, if we are then told that those people will be ourselves, we are horrified—we *especially* regret this. Thus, individuals might care to some extent about a future in which individuals have become group entities of certain sorts; indeed, it might even be desirable in some sense. But we do not and cannot look at such a prospect in the special and especially vivid way we look at future scenarios in which we exist as individuals. This special sense in which we care *particularly* about what happens to us is not engaged by nonatomistic models of immortality.

Since nonatomistic models seem to run afoul of the identity condition, let us instead turn to atomistic models of immortality. In this class there are *serial* and *nonserial* models. In serial models of immortality, the individual in question in some ways lives a series of lives; in nonserial models, the individual simply leads an indefinitely long single life.

The atomistic serial model of immortality comes in at least two versions: the *disjoint-lives serial model* and the *connected-lives serial model*. In the disjoint-lives model, one individual lives an indefinitely long series of lives without internal psychological connections: there are no significant continuities or connections of memory or other psychological states, such as values, beliefs, desires, and intentions, from one life to the next. In this view, the self is some sort of soul or bare particular without any essential mental contents. When the soul enters a new body, the person itself persists, even if there are no remaining memories, beliefs, preferences, values, or intentions. This model recalls the Hindu model of reincarnation. A possible metaphor is the tulip bulb—the different lives correspond to the different plants and flowers that spring from the bulb from one year to the next, whereas the persisting self corresponds to the essential bulb.

But, like the nonatomistic model, the disjoint-lives serial model runs afoul of the identity condition. It is unclear how an individual could recognize a future individual as genuinely identical to himself or herself if there is no psychological connection between the two (including connections of memory). We do not know if it is metaphysically coherent to suppose that persistence of personal identity means the persistence of a bare, psychologically empty soul; there are deep perplexities here into which we cannot go. Even if the model is metaphysically coherent, the identity condition does not seem to be satisfied in the relevant way, a way that makes it possible for us to *recognize* ourselves in the future scenario. That is, even if there is no insuperable ontological problem with the disjoint-lives serial picture, there is an epistemic problem: presented with a description of a future scenario, there is no way individuals can recognize or identify *themselves*. And, if the relevant future person has no psychological connection to the current individual, why should the individual care especially (in the way one cares especially about *oneself*) about this future person? Given this problem, the disjoint-lives model is unappealing—it cannot capture the sense in which we might value especially our own immortality.

Unfortunately, the connected-lives serial model fares no better. Imagine, if you can, what it would be like to lead one life—to go through childhood, adolescence, and all the stages of life—accumulate memories and associated values, and then begin again: go through a second childhood (but with memories of the previous life), a second adolescence (but with memories of the previous life plus the new childhood), and so forth. What would it be like to be a small child carrying memories of adolescence, marriage, raising a family, seeing one's children grow up, and so forth? The model of full or robust psychological connections within serial lives seems either entirely incoherent or entirely unattractive; in any case, it surely does not meet the two criteria. Nor does it seem possible to weaken the psychological connections in any natural or appealing way; in particular, it does not seem plausible that one could have only certain memories (just enough to be able to recognize oneself as a persisting entity) at certain stages of life. This would involve "blackouts" of parts of memory at some stages and not others—an almost stroboscopic and bizarre picture of memory. SF often puts a skeptical valance on this sort of connected-lives serial model. Consider Clarke's *The City and the Stars* (1956). In this novel people are reborn into new bodies without memories of previous lives; then, as they near adulthood, they gradually remember their previous lives. From the perspective of the "new" individual, it would surely be disconcerting to be suddenly flooded by a vast set of old memories of earlier lives; and—more relevant to the issue of immortality—from the perspective of the "old" individual, it would not be pleasant to stop being conscious one day, then reawaken with a new set of memories involving a new childhood and adolescence.

Thus, even though SF novels may claim that a character leads many lives, our ruminations above lead us to call this possibility into question. On closer scrutiny, these novels do not depict characters who themselves lead different lives in the senses required by the serial model. A particular character (say, Lazarus Long) does not lead many lives; rather, *he* leads *one* extended life in which many other people play roles. Many lives become part of his life when they intersect it—but Long himself does not genuinely lead a series of lives. (A life with a series of people need not be a series of lives.)

Our taxonomic trail leads finally to atomistic nonserial conceptions of immortality, of which there are various versions. Primarily, these involve different ways of *generating* or *maintaining* the indefinitely long life, and different ways of viewing the *nature* of the life (pattern and distribution of experiences, relationship to other lives, and so forth).

Let us first consider the different ways of generating or maintaining a nonserial atomistic form of immortality. There are a number of horror stories in which a vampire draws on the life force of another to continue existence. Literature and films have produced many variations on this theme; the vampire does not always follow the Count Dracula formula. Numerous films, for example, depict beautiful young women who seduce young men to feed off their energy; and Oscar Wilde's *The Picture of Dorian Gray* (1897) features a protagonist who remains young while his portrait ages. In E. E. "Doc" Smith's Lensman series the Overlords live off the life force of the Velantians. In one Balzac story, an old man lives off young girls. A recent Stephen King film, *Sleepwalker* (1992), depicts a young man who gains vitality from the innocence or purity of young virgins, whom he kills in order to devour their life force, or souls. Obviously, the topic continues to generate discussion.

In Anne McCaffrey's series comprising *Crystal Singer* (1982), *Killashandra* (1985), and *Crystal Line* (1992), humans have developed a symbiosis with a spore, which makes them extremely long-lived. Unfortunately, they must periodically return to the planet of the spores to avoid a terrible death. (This somehow resembles the need to visit one's parents regularly—at least in our families!) In McCaffrey and Jody Lynn Nye's *The Death of Sleep* (1990), the protagonist, who engages in cryogenic sleep, ages only four or five years in seventy-two. Another type of life prolongation is envisioned in Hugo Gernsback's *Ralph 124C 41+: A Romance of the Year 2660* (1925), in which a man reacts to a scientist's revival of a dead dog by exclaiming, "I only regret for myself that you had not lived and conducted this experiment when I was a young man, that I might have, from time to time, lived in suspended animation from century to century, and from generation to generation as it will now be possible for human beings to do."[4] This would not be continued conscious existence with stroboscopic memory, but rather stroboscopic consciousness of a certain sort. In some novels, cloning gives characters a form of immortality. For example, in Heinlein's *Time Enough for Love* (1973), Lazarus Long is more or less cloned as his own daughters.

Another biological method of achieving immortality consists in socalled body transfers, which presupposes the falsity of the "bodily identity" criterion of personal identity. In *The World of Null-A* (1948) and *The Players of Null-A* (1956), by A. E. van Vogt, Gosseyn's consciousness transfers from one body (when it is destroyed) to another. As long as there are bodies, he can exist forever. Of course, conceptually one can distinguish between various sorts of body transfers. In some cases the brain is transferred to a different body. In others the brain itself is not transferred, but the mental state is, as in the film *Invasion of the Body Snatchers* (1956); in some of the latter sorts of cases, there can be teleportation as well as mental transfer.[5]

There are also rather less exotic (though by no means mundane) biological methods of generating and maintaining immortality, as portrayed in Mary Shelley's "The Mortal Immortal" (1910) and Larry Niven's *Ringworld* (1970), *Ringworld Engineers* (1979), and *Protector* (1973), all of which feature immortal beings. In Shelley's story, a young apprentice drinks the creation of his master and becomes immortal. In Niven's books, individuals live for centuries by using a drug especially tailored for their chemistry; without the drug, they die. Any human who eats the Spice of Life becomes a Pak Protector. Human Protectors undergo a physical change that makes them almost unrecognizable as human and a mental change that makes them protect whatever society they are in at the moment. These beings seem to be biological analogues to Isaac Asimov's robots, and they follow laws (instincts, in this case) similar to his Laws of Robotics.

There are also nonbiological methods of generating and maintaining immortality. In *Neuromancer* (1984) William Gibson creates a kind of human immortality by allowing the transfer of human mental states to computers. In Gregory Benford's *Great Sky River* (1987) the transfer is accomplished through the insertion of computer chips into the human, resulting in a combination of biological and mechanical capabilities: though the body may die, the "mind" continues. These procedures involve mental transfer ("downloading" of the "mind") not accompanied by actual brain transfer.[6]

Other SF authors increase human longevity or create immortality by augmenting or supplanting normal human biological capacities through mechanical means. In McCaffrey's *The Ship Who Sang* (1969), a future society trains deformed but mentally functional babies to work in cyborg-type bodies if the parents so choose. This falls under the rubric of cyborg-type models of generating and maintaining atomistic nonserial immortality. In other works, robots are created and then allegedly made sentient. Their mechanical nature makes them more or less immortal. Thus, in Asimov's Robot and Foundation series, Daneel first acquires a feel for human phenomena and then leans more and more toward the human, becoming telepathic to get a better insight into human nature and reasoning. Finally, he makes plans to transfer his knowledge and memories (which in a robot are also his essence) to the brain of a Solarian child, thereby becoming mortal. But it is a prolonged mortality because Solarians, like all Spacers, live three or four hundred years. Further, if he can perform the operation once, he can do it again, particularly because this child is a hermaphrodite who will produce at least one offspring that is for all intents and purposes "itself." So, unlike Andrew Martin in "The Bicentennial Man," Daneel leaves his "option" of immortality open.

One other nonbiological way to produce immortality (one might call it "relativistic" immortality) involves time travel, as in Joe Haldeman's *The Forever War* (1974), in which time travel paradoxes are manipulated to achieve a sort of immortality.[7]

Having briefly surveyed the methods of generating and maintaining immortality (in particular, atomistic nonserial immortality), we now turn to the *nature* of immortal lives—their relationship to other lives and the pattern and distribution of their experiences.

First, consider a kind of solipsistic model. Heinlein's "'—All You Zombies—'" (1958) features an endless temporal loop in which the main character is a man who travels in time. But the pattern of his time travels indicates that he is in fact his own father, mother, and baby. There are other, nonsolipsistic, conceptions of the nature of atomistic nonserial immortality. One posits the "lone immortal" who lives among other individuals, all mortals. There are at least two versions of the lone immortal model—one in which the lone immortal is known by (certain) others to be immortal, and another in which the immortality is a secret. Such models appear, respectively, in Asimov's *The End of Eternity* (1955) and Shelley's "The Mortal Immortal." In another conception the immortal is not alone—perhaps others are immortal, as in *Methuselah's Children*, or perhaps everyone is immortal.

We have found problems with all models of immortality except for atomistic nonserial approaches. Nonatomistic models do not seem to meet the identity criterion, and some atomistic models—in particular the connected-lives serial models—run afoul of the attractiveness criterion (if not also the identity condition). But what about the atomistic nonserial models of immortality? Surely some methods of generating and maintaining immortality (such as feeding off the blood and vitality of others) make the resulting immortality less attractive. And some pictures of the nature of such immortality (such as the solipsistic model) make immortality unappealing. But not all methods of generating immortality are similarly problematic, and not all concepts of the nature of such immortality are straightforwardly problematic. Is there something about the nature of atomistic nonserial immortality that renders it, on reflection, *necessarily* undesirable?

Though some philosophers argue for this undesirability,[8] some SF models are not so pessimistic. A common trait in science fiction is its positivistic faith in the ability of technology to accelerate the moment in the process of history when desirable immortality can be experienced. And today, there is already the hope that the human life span can be extended (through cryonics, for example) long enough to allow us to outlive the immediate causes of death and in a sense live to see the dawn of immortality. Yet SF has negative models, too, and can be every bit as critical of positivist aspirations as are many philosophers.[9] One brief example: though some SF novels depict efforts to achieve immortality through transformation into robots or mechanical beings, perhaps an equal number offer the opposite maneuver: a reverse immortality, or "Pinocchio Syndrome," in which an immortal strives to become mortal (not to die, but to become "subject to mortality"). Somehow, even facing the prospect of immortal existence, human (mortal) qualities still retain such value that they are worth the reversal.

Despite a certain symbiosis between models in SF and philosophy, science fiction may be the more open to the possibility of transformation of the human body and life span. But in the end, is SF any more *willing* to abandon human limits? That vast and intriguing question is, unfortunately, beyond the scope of this essay.

Notes

1. Bernard Williams, *The Makropulos Case: Reflections of the Tedium of Immortality* (Cambridge: Cambridge University Press, 1973), 82–100.

2. We see such concern expressed in Robert A. Heinlein's "Waldo" (1942) and Isaac Asimov's *The Gods Themselves* (1972), in which an alternate universe is discovered and energy is drawn from it, thus invalidating the law of the conservation of energy and avoiding entropy. In Poul Anderson's *Tau Zero* (1970) the universe contracts until there is too much energy contained in too small a volume and the contracting universe explodes to begin the process of expansion again. In Gregory Benford's *Timescape* (1980), tachyons—particles that travel faster than light—can make universal wave functions split into two or more universes if a causal paradox is created by the tachyonic interaction. These works all depict science fiction's underlying concern with the mortality of the universe.

3. Greg Bear, *Blood Music* (New York: Ace Books, 1986) [*BM*]; Arthur C. Clarke, *Childhood's End* (New York: Ballantine Books, 1980); Robert A. Heinlein, *Methuselah's Children* (New York: Signet Books, 1958) [*MC*]. Later page references are to these editions.

4. Hugo Gernsback, *Ralph 124C 41+: A Romance of the Year 2660* (New York: Frederick Fell, 1950), 65.

5. For various examples of this, along with an incisive and comprehensive philosophical discussion of the nature of personal identity, see Derek Parfit, *Reasons and Persons* (Oxford: Clarendon Press, 1984).

6. See Rudy Rucker, *Software* (New York: Ace Books, 1982).

7. For a philosophical discussion of time travel paradoxes, see Paul Horwich, *Asymmetries in Time* (Cambridge: MIT Press, 1987).

8. See Williams, *The Makropulos Case*. For a critical discussion of Williams's work, see John Martin Fischer, "Why Immortality Is Not So Bad," *International Journal for Philosophical Studies* 2 (September 1994): 257–70.

9. See the essay by S. L. Rosen in this volume.

From the Sublime to the Ridiculous:
Immortality and *The Immortal*

James Gunn

I can trace the origin of my novel *The Joy Makers* (1961) to the chance reading of an article on "feeling" in the *Encyclopedia Britannica*. The origin of *The Immortals* (1962) is less certain. In 1954, when I was freelancing full time, I was exploring ideas that could be developed as novelettes or short novels and later combined into novels. This was the origin of the principle later codified as Gunn's Law, which in its simplest form says, "Sell it twice!" and in its more philosophical version states, "Nothing is worth writing unless you can use it more than once."

In these days, when novels can become best-sellers and advances of $50,000 to $100,000 are common, and $500,000 to $1,000,000 or more is not unheard of, Gunn's Law is not as relevant, but in the simpler and poorer days when the law was conceived, I had just spent six months writing two novels for advances of $500 each, of which $250 went to Jack Williamson, the coauthor of *Star Bridge* (1955).

In 1954 I was at work on three short stories that eventually would become parts of books: "The Hedonist," which became the central portion of *The Joy Makers*; "The Cave of Night," which became the opening of *Station in Space* (1958); and "New Blood," which became the first section of *The Immortals*. Though I did not know it at the time, 1954 was a very good year.

When I started writing, I had no more insights into immortality than any other longtime reader of science fiction. I knew, of course, about *Gilgamesh*, Methuselah, the Elixir of Life, and the Fountain of Youth. I had read many works dealing with longevity or knew of them from J. O. Bailey's *Pilgrims Through Space and Time,* including Jonathan Swift's *Gulliver's Travels* (1726) with its Struldbruggs, Charles Maturin's *Melmoth the Wanderer* (1820), Honoré de Balzac's *Elixir of Life* (1833), various tales of "the wandering Jew," H. Rider Haggard's *She* (1886), H. G. Wells's "The Story of the Late Mr. Elvesham" (1896), Bernard Shaw's *Back to Methuselah* (1921), Karel Capek's *The Makropoulos Secret* (1922), Olaf Stapledon's *Last and First Men* (1930), James Hilton's *Lost Horizon* (1933), and Aldous Huxley's *After Many a Summer Dies the Swan* (1939). All these suggested the deep hold on the human imagination that dreams and fears of longevity have maintained over the years. But with few exceptions these are literary treatments, useful only for insights on the human condition, not for defining the possibilities of immortality. The more provocative predecessors came from science fiction itself, particularly Robert A. Heinlein's *Methuselah's Children* (1941, 1958) and Isaac Asimov's *The Caves of Steel* (1954), which treat longevity as a topic for legitimate speculation. Like any different way of looking at a familiar theme, science fiction can rejuvenate old ideas by injecting new viewpoints, in this case pragmatism. As Asimov showed with his reconsideration of the robot, science fiction says, "Yes, that's all very well. But how would it really work?" One of science fiction's insights is that the way things work determines how they shape human behavior.

I cannot remember why dealing with immortality occurred to me, but once it did, I moved to the next stage in the science fiction writer's approach: research. How might immortality be achieved? I found various theories about why people age, but the one I liked best—for its narrative possibilities—was that people age because the circulatory system is inefficient, does not provide adequate food for the body's cells, and allows by-products to build up. The cells then develop the inefficiencies that we call growing old. If that were truly the cause, the answer to aging might be simply an improved circulatory system. It was a simple step from there to speculate about a mutation that might provide its carrier(s) with better arteries, better blood, or both.

What made the novel possible, as always, was an imaginative leap: what if that "improvement" was in the blood supply itself, some blood fraction that actually enhanced the circulatory system and the cells it nourished? What if that blood fraction was one of the gamma globulins—which provide passive immunity to diseases (as shown, for example, by the inoculations given pregnant women exposed to German measles)? The immortality factor as a gamma globulin or something similar suggested three stimulating possibilities: first, the metaphorical value of the immortality factor as an immunity to the "disease" of death; second, the possibility of transferring such immunities through blood transfusions; and third, the passivity of the immunity—gamma globulins provide protection only for the thirty to forty-five days that the transfused factors themselves survive. The last speculation was critical for my concept of the novel. The story would have been far different if the rejuvenation were permanent, as some characters in the novel at first thought might be the case. Temporary effects would demand further transfusions that could endanger the survival of my immortal man, Marshall Cartwright. I could have decided arbitrarily that the process would rejuvenate only temporarily, but the essence of the naturalistic science fiction approach demands outcomes shaped by plausible means.

I admit freely that the mechanism of the immortality factor in the blood has more support from metaphor than logic, but it has at least the sanction of theory and the natural associations of blood with life and health. It avoids the magical transformation of Shangri-La and the romantic cliché of the princess played by Margo wrinkling to death on the icy slopes outside the mysterious Tibetan valley.

Brian Stableford, in *The Encyclopedia of Science Fiction*, categorizes treatments of immortality into those that consider it a blessing and those that consider it a curse, between "limitless opportunity" and "the ultimate stagnation and the end of innovation and change."[1] This is a reasonable division, but not the only one. Approaches to immortality also could be divided between mainstream fiction and science fiction. The mainstream, for instance, would focus on the individual reactions of those who have immortality and those who do not. Science fiction treatments, though, would deal with strategies to achieve immortality, or with its consequences, or with its implications for society or the human species. What directed my approach from the beginning was John W. Campbell, Jr.'s, suggestion that authors take something that seems universally accepted and inspect its premises for logical flaws. Stableford suggested that stories portraying immortality as a curse may be tainted with sour grapes, and I agree. I did not for a moment buy the idea that people would not choose immortality if they had a chance; in Stephen King's miniseries *Golden Years* (1992), a woman's protestations that she does not want to be young again ring false. But the idea that someone with the elixir of youth in his blood might be drained dry by others who covet it gives immortality a quality of desperation.

These were just starting points, however. My real concern was with what people like Asimov call "not the prediction but the consequences"— not the automobile but the traffic jam, not radio but soap opera, not the income tax but the expense account. I wanted to consider what would happen to society if immortality became possible. "New Blood" describes the discovery of Marshall Cartwright and his life-giving blood; "Donor," the results of a fifty-year search to find Cartwright or his descendants; "Medic," the later expansion of medical centers to occupy half their metropolitan environments, the longevity of a few, and the impoverishment and limited life spans of the many; and "The Immortals," the short novel from which the novel took its title, the world several hundred years later controlled by long-lived hereditary rulers while the rest of the population endures lawlessness and lack of concern for human life.

Bantam published the novel in 1962, and four years later my agent notified me that "a couple of guys want to take an option on the television and movie rights." Robert Specht was employed in Bantam's West Coast office when he took home *The Immortals* one evening, but in 1966 he and Everett Chambers were the story editor and producer for the television series *Peyton Place*. We signed a two-year option, and it took all of that and more. Chambers dropped out but Specht persisted. Finally, when ABC announced plans in late 1968 for its *Movie of the Week* series, *The Immortal*'s time arrived. When I learned that people were interested in the movie and television rights, I could not at first imagine how anybody could make general entertainment out of a story about the deterioration of the social bond as a result of the discovery of immortality. But when I saw the screenplay and later the television movie, I understood.

Hollywood took out the science fiction and left in the chase. *My* immortal man was a drifter who sold his blood to buy wine. When a doctor told him what kind of blood he had and advised him to get lost and father lots of children so that humanity would eventually gain the benefit of his genetic good fortune, Cartwright understood and disappeared. He was not seen again, except for a glimpse in "Donor," until the end of the novel. He was a bum, but he was not stupid. The screenplay changed his name to Ben Richards to avoid confusion with the Cartwrights on *Bonanza*; more important, it made him a hardworking citizen, a test-car driver who donated a pint of his blood to save his dying boss. And Richards, played by Christopher George, became the hero of the film and series as he was chased around the country by rich and powerful men who wanted to dip themselves in the fountain of youth that was his blood. Immortality was no more important to the film and series than possession of a state secret or a treasure map would have been. ABC and Paramount saw it—as a script reader for Twentieth Century Fox said in an analysis I saw—as another excuse for a chase story, like *The Fugitive*, whose long run had recently ended. The fact that Richards was a test driver also provided the rationale for lots of car chases, the sort of thing that had made a hit of the recent film *Bullitt* (1968).

The Immortal was reasonably successful as a television movie. It was originally scheduled to be the first in the *Movie of the Week* series but was later moved to second. Since the success of a new series depends on early reactions, Paramount may have put extra effort into the production: the cast was good—George, Jessica Walters, Barry Sullivan, Ralph Bellamy, and Carol Lynley—and the experienced Joseph Sargent directed. The movie got a full-page ad in the *New York Times* and half-page ads elsewhere, earned good ratings, and was authorized as a series for the 1970–71 season.

About this time, a friend recounted to me a theory he had read that television programs programmed by opposites. *The Beverly Hillbillies* dealt with the comic adventures of a rural family that moves to the city; *Green Acres* dealt with the comic adventures of a city family that moves to the country. In such fashion, *Run for Your Life* in the preceding season featured a man running around the world because he was about to die; *The Immortal* featured a man running around the world because he was going to live forever. The fall preview issue of *TV Guide* called the series "Run for Your Blood."

I tried to influence the series from a distance, writing to Specht about not making it a "cookie-cutter" series and suggesting that science fiction writers be hired to work on scripts, but a newspaper columnist reported the show would be played for adventure, and I learned from Specht that ABC had vetoed the use of science fiction scriptwriters. As a matter of fact, Specht told me, Paramount and ABC not only did not want to hear from me—they did not want to hear from him either. When his agent answered a studio inquiry for a story editor by suggesting Specht's name, the Paramount executive asked, "Who's he?" Learning that Specht had written the script for the movie of the week, he hung up quickly.

As it turned out, I met the producer of the series before it went on the air. Through the intercession of a Wichita, Kansas, ABC station manager, I had lunch with Tony Wilson on July 5, 1970, and was pleasantly surprised by his attention to my ideas. He asked if I would like to write for the series if it went to a second season, saying his writers could not come up with any ideas about the kind of plateau a man such as Ben Richards might reach. He promised to mail me a couple of scripts. He surprised me again; he did.

I wrote a seventeen-page analysis of the show for him, pointing out the inanities in premise and scripts and the lost opportunities to say something dramatic and meaningful, and suggesting some new avenues that would be much more productive. I noted, for example, that Richards was an experienced driver and often had better equipment than his pursuers, but he was always getting caught. Sometimes he ought to get away. I concluded with a description of the plateau Ben Richards might reach: he could get smarter. He was a test-car driver who kept returning to situations involving cars, and his pursuers were tracking him down by collating information about new race drivers or mechanics. Why did he not hide himself where people leave no records—in the ghetto, perhaps—and never go near an automobile? His pursuers were no smarter, of course. They kept driving up in easily identifiable black Cadillacs or Lincolns, giving Richards a chance to escape in the nearest automobile and the series an opportunity for another chase. Wilson thanked me for my analysis and said he was using it with his writers. I had at least one practical impact: in an episode whose script I had commented on, Richards pulled away from his pursuers, and one turned to the other and said, "After all, he is a test-car driver." But by that time the series was going under and Wilson had been replaced.

As I have since come to realize, however, the problem with the series was not simply the breach of Mark Twain's admonition against playing crass stupidities on readers or people in the tale—what James Blish called the "idiot plot"—but mainstream sentimentality. Science fiction has been accused of being cold and unfeeling, but this is a side effect of its concern with ideas. If people do not behave rationally, the ideas never get tested. A scene in the TV movie illustrates the difference. Richards has just been informed by Dr. Pearce that the immunity factors in his blood rejuvenate recipients only temporarily, and he is the only source. As in the novel, Dr. Pearce advises Richards to "run, you and your fiancée, lose yourself somewhere before Braddock and everyone else learns about you."

Richards replies, "I've been given this unique gift. Am I to keep it selfishly to myself? What about all the people out there who might be saved, not just by me but by the knowledge that might come out of me?" There is more, but the sentimentality, the lack of realism, precludes the possibility of considering how immortality might really function in society.

Everything happens as Dr. Pearce predicts. The point is not that matters might not have worked out similarly if Richards had taken Dr. Pearce's advice, but that the treatment of the idea would have achieved an edge of reality that focused on the idea, not the human inability to think clearly. But then, the idea of immortality was only the McGuffin in this series.

I could point to other moments in the film and series when the stories take shortcuts through logic, often justified in terms of human feelings. Such matters are not unique to *The Immortal*, of course. In Stephen King's *Golden Years*, a kind of updated version of *The Immortal*'s chase story, the script resorts to the same sort of idiot plot. Williams, a man who grows younger after a laboratory accident, is escaping with his wife from ruthless pursuers. They are being aided and guided by the laboratory's security chief, a woman who was a former agency partner to the director of the government group that is chasing them; she is experienced and shrewd and has made good decisions up to this point. Then she asks the Williamses which direction they want to go. Mrs. Williams says she and her husband have a daughter in Chicago and she wants to go there.

A viewer would want to say, "No! No! Go anywhere but Chicago. They'll track you down that way." But the agent, who has the opportunity to say "that's the first place they'll look," goes along without protest. That, I submit, is not a recognition of the part that emotions play in our decisions, but lazy writing.

I might add two footnotes to the short-lived saga of *The Immortal*. Before the series went on the air in the fall of 1970, Bantam and ABC wanted to publish a novelization of the screenplay; they had to get my permission—and give me a third of the royalties—because of my original contract with Bantam. When I asked why they did not simply reprint *The Immortals*, I was told that there were a lot of differences between the novel and the film. "You're telling me!" I responded.

But I finally agreed. And when Bantam could not find anyone else to do the novelization, I agreed to do that as well. I wrote it in seven days, and when I told Bantam editor Eileen Lottman that I could not make it any longer than 150 manuscript pages, she responded, "That's all right. We'll use big type." When the novelization came out and I was revealed as perhaps the only author who has ever written the novelization of the script made from his own novel, the director of special collections at the University of Kansas called it "cruel and unusual punishment."

I also wrote an article about my experience for *TV Guide*, published as "An Author Watches His Brain Child Die on Television: Oddly Enough It

Was Called 'The Immortal'." In it, I tried to analyze what had happened to the series in the context of Hollywood's traditional treatment of science fiction ideas. Ironically, I got more fan mail from that article than from all my other writing—some 125 letters. As a further irony, many letter writers misunderstood what I had written, called *The Immortal* the best show on the air, and mourned its cancellation. Looking back on it now in the context of what has been broadcast since, perhaps they were right. A two-part article about the series appeared in *Starlog*, and in connection with answering questions about it, I reviewed the film (plus a Chinese version made in Hong Kong) and a couple of episodes, and perhaps I was too critical of it—not as science fiction, which it wasn't, but as television entertainment.

To my knowledge *The Immortal* had no discernible impact on written science fiction, which, undisturbed by television's brief and undistinguished treatment of the idea, has kept exploring the issue of immortality. One aspect that is always important in literary treatments is how the immortality is achieved. If it is a gift from the gods, they must be bribed or propitiated; if it is a secret wrung from nature, we must consider what price to pay for that knowledge and what price will be exacted afterward in the changes it will bring about. Between these are the kinds of immortality achieved as side effects of other, more central issues, such as the longevity of vampires. Norman Spinrad offered immortality at the cost of the lives of black children in *Bug Jack Barron* (1969), Robert Silverberg described another kind of survival in "Born with the Dead" (1974), and John Varley, in a series of stories, most directly in *Steel Beach* (1992), treats longevity through cloning and memory storage, as well as computer-directed reconstruction, as casually as changes in other bodily aspects, including sex.

The most significant additions to considerations of immortality in recent years are computers, cryogenics, and nanotechnology. The first novel in Frederik Pohl's Heechee series, *Gateway* (1977), begins with "Full Medical" treatment as an extrapolation of current transplantation techniques, but later novels move on to a possibility that has been used frequently in other recent texts: survival inside or outside a computer as a computer program or an electronic being. One sees such immortality, for example, in William Gibson's Sprawl trilogy, which begins with *Neuromancer* (1984).

Cryogenics, not so much immortality as suspended mortality, leads in the direction of calculated benefits and what people are willing to spend and endure for a remote possibility that is better than no possibility at all. A huge depository of frozen bodies is a background element in Juanita Coulson's *Tomorrow's Heritage* (1981), and a recent examination of the state of present-day cryonics can be found in Sterling Blake's *Chiller* (1993).

Nanotechnology raises the possibility of biological computers remaking the body from within. When the idea is explored for potential consequences rather than as a device to obtain a particular end, narratives consider topics like symbiosis, as in Ben Bova's Voyagers trilogy, and even parasitology and the subjugation or remaking of our species, as in Greg Bear's *Blood Music* (1985). It is interesting that blood, as in "New Blood," remains involved, and that one major and continuing preoccupation of science fiction is still the ways things work.

To many, then, it will seem that I am offering an old and familiar morality play: science fiction examines issues in a thoughtful and imaginative fashion while television reduces everything to mindless pablum. But I do not think that is the whole story; after all, there were television series in the 1960s—the obvious short list would include *The Twilight Zone*, *The Outer Limits*, *Star Trek*, and *The Prisoner*—that showed moments of intelligence and insight. The series based on my novel did not *have* to become a formulaic chase story.

I am reminded of what John W. Campbell said in "Non–Escape Literature": while "the essence of 'main stream literature' is that There Are Eternal Truths And Nothing Really Changes," science fiction embraces the notion of change. It is written for people "who have the unusual characteristic of being able to enjoy non–escape literature—who can look at a problem that hasn't slugged them over the head yet, and like thinking about it."[2] Perhaps that is why *The Immortal* came out the way it did. More than other developments depicted in television science fiction, human immortality would demand far-reaching fundamental changes in virtually all aspects of our behavior and institutions. Spaceships and robots are, after all, only different methods of travel and performing work, but immortality strikes at the heart of what we consider the human condition. It is both a dream fulfilled and a threat to continuity. One basic premise of science fiction, as it is in naturalism and Marxism, is that behavior is the product of environment. Science fiction's corollary is that intelligence allows people to recognize the process and, as in Asimov's Robot novels, choose to break their conditioning. But the traditional culture represented by television and its audience, as Campbell suggested, views human nature as fixed. So, limiting immortality to an individual and preoccupying him with endless pursuit meant that the series never had to deal with the larger, more frightening issues raised by human immortality. *The Immortal* may have adopted the format of the chase story because, in a metaphorical sense, the producers were running away from the idea of immortality.

That is not to say that science fiction has produced the definitive novel on immortality. All our works have limitations. Some texts portray, like the series, one individual who has become immortal, like Clifford D. Simak's *Way Station* (1963) and Roger Zelazny's *This Immortal* (1966); others, like *The Immortals*, Jack Vance's *To Live Forever* (1956), and Simak's "Eternity Lost" (1949), depict immortality as an exclusive privilege of an elite. I did not want to deal with the society-wide changes produced by universal longevity; that, as they say, would have been another story. The end of *The Immortals* suggests what that story would have been:

> Harry nodded, but still he waited. It would take a strong man to go out into a world where immortality was a fact rather than a dream. He would have to live with it and its problems. And they would be greater than anything he had imagined.
>
> He moved forward to begin the search.[3]

Few stories other than Heinlein's *Methuselah's Children* recognize that the development of immortality for a few would generate irresistible demands for universal immortality; and few stories attempt to explore the ramifications of such a development. Even Heinlein's later novels focusing on Lazarus Long and his circle fail to wrestle with that problem. It would be fair to say, though, that, as in my case, authors recognize the problem even if they may not be ready intellectually or emotionally to explore it. The closest approach may be found in Poul Anderson's *The Boat of a Million Years* (1989), which traces a group of genetic immortals through many lifetimes until their adaptation becomes universally available and transforms society in remarkable ways.

Perhaps the best description of our efforts to comprehend immortality is that it is a long road stretching in front of us. Despite its frenzied movement, the series *The Immortal* took only one small step on that road. Science fiction literature, which is much more daring and comprehensive, has traveled only a bit farther. Readers are still waiting for the definitive literary consideration of human immortality. Let us hope that they won't have to wait forever.

Notes

1. Brian Stableford, "Immortality," in *The Encyclopedia of Science Fiction*, ed. John Clute and Peter Nicholls (New York: St. Martin's Press, 1993), 616.
2. John W. Campbell, Jr., "Non–Escape Literature," in *Collected Editorials from Analog*, ed. Harry Harrison (1959; Garden City, N.Y.: Doubleday, 1966), 228, 231.
3. James Gunn, *The Immortals* (New York: Bantam Books, 1962), 154.

Longevity as Class Struggle

Fredric Jameson

The topic of this paper and volume is also a matter of some personal gratification because it allows me to indulge in the chance to talk about one of my favorite books from very long ago—an occasion that might never have arisen otherwise, at least in the normal span of our current lifetimes. George Bernard Shaw's *Back to Methuselah* was published in 1921, at about the same time as Karel Capek's unrelated *The Makropoulos Secret*. Meanwhile, one character in Shaw observes in passing that H. G. Wells "lent me five pounds once which I never repaid; and it still troubles my conscience."[1] We are, with Shaw and perhaps even with the "nonsynchronously synchronous" Capek, still in the afterwash of that late Victorian age in which science, doubt, and vitalistic philosophy met to produce the very first modern science fiction; and I might say, as someone who has always spoken against the legitimization of popular subgenres by high literary respectability (i.e., Dashiell Hammett compared to Fyodor Dostoyevsky), that in my opinion there are genuinely science-fictional pleasures coursing through the epic text of Shaw's "metabiological pentateuch," which some might still be tempted to identify with the canon.

It is questionable, however, whether the canon is yet ready to return to Shaw; or whether Michael Holroyd's immense biographical efforts, or the current Irish revival—more specifically the Oscar Wilde revival—or even the heliotropic turning of the collective imagination back to the belle époque and the age of the Second International are sufficient to make Shaw's art again available to us. This is to say that we may still harbor some deeper doubts or hesitations about the cryogenic revival of this figure, just as we may entertain them about Robert A. Heinlein, whose garrulous and didactic longevity has so much in common with that of the socialist playwright. To acknowledge Shaw as our Bertold Brecht (at least for the stage; in verse it is rather W. H. Auden one would like to acknowledge as Brecht's English-language approximation) is then to reckon in another way with the possibility that after Brecht we may no longer need a Shaw. Still, in the uniquely apolitical atmosphere of Anglo-American literature (where the other rival for assuming some genuinely Brechtian intellectual role may well turn out to be T. S. Eliot himself), it is always instructive to examine the extraordinarily rich practice of one of the few great political artists of modern times: it has been said, indeed, that few things contributed so fundamentally to the cultural preparation for the Labour Party's victory in 1945 as Shaw's tireless propaganda for socialism, which took the form of secondary figures in the great plays whose tirades gradually domesticated, respectabilized, and legitimized that terrifying ideology in the British middle classes.

Back to Methuselah, though, makes it clear that the implacable critique of middle-class hypocrisy in general and the English national character in particular (which an Anglo-Irishman was particularly well placed to articulate) was also a fundamental cultural and political act: something we can perhaps appreciate all the more in the superstate today, from which all lingering and nagging or garbled approaches to some self-knowledge about American vices of national character, let alone original sin, have been triumphantly expelled. One must also appreciate the fable whereby the last genuine remnants of true ethnic or group consciousness—the Irish and the Jews—abolish themselves as cultures on the shattering contact with the long-lived, whose proximity and existence—this is one of the fundamental themes of the play—inspire a well-nigh fatal "discouragement" in normal short-lifers like ourselves. But this running political commentary—including a great deal more on the British parliamentary system, which is no longer necessarily of interest to us, along with some remarkable developments on war and aggressiveness from Cain to Ozymandias and the Napoleons of the far future—can serve to illustrate the formal and structural peculiarities of the Shavian play, where much can be added in passing of a seemingly extraneous or digressive nature, and the mesmerizing experience of sheer unbridled talk itself can laterally, as it were, allow any number of supplementary topics to be carried into the spectatorial consciousness along with the official subject of the play. "There has to be something to eat and drink on every page," Flaubert once said by way of characterizing the drive for heterogeneity he felt at work within his own will to style.

Meanwhile, the all-inclusive nature of the monuments of high modernism, their vocation to become the Book of the World, also seem echoed, but idiosyncratically, in this Shavian method, which seems to consist in affirming a whole list of his own idiosyncrasies, of which the ideal Shavian spectator expects—nay, demands—a full recapitulation in every new play.

We are not interested in those idiosyncrasies today (too bad for us!), but it is worth underscoring a single extraordinary moment in *Back to Methuselah*, what Brecht might have called a *gestus*—the shaping of an act or an event into a gestural form that speaks in its own new language— before using this particular fantasy about longevity or immortality to gauge and bring out the specificities and the differences of the other, more modern versions we will have to deal with later on. As any schoolchild knows, *Back to Methuselah* begins in the Garden of Eden. From there, four additional full-length plays (a cycle that evidently owes something to Richard Wagner) lead us to the Utopian condition of a "summer afternoon in the year 31,920 A.D.," or, following the title of this concluding play in the cycle, "As Far as Thought Can Reach." Not the least fascinating aspect of its dramaturgy—occasionally the cycle is actually performed—is the suggestion of recurrence implicit in the use of the same actors for later and later roles, so that the first family of Eden turns up in the proper nonconformist British drawing room of the 1920s, the still exceedingly British world government of the twenty-second century, the world of A.D. 3000 dominated by powerful and mysterious long-lifers who have segregated the short-term people in other parts of the globe and serve as their oracles, and on into some ultimate Utopian state in which sexual relations have ceased and humans are born fully grown from eggs, and with but three or four years to live a normal, "childish" life before acceding to the unlovely isolation and wisdom of the condition of the Ancients, who long only to do away with their bodies altogether and attain the immortality of pure thought. One may incidentally feel that Shaw's physical puritanism is not much more repellant than Heinlein's hearty and obligatory hedonism; maybe neither value has that much to do with sex after all. Indeed, I am going to argue that as a general rule, at least in these works, the official subjects can mask a less obvious but deeper one, which it is the task of the critic and the interpretative process to draw out.

Shaw takes what one may want to call a Christian Scientist attitude toward biology, and perhaps even toward politics and metaphysics as such: in these last areas, it would be easy to diagnose his attitude as the expression of a kind of Fabian or social-democratic idealism, which would reflect a characteristic overestimation of reason and persuasion and an equally characteristic underestimation of ideology, unconscious drive, and the role of violence in human history. That is just the kind of idealism one would expect to find as the working ideology and legitimation of the practice of one of the great political orators of the twentieth century; but in Shaw it is by no means as one-dimensional an idealism as this account might suggest. Indeed, his view of choice dovetails well with the requirements of a theatrical aesthetic (with its structural premium placed on speech and dialogue) and opens a mediatory dimension between base and superstructure of a more distinctive and unique kind.

For Adam "decides" to live for a thousand years at the moment when words and concepts are being invented for the first time: his freedom to choose his own life span is part of that first unnamed freshness of the universe, and incidentally coordinates the theme of longevity with that of language and figuration, as we shall see below. But it is with the second moment in the process that we are most concerned here. For in the most characteristically Shavian fashion this first play or moment of the pentateuch, in the Garden of Eden before the Fall and then several centuries later, is succeeded by a new moment staged in the quintessential British drawing room, on Hampstead Heath, peopled by the two cranks of the title ("The Gospel of the Brothers Barnabas") along with their families and assorted typical British politicians of the interwar period. It is indeed the conviction of the brothers that politics, as they are still practiced despite their disastrous consequences in the Great War a few years earlier, can only be reformed by biology, but of an unusual kind: "Our program is only that the term of human life shall be extended to three hundred years," and "our election cry," the flapper adds, "is 'Back to Methuselah'" (BM 77).

Faced with this possibility, the politicians rearrange their platforms and electoral strategies and the curtain falls. It is about the next evening that I want to talk primarily and to some purpose. This play, or subplay, is significantly entitled "The Thing Happens": a description that parlays the immediate representational motif—in this case whether people will live longer, or indeed forever—onto a higher level of symbolic abstraction. As far as the longevity motif is concerned, it always involves a basic representational dilemma: How can you show that people have begun to live longer? At what point can longevity become visible in the narrative itself? It is all very well for us to look back across Lazarus Long's long life. From the outset, virtually by definition, we know that the "thing" has happened to him. But we and the writer are more often in the unhappy position of

Emperor Rudolph II of Bohemia, who first tries the Makropoulos secret out on the inventor's daughter in 1600 and then goes mad. "How," as she puts it three centuries later on the modern stage, "how could he be sure I was going to live for three hundred years? So he put my father in a tower as a fraud and I ran away with everything he had written to Hungary or to Turkey, I don't remember which."[2]

How indeed? How do you make an event out of such a condition, whose features consist in suddenly beginning one day to wonder why after so many years a friend or acquaintance has not seemed even to begin to change or grow old? It is by comparing newsreels of the drownings of a number of famous people that Shaw's short-lifers discover their astonishing physical similarity, much as though we were to discover that Alexander the Great, Christopher Marlowe, and, say, James Dean all looked suspiciously like the same person. At the very least this would tend to convert the immortality or longevity drama back into a kind of detective story—something it most notably is in Capek's play. In a moment, I want to trace the consequences of this representational problem or dilemma out in two different directions: namely, on the one hand, the reason why the long-lifers feel the need to disguise their unusual destinies; and, on the other hand, the question of time itself, not merely how one might represent an expanse of human time of this magnitude but what it would feel like existentially and to what degree the inner experience of the long-lived might be imagined to be radically and qualitatively different from that of the normally mortal—would there, for example, be many more volumes full of Proustian *madeleines* and *souvenirs involontaires*?

But this particular representational problem—the palpable difficulty in finding an objective correlative or narrative figuration for the disclosure of longevity or immortality—suggests some more fundamental interpretative and hermeneutic lesson. In the following pages we will act methodologically as though a principle exists according to which the ostensible content, the manifest topic or subject matter, always masks a deeper one of an entirely different nature. Some such principle is probably always at work in the hermeneutic process since interpretation would not be required if the work always said exactly what it meant. Interpretation seems called for in the present instance by the nagging suspicion that the longevity motif may be a cover or blind for something else.

This is a point that might be illustrated the other way around by the thematics of death, more specifically by meditations on its meaning: Simone de Beauvoir (but also Ernst Bloch, I believe, in a very different philosophical context from Sartrean existentialism) has argued that since death is meaningless in the first place, such meditations, despite their evident charge of affect, cannot be expected to lead anywhere; they are reveries in a void that in reality capture and express feelings and anxieties of a very different (nonexistential) kind. The interpretative hypothesis would then suggest that the theme of death—thinking about it, experiencing the death anxiety—invariably serves as a cover and vehicle for deploying the fear of something else (for de Beauvoir, the fear of having wasted one's life, regret at not having lived).

What we must now conjecture is whether something similar could be advanced for the immortality or longevity plot: whether its anxieties too might stand, in the conscious mind, as substitutes for some more concrete and fundamental worry and fear—some deeper contradiction—at issue in the unconscious. With the possibility of such a hermeneutic reversal, I come back to the most stunning development in Shaw's narrative. In "The Thing Happens," set in the year A.D. 2170 in the office of the president of the world system, which is located in the British Isles, members of that government—some of whom look suspiciously like the politicians in the previous twentieth-century governmental system and are indeed their descendants—slowly discover that two of their number, the Archbishop of York and the Domestic Minister, Mrs. Lutestring, are in reality very different from themselves and prove to have lived for over two hundred years. Who are these two people? They are evidently not the political leaders (whose descendants we have actually witnessed here, still in charge of the ship of state after so many generations), nor even the great-grandchildren of the original "inventors," if one may put it that way. They are, in fact, the parlor maid of the house and the fatuous young tennis-playing cleric we remember to have courted the brothers' daughter (or niece), and who offered a singularly pure example of a witless leisure class in its most marginal and secondary manifestations. These, and not the protagonists, the main characters or stars, are those whom the lightning somehow struck. They merely overheard the good tidings, which were meant for a more important public. When Mrs. Lutestring is asked what set her thinking about the new idea of longevity, she replies:

Conrad Barnabas' book. Your wife told me it was more wonderful than Napoleon's Book of Fate and Old Moore's Almanac, which cook and I used to read. I was very ignorant; it did not seem so impossible to me as to an educated woman. Yet I forgot all about it, and married and drudged as a poor

man's wife, and brought up children, and looked twenty years older than I
really was, until one day, long after my husband died and my children were
out in the world working for themselves, I noticed that I looked twenty years
younger than I really was. The truth came to me in a flash. (*BM* 135–36)

And for the Mozartian accents of Shaw's instrumentality, the pathos more
delicate than anything in Capek or Heinlein, there is also a brief expression of regret, in a play whose ruthless indifference to death matches its
idealism: "There was one daughter who was the child of my very heart.
Some years after my first drowning I learnt that she had lost her sight. I
went to her. She was an old woman of ninety-six, blind. She asked me to
sit and talk with her because my voice was like the voice of her dead
mother" (*BM* 135).

Radical chains, the weakest link, the meek shall inherit the earth—such
are some of the more ancient cultural stereotypes that cross the mind confronted with this remarkable development, so unsuspected as to offer the
very figure of sheer unforeseeability and unexpectability as such and in itself. I will use the gestus of this twist in two ways, the first of which has to
do with the nature of causality here proposed to us. It should be clear that
in Shaw, as has already been observed, a kind of Christian Science version
of the "life force" replaces the machinery of the modern or postcontemporary "rejuvenation" technology. What happens when all that is reckoned
back into the contemporary SF narratives we will see in a moment; but it
seems unsatisfactory to attribute the new development to mere voluntarism
or a boundless Enlightenment belief in the power of the conscious mind or
of Reason as such. On the contrary, Shaw here offers us an infinitely more
flexible and subtle vision of the unconscious mind—perhaps even the unconscious collective mind—than we are used to dealing with. Indeed, if
you take the whole stage of part 2 (in which the "gospel" of the Brothers
Barnabas is promulgated) as allegorical representation of that psyche itself,
we have one conscious will—the brothers—earnestly conveying its message to corrupt listeners only too eager for their own part to exploit its
possibilities, while elsewhere in the drawing room distracted secondary
minds catch bits of the freighted rigmarole in passing and a servant passes
in and out of the central stage carrying a tea tray and intent on more menial
business, storing up pieces of conversation for future use. There is a family
likeness here to Proustian involuntary memory, which has no use for overly
conscious acts of attention of the will but takes in its bounty of experience
laterally, as it were, and by way of afterthought: indeed, Proust also prom-

ises a kind of increase of life, but by adding to the conscious life span all those secondary lives we had no time to notice we were also living simultaneously with the first, official one. Walter Benjamin's notion of distraction and Brecht's idea of the musing, reflective distance of the judicious, smoking theater spectators of his pedagogical dramas, from which Benjamin's idea itself develops, also merit a mention here, for future comparison. So also do current neopragmatist reflections about belief itself and the peculiar level at which it operates: a postmodern substitute for the roles played by the more modernist Freudian notion of the unconscious and the Marxist notion of ideology.

Another figure from the 1920s, though, seems closest to Shaw's intricate conjuncture of the unpredictable and unforeseeable with the inevitable, and it will move us on to the second remark I had in mind to make about this episode. This is the famous image, which we owe to Victor Shklovsky, of the "knight's gambit," the knight's nonlinear jump across the chessboard that awkwardly seems to rebuke, in a vaguely premonitory or Utopian fashion, the more traditionally graceful yet prosaic moves of the other pieces. The most richly inventive of the Russian Formalists, Shklovsky wanted to dramatize by this figure an idea that was dear to all of them and had to do essentially with literary history—namely, that this last does not proceed from father to son (nor even, one supposes, from mother to daughter) but rather from uncle to nephew. The development of forms and genres is thus discontinuous and teleological all at once: when one is brought to fullest development (and by definition exhausted), what takes its place is not the successor or epigone but rather a marginalized and hitherto popular form that springs into place as a new space for formal and artistic development and evolution. So also with Shaw's characters: it is not the ruling class or its politicians but the poor, ignorant, and undeveloped who are the recipients of the new message. "I was too ignorant to understand the thing was impossible," the former chambermaid tells us. And in some similar fashion Georg Lukács, also in *History and Class Consciousness* (but following the first published articles of Marx himself), posits the richer human and intellectual and cultural potential of people who have been denuded of everything, who have not inherited the standard culture or undergone the standard educational formation—indeed, who have become little better than commodities themselves, reduced to selling their own labor power.

I mention these parallels in order to complete the second move demanded by this interpretative process, which is to suggest that at least in this case, the longevity drama is not "really" about longevity at all, but rather about something else, which can a little more rapidly be identified as History itself. It is History (not merely literary history) whose *telos* moves according to the knight's gambit; and the power of Shaw's play is to have given body to that within the extraordinarily limited and genteel confines of the bourgeois drama and the bourgeois drawing room. The title of this episode, "The Thing Happens," then, can already be seen in advance to fling the whole drama of unexpected longevity onto a higher plane of abstraction, where it stands for the Event itself, the Event in collective history, that radical act we often, for want of a better term, call revolution—a sudden collective movement of the people that can never be predicted in advance, that strikes the least likely place and the least likely collective agents or actors, that cannot be prepared by arrangements of the conscious will, but that is surely prepared in other subterranean if not unconscious ways. Benjamin sought a different kind of figuration for this ultimate Event of our collective social life, this ultimate mystery, when he had recourse to the language of the messianic, trying thereby to convey—against linear notions of historical accumulation and progress (which he attributed to the Second and Third Internationals fully as much as bourgeois thinking)—the way in which the Messiah arrives at the most unexpected moment, through some small lateral door in the historical present. It is a supreme event that has nothing whatsoever to do with anything that went before, or even that transpired in the seconds immediately preceding the unfolding of this new reality. In Shaw, the break is less absolute. There is preparation of a cultural and intellectual kind; seeds are sown, but the thing happens in seeming independence of all that. I want to explore the possibility that the longevity plot is always a figure and a disguise for that rather different one which is historical change, radical mutations in society and collective life itself.

As to why this is so, why everything has to mean something else, in this particular case the hermeneutic principle—for this is ultimately at stake in allegorical interpretation as such—can be defended locally in terms of the experience of longevity itself, about which our books tell us uniformly that nothing whatsoever is to be said. This emptying out of the very figure of long life, the absence of content at the core of the narratives we are examining, can be said, if you do not mind a rather different philosophical reference, to exemplify a fundamental Nietzschean doctrine about the irreducibility of the present. We will let Heinlein field this one, which is the discovery by the short-lived Dora, who is if anyone the principal woman protagonist of *Time Enough for Love*:

> Long ago, three or four years at least, shortly after I figured out that you were a Howard, I also figured out that Howards don't really live any longer than we ordinaries do. . . . We all have the past and the present and the future. The past is just memory, and I can't remember when I began, I can't remember when I *wasn't*. . . . So we're even on that. I suppose your memories are richer; you are older than I am. But it's *past*. The future? It hasn't happened yet, and nobody knows. You may outlive me . . . or I may outlive you. Or we might happen to be killed at the same time. We can't know and *I* don't want to know. What we both have is *now*.[3]

It is a discovery that, later on, Lazarus Long will summarize as follows: "Each individual lives her life in *now* independently of how others may measure that life in years" (*TEL* 398). One may wish to nuance the account and point out that, typically for the bourgeois philosophical position, Dora overestimates the past and underestimates the future, something Shaw's next evening, or subplay ("The Tragedy of an Elderly Gentleman"), makes clear. "It is not," Zoo tells the elderly gentleman in question (a short-lifer, or ordinary), "the number of years we have behind us, but the number we have before us, that makes us careful and responsible and determined to find out the truth about everything" (*BM* 183). And indeed, Shaw insists over and over again on the idea that not the accumulation of past memories and experiences piling up, but rather the perspective of having to live for several hundred years more makes up the difference and "wisdom" of the long-lived. We will return to this difference when we raise the issue of the psychological, and in particular the issue of boredom versus "discouragement."

For the moment, however, it is the narrative consequences of the matter that I want to underscore: for if Dora is right, then from any existential point of view there can be no essential difference between the experience of the short-lifers and that of the long-lived, and the Emperor Rudolph was quite right to go insane, like a theatergoer who is told he will have to wait another thirty years for the play to be finished. This is why the sheer experience of the present—which Heinlein discovers and reinvents in the passages I have quoted—can play no part whatsoever in his novel and occupies less than one page out of six hundred. Longevity is thus, as I have tried to suggest, a pretext for doing something else: in Heinlein's case, among other things, it serves first as a structural frame for interpolated stories—just as the Russian Formalists claimed about *Don Quixote* years ago. Don Quixote, Shklovsky argued, is not a character but the "motivation of a device," the pretext for stringing together a host of interpolated stories, novellas, and anecdotes, in the process of which this pretext is reified and turned into a character in its own right. So also Lazarus Long, who may then be looked at from two different perspectives. From one standpoint indeed, the project may be seen as the equivalent of a modernist one for Heinlein. That is to say, and whatever the differences, this ultimate project is designed to be all-inclusive and interminable in the most literal sense, and it thus fulfills the existential requirement and function of the archetypal modernist projects in Mallarmé or Joyce or Proust: that they completely absorb everything contingent about human existence, that they give you something to do for the rest of your life and thereby make every accident and every stray moment of that otherwise uneven and unjustifiable sequence of days and years supremely meaningful, by virtue of the project into which it can be incorporated (not necessarily in any basely autobiographical way). The theme of boredom that I anticipated above—the boredom of Utopia, the tedium of acedia of the long-lifer—now acquires a somewhat different and unexpected resonance, as that which threatens the modernist project and risks falling out of it into a random unjustifiability that the project cannot redeem or transform. The banal form of this is, then, the possibility for Heinlein to fill up book after book of Lazarus Long stories.

The content of those stories, however, moves us on to a somewhat different aspect of the matter, which is the pedagogical strain Heinlein shares with Shaw, but which in the American is more fundamentally related to a kind of cult of experience (in Shaw it is based on an impertinent assumption of difference and sheer genius). As is the case with the oldest realists in the tradition, much storytelling in Heinlein (or at least much of the later storytelling) seems to be based on the pleasure of sheer know-how, from which there flows the more multiple pleasures of sheer explanation (how to set up camp in the wilderness, how to outsmart your enemies, how to invest in galactic stocks, be an interplanetary trader, raise a family, and so forth). All of this can perhaps be resumed under the notion of assuming the paternal function—or better still, of combining that function with primal narcissism. It explains why, if Shaw's parable is really about History, Heinlein's is about the Family (and I do not mean to deny the link he makes between rejuvenation and the starting up of multiple new families).

But all of that in turn is based on what Jean-Paul Sartre long ago in *Nausea* denounced as the "ideology of experience," the idea that we learn from the past and that the older we are and the more experiences we are supposed to have had, the more we know and the more suitable we become for occupying a paternal function that consists in explaining things interminably and in showing off our infinite know-how. Late Heinlein, then, confronts us with the interesting question of what narrative really is: not so much what storytelling really is as what the story in storytelling might or might not be. When I show someone how to repair a car engine or put up a tent, is that a story or the material for a story? The answer must be that the lesson becomes a story only when I am able to show myself in the act of giving the lesson in the first place. Longevity is then the excuse, not for lots of lessons so much as for lots of stories about those lessons.

But early Heinlein was clearer about another displacement or consequence of the longevity plot, which we already encountered in Shaw at the end of "The Thing Happens" and with a certain reversal then in full force in the next drama of the pentateuch, "The Tragedy of an Elderly Gentleman," to which I have already referred. The motif of longevity or immortality, I have suggested, must always necessarily mean something else to acquire narrative content; but there is a second set of consequences that flows from the choice of the cover motif itself. This new set of narrative consequences has to do with the coexistence of long-living characters with the older, shorter-lived kind, so that the new, semiautonomous, independent story that coexistence begins to tell, in all the versions that are conveniently consulted under the rubric of immortality or longevity, becomes a story that can only be identified as that of class struggle.

What immediately happens in Shaw, for example, is that on discovering long-lifers in their midst, the politicians of the world state make plans to kill them all. Heinlein's *Methuselah's Children* (1958) is then the classic story of this persecution. In it, group fear and envy transcend the dynamics we generally associate with the backlash against race or gender or ethnic markings and attain the proportions of a kind of existential panic very similar to class panic itself. For now it is not merely that the *jouissance* of the alien group—its collective cohesion, the intensity of libidinal gratification this cohesion produces—seems far greater than my own and incites me to the kind of envy that, as Slavoj Zizek has shown,[4] underlies the backlash formations. Now, in the case of long life itself, my very existence as an individual and a group is called into question, and a political mobilization of a necessarily more cynical or lucid kind results, one that cannot be disguised, legitimized, or mythologized by fantasies about race or gender. This development can be seen, if you like, as the coming to the surface of that deeper historical content we first posited: if the longevity plot is really about radical social change, then its working out is bound to involve the violence and collective convulsion of just such struggles as we begin to find inscribed here in a second moment. The modern developments of the genre then show the narrative consequences and possibilities of this content, as we will see.

But it is perhaps worth concluding with Shaw at this point, using a few final observations about *Back to Methuselah*, to develop another motif neglected until now—namely, the matter of the boredom of eternity. *Time Enough for Love* begins indeed with Lazarus's well-nigh terminal depression at the thought that as he had already done everything conceivable (in a life span of some two thousand years) there was no point to living any longer. It is something that the novel then seeks energetically to cancel—narratively, by way of the frontier motif itself; formally, by way of the *Thousand and One Nights* compendium; and libidinally, by fantasies about clones (and probably about bisexuality). The biographical old age of Shaw himself, who, haunted by Jonathan Swift's Struldbruggs, longed to die as passionately as T. S. Eliot's Cumaean Sybil, would seem to document the plausibility of the complaint. But we must decline to endorse this stereotypical wisdom and must rather insist that boredom itself, like the fear of death, is always the disguised expression of something else. This becomes much clearer when we adjust the valences from the individual to the collective, when the complaint about the boredom of Utopias can much more clearly be seen to be so much propaganda for the excitement of market competition.

What is more interesting in Shaw's play is the displacement or inflection of the boredom motif toward what he calls discouragement, the morbid and suicidal quasi-physical feeling short-lifers experience in the presence of the long-lived, who have by now become, in the fourth play of the pentateuch, virtually a different species and are in the last play, or ultimate Utopia ("As Far as Thought Can Reach"), transformed into an oviparous life-form that sheds most of its bodily, formerly human, interests after the fourth year (the "boredom" of this now being remotivated as a kind of childishness). Discouragement, however, marks a kind of reversal of the power relations not unlike the great "thought-experiment" of H. G. Wells's *The War of the Worlds* (1898), in which the genocides of colonial peoples are redirected on Europe itself so that the "civilized" can learn what it feels like for a change. Here too the short-lifers—our own species—have lost the class struggle with the alternate society and the alternate Utopian beings; and the cultural envy of the traditional ruling classes has given way to the pain of the vanquished. It is the obverse of Shaw's picture of lateral or preconscious conversion; here too discouragement is both physical and a matter of deeper preconscious awareness and conviction that has little enough to do with the conscious mind. It is indeed one of the grand and dramatic merits of SF as a form that it can thus win back from the sheerly psychological or subjective such expressive powers of pathology—depression, melancholy, morbid passion—and place this material in the service of collective drama; but it may not be so important to insist, for insiders, on what must be stressed for the benefit of outsiders to SF as such: namely, that the unique new possibilities of this representational discourse—which has come to occupy something of the functions of the historical novel in the beginning of the bourgeois age—are social, political, and historical far more than they are technological or narrowly scientific.

Still, it is in the direction of science and technology that the longevity plot leads in our own time, and I will conclude with a few comments on the distinctiveness of the latest, post-Heinlein, fortunes of the genre—a characterization I scarcely mean to be understood in purely chronological terms, since books like Robert Sheckley's *Immortality, Inc.* (1958), Clifford D. Simak's *Why Call Them Back from Heaven?* (1967), and Robert Silverberg's *To Live Again* (1969)—all from the 1950s or 1960s—precede *Time Enough for Love* in linear time at the same time that they largely anticipate and foreshadow a novel like Joe Haldeman's *Buying Time* (1989), which I take to be characteristic of current contemporary or postcontemporary works in this particular form.

Paradoxically, the new narrative mutation is now far better equipped to navigate the problem of representing longevity as an event by the way in which the question regarding the appropriate contemporary technology is appealed to as a stand-in or substitute for the thing itself. Thus, in Haldeman, the rejuvenation process itself, which might be expected to entail the corniest battery of traditional SF wonder-working medicines and machinery, is displaced by two innovations: it needs to be renewed every so often, and at each renewal one's entire fortune must be given to the corporation (whence an interesting subplot of an investment nature emerges). The absence of medical and technological details is motivated, however, as it already was in Heinlein (whose delight in village explanations did not that way lie), in this manner: the whole thing is so agonizingly painful that the subject represses all memory of it. I suppose that the most graphic way of handling this properly technological moment is the idea of changing bodies, as in Sheckley (or even, secondarily, in Silverberg); but that brings us close to fantasy and the occult, as indeed the survival of the category of zombies, poltergeists, and the like in Sheckley's novel testifies (in a virtually autoreferential comment). The most chilling representation of the subject is therefore one in which the camera ensures a kind of documentary objectivity: I refer to John Frankenheimer's great film, *Seconds* (1966), in which the embarrassing political questions—Where do the bodies come from? How is the organization itself structured?—receive the grimmest answers. But there can be no doubt that the ultimate displacement is one in which longevity and immortality are represented by their opposite, and the virtually nonnarrative idea of living forever is made into a story you can tell by way of the deep freeze that precedes it (sleep or suspension now taking the place of living as a narratable event). It remained for Philip K. Dick's *Ubik* (1969) to produce in advance something like the metanarrative of this now conventional narrative and raise visceral questions about our vulnerability during this half-life condition, questions that are themselves, as we shall see, displaced political ones.

For it is finally the political overtones that save the new paradigm from regressing into some older science-and-technology SF paraphernalia of an outmoded Golden Age type. The idea that, in the deepening conservatism of the Reagan years and beyond, SF has regressed into more exclusively scientific interests (or better still, that, in a kind of Eliot-like dissociation of sensibility, its energies have been divided between just such a return to science, on the one hand, and a surrender to multivolume fantasy production, on the other) seems a plausible enough assertion, which it would nonetheless be advisable to nuance. For I think that the contemporary fascination with hard science tends to be as sociological as it is epistemological, and this not least because of the massive co-optation of pure science in the United States by business and defense research of all kinds. But this means that if we are interested in contemporary science, it is not only in the theories but in the very mechanics of experimentation—the grant procedures, the lobbying whereby the necessary laboratories (which can range from a giant celestial telescope to expensive underground shooting ranges for rare electrons) are funded. And this leads on finally to an interest (still sociological) in the psychology of the newer scientists who have, perhaps since *The Double Helix*, begun to replace traditional artists as the characterological disguises and distorted expressions of the representation of what Utopian, nonalienated work might look like. But, clearly enough, in the moment we become interested in scientific activity as a collective or guild matter, in terms of professionalism and socially determined psychological dispositions and aptitudes—in other words, in yuppie science, if I dare put it that way—in that moment we are not far from the convulsive reappearance of general politics as such.

How could it be otherwise in a situation in which the most intimate psychological problems of geriatric care and contraceptive medicine, and the still exceedingly physical matters of the homeless as well as of the massive and systematic administration of drugs to elderly and psychiatric patients, are everyday media concerns; in which the salaries of what are euphemistically called health care providers are debated with as much acrimony as the yearly bonuses of the great business executives; in which the privatization of hospitals becomes a matter of profit and business, and investment is solicited for the so-called health industries as a whole? In this atmosphere, not only are the arrangements of all professional guilds, including those of the scientists, drawn back into an instant micropolitics, but the kinds of political privilege specifically suggested by health care can only be magnified to panic levels by the addition of the chance that one might be selected to live forever, presumably on the basis of a cash down payment.

It has been said that one of the most remarkable political revolutions, one of the grandest moments in the history of human freedom, occurred on that day in the Egyptian Fifth Dynasty (in the third millennium B.C.) when immortal life, hitherto the privilege of the elite, was extended to the Egyptian population as a whole. If this is so for a phantasm, so will it be for a scientific fantasy in which the representation of long life for a few is bound to raise the inevitable issue—a most embarrassing one ideologically, but a happy, welcome, and productive one on the level of narrative construction and storytelling—of the attitude of all the others to this ultimate form of special privilege. Free enterprise ideology in the United States was always stimulated by the fantasy that under the rules of the game you (or your children) had the outside chance to strike it rich; but the new fantasy of extended life can no longer be used that way; it now serves a divisive ideological function of excluding the anonymous demographies of the only-too-mortal.

For fantasy is also a harsh mistress and includes its own ironclad reality principle. You cannot satisfactorily daydream about living forever without first settling the practical matter of how those who do not live forever are going to be handled: fantasy demands a certain realism in order to gain even provisional or ephemeral libidinal and aesthetic credit, and this is indeed the deeper truth-mechanism of narrative itself (and the source of the adage about trusting the tale rather than the teller and his own personal ideology). However a story may originate in private wish fulfillment, it must end up disguising its private subjectivity and repairing all the non-functioning machinery,[5] building a village behind the Potemkin façade, dealing with the sheerly logical contradictions the Unconscious has left behind it in its haste—in short, shifting the attention of the aesthetic spectator from the gratification of the wish to its far less appealing preconditions in the real, and thereby becoming in the process transformed from the expression of an ideology to its implicit critique.

In the case of longevity or immortality, I would not want this critique to be taken in any moralizing sense. I am indeed astonished and appalled at the degree of residual moralism still inherent in this topic: it surely has some relationship to the traditional anti-Utopian motif of ultimate boredom I referred to, although the scarcely veiled motivation of this is political and thereby a little less complicated than the insistence of so many writers on the subject that it would be evil to live forever, that true human existence requires a consent to mortality, if only to make room for our children's children; that hubris and egotism are to be denounced as prime elements in this particular fantasy about the supreme private property, not merely of having a self but of having it live forever. All that may be so, but I would be very embarrassed to argue it this way, and there is certainly an aroma of *ressentiment* or sour grapes to be detected in this extraordinary puritanism, which may simply reflect the great facility accorded to writers by simple religious and ethical paradigms, as opposed to the more strenuous business of imagining the social itself.

I conclude by suggesting two levels of the political in recent SF longevity paradigms: on the more global level, what is reflected is clearly the increasing class polarization of the advanced countries of late capitalism (in the United States, we are told, 1 percent of the population now owns 80 percent of the wealth). On this level, it does not seem far-fetched to argue that the motif of some special privilege of long life offers a dramatic and concentrated symbolic expression of class disparity itself and a way to conveniently express the passions that it cannot but arouse. But here one would want to add in something of the history of the form and suggest that the new paradigm marks a modification of the older, only-too-familiar near-future paradigms of overpopulation, ecological disaster, and the like. The longevity novel would thus stand as an enlargement of the possibilities of the near-future subgenre, deploying the attempt to imagine future technologies in the service of the expression of deeper and more obscure fears and anxieties.

The hermeneutic model we have proposed above—deeper meaning hidden within the text, behind, below the surface, like an "unconscious" of the text that needs to be interpreted out—is no longer a very popular one in this age of surfaces and decentered, textualized consciousness. Another model may therefore also be suggested, namely that of allegory: a structure in which a more obscure train of thinking attaches itself parasitically to a second, an-other (*allos/agoreuo*) line of figuration, through which it attempts to think its own, impossible, as yet only dimly figured thought. So it was by way of death and existential anxiety, along with the fantasy of living forever, that Shaw's play tried to think through its imperial content, at the very moment of the agony of the British empire itself: by way of similar affective content, but at another time and in another place, that Heinlein invoked fantasies of the family and the frontier, and attempted to produce high-technological and far-future images of both as viable forms. In the most recent SF texts on longevity, however, what seems to be the deeper secondary line of reflection and allegorical intellection is the increasing institutionalization and collectivization of late modern or postmodern social life, as that seems primarily embodied in the vast transnational corporation, bigger than most governments, and virtually impossible to modify or control politically.

In this material, for the moment at least, the political dilemma is at one with the representational one: the problem of bringing the great corporations under political control is the same as the problem of mapping their presence in our daily lives, of perceiving them, of giving them expression and articulation of a narrative as well as a cognitive type. In earlier periods of SF (to limit ourselves to that prescient registering apparatus), the great corporations coexisted with small businesses and their more humane ethos, as in Philip K. Dick for example, or else called forth over against themselves individualistic rebels and heroes of a classic populist-style revolt, as in Frederik Pohl and C. M. Kornbluth's *The Space Merchants* (1953). In our particular longevity subgenre, it is surely Norman Spinrad's remarkable *Bug Jack Barron* (1969)—a high point of a certain 1960s narrative ethos and still full of surprising vitality—that marks the exhaustion of the paradigm of heroic revolt, beyond which, however, there stretches the faceless anonymity of the multinational or transnational corporation of the present day, as that began to emerge after the winding down of the Vietnam War (in the Allende coup, for example).

But it is precisely that anonymity that poses questions not merely for narrative—problems of agency and actant of anthropomorphism and personification, indeed of event and diegetic change—but also for political praxis as well. The transnational structures have of course found a different kind of expression in the sheer euphoria and delirium of cyberpunk, where their cybernetic networks are affirmed with all the excitement of the high and the nonstop production of new language and new figuration. It may not be inappropriate, then, in closing, to see the new longevity narrative as the other face of that, the bad trip, the obscure and deep-rooted depression in the face of an uncertain future, in which the function of immortality is only to revivify images of death.

Notes

1. George Bernard Shaw, *Back to Methuselah* (New York: Brentano's, 1921), 131. Later page references in the text preceded by *BM* are to this edition.
2. Karel Capek, *The Makropoulos Secret* (1922; Boston: International Pocket Library, 1975), 81.
3. Robert A. Heinlein, *Time Enough for Love* (New York: Berkley Books, 1973), 283. A later page reference in the text preceded by *TEL* is to this edition.
4. See Slavoj Zizek, *For They Know Not What They Do* (London: Verso, 1991).
5. The classic analysis remains Sigmund Freud's "Creative Writers and Day-Dreaming," in *The Complete Psychological Works of Sigmund Freud*, vol. 9, translated under the general editorship of James Strachey, with Anna Freud, Alix Strachey, and Alan Tyson (1908; London: Hogarth Press, 1959), 141–53.

Part II

Science and Immortality

The Immortality Myth
and Technology

Steven B. Harris

Since the 1960s, when Joseph Campbell's *The Hero with a Thousand Faces* (1949) was read on many campuses, and since Campbell's 1988 interviews with Bill Moyers made his work more popular, people have looked at mythology in a new light. We thought we knew what a myth was: a weird story that people in *other* cultures told. *Our* stories were "religion" or "scripture" and were not weird at all; in fact, Joseph Campbell (with tongue firmly in cheek) once defined myth as "someone else's religion."

Myth is not only religion, of course; it is something more inclusive, broadly encompassing such things as rituals and beliefs. But myth is especially the collection of stories we tell to give ourselves a narrative psychological framework with which to deal with the world. In that larger sense, myth includes (but is not limited to) any story that answers the difficult questions of life:

> Who am I?
> Where did I come from?
> Where am I going?
> What is the far future going to be like?
> What is expected of me?
> Who are the heroes? (What is the Good? What defines *Cool*?)
> What is going to happen to me when I die?

People need to have answers for these questions (even if the answers are insupportable fantasy), because excessive worry about them may detract

from basic survival efficiency. Psychology experiments show that compared with objective assessment, people with normal, "healthy" mentali-
ties consistently *overestimate* their own abilities and strengths, while de-
pressed people are more realistic in such judgments. Why would nature
saddle our species with a normal mental state that provides an unrealistic
worldview? The answer may lie in the fact that anxiety saps strength and
ruins performance (as Olympic athletes know), so it may be worth a small
cost in objectivity to be rid of it. Thus a major function of myth (and
human culture) is to relieve anxiety by answering unanswerable questions.
Karl Marx called religion the opiate of the masses, but perhaps he would
have said today (given modern pharmacology) that religion is the Valium
of the masses. The same can be said of superstition—another name for
"other people's religion."

Of course, there is also much art in myth. Myths are not factual, but
that does not mean that in some sense they are not true. As Campbell reminds us, all metaphors are in the narrow sense lies (the Moon is not *really*
a ghostly galleon tossed on cloudy seas). Myths are metaphors—metaphors for something that cannot be said another way; they are stories that
speak to the old and basic part of human consciousness that holds cultural
programming.

Mythic stories resemble (to adopt a technical metaphor) the programming in "read-only memory" chips of a computer—programming that is
more or less permanent. Once one is culturally programmed the first time,
one is programmed for good; and after a certain age, new cultural myths
will sound foreign. As missionaries can attest, mythic reprogramming
may not be completely successful because of this effect. The same effect
appears when people lose faith later in life—remember Bertrand Russell's
thesis that Catholic atheists are quite different from Protestant atheists.

Much of our cultural programming is in stories, and at least since
James Joyce's idea of the "monomyth," one can argue that there are only a
few basic stories and all good tales are variations on them. The love story,
for example, in all its permutations, never seems to pall if told well. There
are creation myths, including a cycle of myths involving feminine forces
and goddesses (as Robert Graves reminds us), that seem important in artistic inspiration. On the masculine side, there are stories of the mythic
hero, an often semidivine, usually male adventurer on a quest or journey
to win some victory before returning home with the power he has won.
(The traditional hero, both masculine and admirable, is now out of fash-

ion in university English departments, but Campbell's paradigms work best for the science fiction themes we will cover in this essay.)

Though the hero may be semidivine, many tales insist that he is at least partly human, and thus mortal. The rules of conduct are manifestly different for gods, who are beyond morality, and many Greek myths about divine behavior (especially as retold in Latin) are as amoral as modern soap operas. Morality and the question of "the Good," however, are important for mortal humans (who have a limited time to learn from mistakes), so the tale of the mortal hero is often a morality play. Such tales are often stories of a mortal human who manages, as a hero, to make of himself something more. (The god-heroes in Eastern literature show us that no rule is without exceptions.) Since the hero is usually mortal, one of the oldest and most popular of the hero myths is of the hero who seeks immortality. These myths, and the way they (as cultural programs) have been employed to deal with the psychological challenges of real and anticipated advances in technology and medicine, form the subject of this essay.

Tales of resurrection have probably been around for as long as people. Neanderthal graves have been found to contain food and tools, which would have been included only if people thought the deceased might one day need them. We can infer from this that Neanderthals had a fairly complex language, since it would seem impossible to communicate something as abstract as "life after death" with grunts and barks. By this loose reasoning we can also guess that Neanderthals even had a culture, and that their culture told immortality stories.

The oldest written story known is the five-thousand-year-old Sumerian tale of a hero-king seeking immortality—*Gilgamesh*. Heroes can be semidivine as well as royal, and King Gilgamesh is two-thirds god and one-third man. His human part makes him mortal, and, realizing that he is one day going to die, he starts looking for the secret of life. Although he comes tantalizingly close to immortality, he finds he cannot have it, and Gilgamesh becomes the first tragic hero.

Almost every culture has a divine but mortal hero in search of immortality (though he is usually more successful than Gilgamesh), and I can mention only a few here (Adonis, Tammuz, Dionysus, etc.). One of the most important, however, is Osiris, a god who came to Egypt to be a teacher but was assassinated and dismembered (though fully divine, gods may still be vulnerable). Reassembled by his divine brother Horus, Osiris becomes God of the Dead. His sacred name is used in the ritual in which the dead journey through the underworld to be immortally reunited with the breath of life. Egyptian society was the first to link immortality and resurrection with human technology—here, the technology of mummification—but application of the technology was ritualistic and thoroughly religious.

The biblical Pharisees believed in the resurrection of the dead—as the Sadducees did not—and the myth of the resurrected hero was, according to Matthew, present in Palestine in the time of Jesus. In Matthew 16:14, Jesus asks the disciples what people are saying that he (Jesus) is. They reply in part that some people think he is really John the Baptist—who had been beheaded by this time (Matthew 14)—so the poor disciples are here repeating the equivalent of a modern tabloid story: a myth of a popular hero who is killed and comes back to life again to work miracles. And all this is (according to Matthew) *before* Jesus' crucifixion. Thus, even those who take the New Testament literally must admit that mythic folk stories of the return of a popular dead figure were as widespread then as they are now.

In fact, resurrected hero stories occur in all cultures. When the Jesuit missionaries of the Roman Catholic church reached the New World, they found that some of the natives' resurrection myths were so close to the Christian one that they believed the stories to be the work of the devil. A more Jungian view is that these archetypal stories reflect the way the human collective unconscious (or, if you prefer, neural architecture) is constructed. In other words, if we humans do not have a God-shaped place in our souls, we may have a "resurrected-hero-myth-shaped" place in our psychological makeup.

What happens mythologically when the resurrected person is not a hero and no official religious process is involved? There has always been a darker side to resurrection stories. It may be fine, even expected, for kings and demigods to return from death; but people do not always want the same for more mundane relatives, particularly in times and areas where resources are scarce. The possibility that the dead may return is a source of anxiety, and it is the social function of myth to deal with it. In mythology, the newly dead (unless royal) are always dangerous unless properly dealt with, and they may continue to give trouble to the living until they have completely decayed to safe bone. It is common in many cultures, in fact, to ritually treat a new corpse to ensure that it stays in the grave and does not become a revenant.[1]

Many mal-resurrection myths probably stemmed from misunderstandings of what happens to unembalmed human bodies after burial. We now know that natural decay processes can make corpses look fatter. The dead may exhibit a discharge of blood from the mouth, and the skin may briefly appear more, not less, lifelike. Unsophisticated people who saw these changes might have inferred that the corpse had been out and about, feasting on blood.[2] A collection of such stories loosely inspired one enduring personification of evil immortality and resurrection—Bram Stoker's *Dracula* (1897).

The walking mummy of the Boris Karloff movie *The Mummy* (1932) is a close relative of the vampire. In mythic terms, resurrection from death is possible, but without a standard religious mechanism, or at least a royal or divine hero-patron (like Osiris or Jesus), such resurrections are evil and can be expected to produce monsters. In the case of the vampire and the mummy, the creature roaming about is a living dead man who is no longer the original person but rather a transformed and murderous demon. In fiction, as in myth, the general message to the public about coming back from the dead is: "Do not try it without the religious seal of approval."

Before returning to mal-resurrection, we must consider a second theme—technology and medical progress. A critical element in science fiction is the speculative impact of technology on people and culture, and technical progress and its implications have made the mythic vampire and his cousins more immediate in our time. Dracula and the mummy are rather recent figures in the history of horror, and as immortal personifications of mal-resurrection, they are recognizably the literary grandchildren of Mary Shelley. Long before Shelley, however, came certain developments in resuscitation that made people think differently about nonreligious resurrection.

Historically, mouth-to-mouth resuscitation is suggested in the Bible (II Kings 4). Though the story is a bit garbled and like an earlier story of a child's resuscitation (I Kings 17), both stories contain descriptive elements of chest compression; there is clearly something more than mysticism going on here. For centuries, however, the Western world made little progress in the matter. In the Middle Ages, when most advances in medical science were made by Moslems, Arabic medical books told a little-known secret passed down from midwife to midwife: if one blew in the nostrils of a stillborn infant, it sometimes began breathing. We know that Arab physicians experimentally attempted to resuscitate corpses with bellows, but word of this work was not widespread either.

The development of the printing press in the fifteenth century changed everything. Suddenly written knowledge was relatively cheap to own. Science, whose treasure trove was a wealth of boring experimental detail that did not lend itself to oral tradition, particularly benefited from the invention. In fact, soon after the invention of this key device there came not only the Renaissance and the Reformation but a scientific revolution as well.

One of the major books of the scientific revolution was Andreas Vesalius's (1514–64) atlas of the human body, which included techniques for resuscitating asphyxiated dogs with bellows. The implications were clear. Paracelsus (1493–1541), an alchemist and perhaps the greatest physician of his age, was said to have tried resuscitating a corpse using bellows, a trick he may have picked up from Arabic medical writings. Doctors eventually learned (possibly from laymen) that simple mouth-to-mouth resuscitation sometimes worked on recently asphyxiated adults as well as on newborns.

By the 1740s, several cases of successful mouth-to-mouth resuscitation had been reported, the most famous of which was Tossach's 1744 report of the resuscitation of a clinically dead coal miner (no breath or heartbeat) who had been overcome after descending into a burned-out mine. By the 1760s, in the wake of such reports, some groups advocating the resuscitation of drowned persons had sprung up in Europe. In 1774 a society was founded in London to promulgate the idea that "dead" people in some cases were not dead. Called, after a bit of experimentation, the Society for the Recovery of Persons Apparently Drowned, the organization quickly evolved into the Humane Society (still later, with official patronage and funding, it became the Royal Humane Society, which it remains to this day).

The Humane Society advocated techniques that were highly advanced. Three months after its founding, for example, a society member had the opportunity to minister to a three-year-old child named Catherine Greenhill who had fallen from an upper-story window onto the flagstones below and was pronounced dead at the scene. The member, an apothecary named Squires, was there within twenty minutes, and history records that he gave the clinically dead child several shocks through the chest with a portable electrostatic generator (!). This treatment caused her to regain pulse and respiration, and she eventually (after a time in coma) recovered fully.

The resuscitation of Catherine Greenhill, probably the first successful cardiac defibrillation, followed earlier suggestions by American scientist Benjamin Franklin and others that electricity might "revivify" the human body—and so it proved able to do in selected circumstances. In 1788 a

royal medal was given to Humane Society member Charles Kite, who not
only advocated the resuscitation of victims in cardiac arrest with bellows
and nasolaryngeal intubation but had also developed an electrostatic revivi-
fying machine that used Leyden jar capacitors in a way exactly analogous
to the DC capacitative countershock of the modern cardiac defibrillator.
(To my mind all these contraptions are as fantastic as devices in a Flint-
stones cartoon, yet they actually existed. A time-traveling physician from
today could not have created a better resuscitation kit with off-the-shelf
technology of the time.)[3] But the amazing progress in medicine in the late-
eighteenth century did not last. From the first, dark images from the
human psyche gathered in resistance to the new ideas. Technology never
intervenes in a major way into human life without creating new anxieties
and social backlash. Resuscitation had its problems.

To begin with, the eighteenth-century discovery that "death" was not a
sure and objective state did not sit well in the public mind. Charles Kite
believed that not even putrefaction was a sure sign of true death, since it
might be due to advanced scurvy (!). However conservative this view
might have been for Kite and his medical agenda, the public had its own
concerns: If one could be mistaken for dead, like Shakespeare's Juliet,
when one was in fact revivable, what did that imply? The answer, of
course, was horrifying. One could be buried alive. Soon after the first
word-of-mouth reports of adult resuscitation began surfacing in the
1730s, French author Jacques Winslow published a book descriptively titled *The Uncertainty of the Signs of Death and the Danger of Precipitate
Interments and Dissections*. Now the real concern with the difficulty of
defining death in a technical age was out of the bag: *What if you got the
diagnosis wrong?*

The realization that "death" was not necessarily *death* inspired Edgar
Allan Poe's psychological thriller "The Premature Burial" (1844); but
Poe, in popularizing the problem for nineteenth-century America, actually
came late to the controversy. In eighteenth-century Europe the fear of premature burial or dissection was not just the preoccupation of writers of
the macabre; whole classes of people were affected, albeit in different
ways. Upper-class persons fitted coffins and crypts with special signaling
devices to alert the outside world in case the occupant should inexplicably
revive. The lower classes had problems, too. Anatomical dissection, long a
part of the punishment for heinous crimes because it denied the malefac-
tor an intact bodily identity and grave, now took on a special meaning. To

wit: it killed. Historian Ruth Richardson describes this incident which took place in the 1820s when a dissecting anatomist at Carlisle prison was killed, and another severely wounded, by friends of an executed man:

> Although . . . an extreme reaction, it was certainly the case that hanging the corpse in chains on a gibbet was popularly regarded as preferable to dissection. What later incredulous commentators seem to have missed or misunderstood was that in eighteenth and early nineteenth century popular belief, not only were the anatomists agents of the law, but they could be the agents of death. Genuine cases were known of incomplete hangings, in which the "dead" were brought back to life, and plans for celebrated corpse-rescues centered on the possibility that the noose had not fully done its work. Folk-tales circulated about famous criminals revived by friends. . . . It was popularly understood that the surgeon's official function and interest in a murder's corpse was not to revive, but rather to destroy it. Dissection was a very *final* process. It denied hope of survival—even the survival of identity after death.[4]

By the early nineteenth century, when the riot over the dissection of the hanged man at Carlisle took place, things had reached a fever pitch. Technology had intruded into the macabre. The horrific potential of the new electromechanical resuscitative technology had its first fruitful literary influence on Mary Shelley, who first had set out to write a ghost story but instead produced *Frankenstein* (1818), a cautionary tale of the technological resuscitation of a monster constructed from pieces of corpses by an experimenter. "Frightful must it be," writes Shelley of her monster in an 1831 introduction to the book, "for supremely frightful would be the effect of any human endeavour to mock the stupendous mechanism of the Creator of the world."[5] Given the spirit of the times, Shelley's story touched a public nerve as though with one of the new electrical machines, and Frankenstein's monster was an instant sensation. In keeping with its archetypal nature, the tale, completed while Shelley was still only nineteen, remains her most famous and enduring work.

After the *Frankenstein* sensation, something strange happened. Shortly after the book's publication, the new enlightened medicine began to go out of favor, and the science of resuscitation suffered on both the technical and mythological fronts for several reasons. Mouth-to-mouth resuscitation was discarded in favor of bellows, the bellows in turn was discarded for technical reasons, and earlier promising methods were never brought back. Once it was discovered that human breath has less oxygen in it than air, no one bothered to ask if the difference was clinically significant;

though there is no proof of art influencing reality here, if one looks closely at what happened it is almost as if the culture deliberately turned its back on the whole idea of revivification.

Electrical resuscitation fared no better than mechanical "respiration" (ventilation). The phenomenon of electricity was quickly transformed into a quack cure by the practice of "galvanism" (passing mild shocks through the body to cure disease), and its reputation was accordingly tarnished. Perhaps even more devastating, the charming new force was transmuted into a powerful and dangerous energy by the giant alternating current transformers of George Westinghouse (maligned for their deadliness in a rival Edison PR campaign) and also by the newfangled American electric chair (1890). Technologies, like people, may suffer from social stigmas. Shelley had originally not specified the method of the revivification of her monster, but her literary friends (she tells us) had been discussing galvanism a few hours before the vision of the monster came to her in a nightmare. By 1931, in electrified America, Frankenstein's monster came to the movies electrically charged, and soon the electric chair was producing its own monsters in the cinema (Karloff's *The Walking Dead* [1936]). Amid these social transformations, therapeutic electric shock, so full of promise in the 1790s, simply disappeared. It did not again come into its own for lifesaving purposes (even for psychiatric purposes, for that matter) until about the same time that resuscitative breathing was being reassessed, *in the middle of the twentieth century.*

For decades after Shelley wrote it (indeed, to this day), *Frankenstein* colored resuscitation as it appeared in science fiction. An exception is Poe's 1845 story "Some Words with a Mummy," which is social commentary rather than horror. The mummy of the story, resurrected by galvanism, is one of a race of ancient Egyptians who perfected suspended animation and used it to travel rapidly through time for pleasure, as tourists and revisionist historians. The tale is one of the first positive stories about suspended animation.

Poe had an antecedent for the idea, for "Some Words with a Mummy" echoes some earlier optimistic thoughts by Dr. John Hunter (1728–93), who in 1766 experimentally froze live fish in an attempt to prove that humans might be able to see the far future by being intermittently frozen for long periods (the fish died and Hunter abandoned the idea). Another scientist who took an interest in suspended animation was Hunter's contemporary, Benjamin Franklin, who not only foresaw advanced treatments for aging as a result of science but in a letter expressed a wish to be preservatively embalmed "in a cask of Madeira wine, with a few friends," to see eventually what might become of his beloved America.[6] Franklin thus was not only one of the first to speculate about seeing the future in this way, he was also the first to see that such thoughts inevitably move one to want to take along some of one's social network. Poe's story and the private views of Hunter and Franklin stand in contrast with the more common and alienating views of long-delayed revival of *single* individuals, a time-travel-to-the-future genre that perhaps began with Washington Irving's dark and poignant "Rip Van Winkle" (1820) and continued with H. G. Wells's time traveler and sleeper.

Poe's other exploration of attempts to bypass the effects of death, written about the same time as "Some Words with a Mummy," is more typically macabre. In "The Facts in the Case of M. Valdemar" (1845), Valdemar dies while in a deep hypnotic trance. So deep is the trance that, although his heartbeat and breathing have stopped, Valdemar's tongue still obeys commands. ("I *have been* sleeping—and now—now—*I am dead*," he states in one of the most famous lines in horror literature.) For seven months this state of suspended animation continues, with the dead body (save for the horribly moving tongue) locked in rigor mortis but basically unchanging. Finally, the experimenters decide to end the trance, and the hypnotized man turns, in less than a minute, into "a nearly liquid mass of loathsome—of detestable putrescence."[7]

In the long-delayed and unnaturally rapid decay of Poe's released hypnotic subject we see the traditional fate of staked vampires, the other escapees of traditional mortality. As H. Rider Haggard's *She* (1886), Oscar Wilde's *The Portrait of Dorian Gray* (1897), and James Hilton's *Lost Horizon* (1933) all show, slowing or arresting the natural aging or dying process can run up a kind of cosmic credit card bill that may later come due all at once, with dire consequences. This suggests a cultural psychological heritage that views death and decay as inevitable forces that, like a bottled-up natural flow or pressure, may produce explosive and terrible results if held in abeyance even temporarily.

To be sure, such cosmic debt does not accrue to Shelley's monster, who does not age. In *Frankenstein*, the price the monster pays for its artificial life is alienation and social ostracism (the monster is horribly ugly). The monster is also neglected and abandoned by its only "parent"—its creator. With few exceptions, however, secularly resurrected figures in fiction usually pay a more direct price for their existence. The same is true of those who direct the reanimation, although (as in W. W. Jacobs's 1902 story "The Monkey's Paw") the ignorant may escape the ultimate price.

After Poe, the next major commenter on scientific reanimation of the dead was that gentle but slightly unhinged dropout from life, H. P. Lovecraft. His first tale, "Herbert West, Reanimator" (1922), is a tribute to Shelley, though it would be some time before Lovecraft was able to explore the psychology of horror as deftly as Shelley. "Reanimator" is the story of a young medical student of a materialist bent who seeks to reanimate corpses with chemicals. He is only partly successful—his reanimated beings are murderous, even if they were good while alive (one demonic monster was a kindly and philanthropic dean of medicine). Like Shelley, Lovecraft carefully never gives any of his reanimated corpses what it takes to be human: those bodies that are whole behave like animals, and those that have human intelligence and understanding are horribly mutilated. West's resurrections, like Shelley's, are mal-resurrections. In the end, West, the creator of the beings, is destroyed by them.

Lovecraft's reanimator stories have artistic and technical problems, and the prose is unusually florid (even for Lovecraft) and rather racist. Lovecraft sought to bury the stories, but with his death they took on lives of their own and were resurrected in many anthologies. There is a curiously archetypal sort of draw in the resurrection story, even if technically it is not up to par; and there is irony in the fact that these stories, which Lovecraft hated, remain his only works to make it to the screen (*Re-Animator* [1985] and *Bride of Re-Animator* [1989]) with reasonable fidelity.

Possibly for escapist reasons, the Great Depression triggered a spate of American films about horror, and in many cases their content was quite scientific and biologically realistic (it was not until 1945 that the smock of the mad scientist passed from biologist to physicist). *Frankenstein* (1931) features Karloff, who also played the title role in *The Mummy*. A few years later, after the success of Universal's *Son of Frankenstein* (1939), Columbia Pictures made five Karloff horror movies with more explicit themes of scientific life prolongation or resurrection. These followed aviator Charles Lindbergh and Nobelist Alexis Carrel's work on an artificial heart, and biochemist Robert Cornish's famous experiments reviving asphyxiated dogs in very much the manner used by Vesalius. (Cornish, in charming 1930s fashion, proposed to test his method on executed prisoners.) In *The Man They Could Not Hang* (1939) a doctor (Karloff) learns how to put humans in suspended animation with an artificial heart machine. The authorities mistake a suspended man for dead (the Juliet problem), and the doctor is sentenced to death. After he is hanged, a student uses the machine to resuscitate him. The revived Karloff is evil and vengeful, however, and tries to kill the people who convicted him. Another scientific resurrection has evidently failed to do anyone any good.

No positive view of scientific resuscitation or life prolongation was portrayed on film until the great Robert Wise movie *The Day the Earth Stood Still* (1951). In it, a humanoid alien named Klaatu visits Earth in a flying saucer, along with a giant robot named Gort. When he attempts to deliver a message to Earth's inhabitants, Klaatu is killed by the army. In a spectacular scene, Klaatu's body is recovered by Gort and returned to the saucer, where it is resuscitated with the aid of machinery inside the ship. Thereupon Klaatu, risen from the dead, is free to deliver his message and ascend to the heavens.

The Day the Earth Stood Still is, of course, a deliberate and shameless· biblical allegory—the resurrected hero myth recast in science fiction terms. Klaatu is a Christ figure (a sly touch is his pseudonym, "Mr. Carpenter") sent from Heaven to warn humankind of its sins. Although his coming is attended by wondrous events and he obviously has superhuman powers, he spends most of his time not with the great and mighty but with common folk and children. His uncommonness is all too apparent, however; Klaatu's teaching of the famous Einstein figure Professor Barnhardt (Sam Jaffe) is as much a personal self-revelation as that of the boy Jesus confounding the rabbis. Eventually, Klaatu does "go public," but this high priest of technology demonstrates his power not by calming the water but by calming and silencing the world's machines.

In keeping with the allegory, Klaatu is finally betrayed and murdered by the very people he came to warn. His body is taken to a jail cell in lieu of a tomb and guarded by soldiers. The cell is opened by a mechanical servant in place of an angel, and there is a resurrection, albeit a technological one. (Patricia Neal is the Mary Magdalene figure, asking the questions for us.) Eventually, his message delivered, Klaatu returns to his ship, which rises into the heavens. An interesting footnote: while sightings of flying saucers actually began in the 1940s, the flying saucer *cults* postdate this film.

The Day the Earth Stood Still is not a typical science fiction movie of its time because the alien beings are not seen as marauding monsters. Even more intriguing is the idea that high technology, as manifested in space transportation, would naturally go hand in hand with prolonged youth (Klaatu is seventy-eight but looks thirty-eight; his people live twice as long as earthlings). Another film of this era, *Earth vs. the Flying Saucers* (1956), also features geriatric aliens, but they come in space suits with built-in bifocals and hearing aids (a better name for the film might have been *Earth vs. the Galactic Nursing Home*). Here, the more conventional idea is that technological life extension leads to Struldbrugghood (the Tithonus Syndrome), hardly an appealing concept.

High technology is linked to advanced resuscitation capability in *The Day the Earth Stood Still*, but not to horror. This absence of horror is archetypally a bit odd, and possibly in consequence the movie was not made without controversy. Screenwriter Edmund H. North's script (an adaptation of a 1940 Harry Bates story, "Farewell to the Master") originally called for the alien Klaatu to be resuscitated by Gort and thereafter to go about his functionally immortal business. Unfortunately, the Breen Censorship Board (an autocratic self-censorship mechanism especially active during the cold war years) was scandalized by the idea of a robot bringing Klaatu to life ("Only God can do that!"). North's protestations that the movie was science fiction, and that the action in question involved genuinely unearthly alien technologies, got him nowhere.[8]

Eventually, a compromise was worked out: Klaatu invokes deity (in the final script Klaatu asserts piously that the power of life and death belongs only to the "Almighty Spirit") and admits his own mortality (the life conferred by the machine is good only "for a limited period" whose duration "no one can tell"—presumably meaning that your mileage may vary). With these changes, the Breen Board, satisfied that it had protected the public from the un-American idea of scientific immortality, withdrew its ban. The scene in which Klaatu explains that scientific resurrection is (in effect) not all it is cracked up to be stands as a monument to popular resistance to casting scientific progress in any form resembling God. (Notably, a similar bit of censorship is seen in the 1931 Frankenstein film: actor Colin Clive's famous words "It's alive!" are followed by the declaration "Now I know what it feels like to be God!" but this last was stricken from the soundtrack, even though the actor can still be seen mouthing it.)

If *The Day the Earth Stood Still* is a contender for the best science fiction movie ever made, it is partly because of its partial reworking of the old resurrection myth. The power of this theme may be gauged by the fact that the enormously successful *E.T.: The Extraterrestrial* (1982) pulls the very same psychological strings (as does the "*E.T.* rip-off" *Starman* [1984]). Again, in *E.T.*, we see the heavenly being visiting Earth with magic life-restoring powers (a glowing finger). Again an unenlightened government sends squads of soldiers to chase the visitor, who all the while is content to spend his time with common folk and children. Again we see the visitor's death and technological resurrection (the only difference being that in 1982 cardiac defibrillation was available, so they put that in). And again there is the ascension to the heavens, this time to heavenly parents. E.T., you see, is only a child.

Since Riverside, California, the site of the Fourteenth Annual Eaton Conference where this essay was first presented, is the cryonics capital of the world, I conclude my look at immortality myths and technology by describing the device of cold storage as seen in fictional and real pursuits of immortality.

Horror writers love the cold, and both Shelley and Poe (*The Narrative of Arthur Gordon Pym of Nantucket* [1837]) employed frozen backdrops to good effect. Later authors followed in this tradition. The first writer to employ cryogenic preservation for monsters was Lovecraft. In his novella *At the Mountains of Madness* (1931), an Antarctic expedition unearths frozen half-animal, half-vegetable creatures from an earlier age. In a now-hackneyed scene (but Lovecraft did it first!), a scientist dissects a creature while others are allowed to thaw unattended. The result is carnage. Later, it transpires that the monsters are an extinct intelligent species who long ago created all life on Earth—not only the familiar forms that led to humans, but also a race of servant monsters that later turned on their creators, Frankenstein style. In Lovecraft, even the monsters are troubled by monsters.

One of the primitive emotional responses Lovecraft seeks to evoke in his fiction is the human dread of friendlessness and isolation. He tugs at our fear, as social beings, of the most horrible and final kind of *alienation*, being cut off from all social contact while still remaining sentient. As I have already noted, this theme goes back to the start of the genre; *Frankenstein* may be more about the horrors of social alienation (child neglect, physical unattractiveness) than the horrors of scientific resurrection. (The Anne Rice vampire novels recently work this theme in parallel—her immortal vampires are alienated not only from our culture, but from their own as well).

Lovecraft, like Shelley (see *The Last Man* [1826]), seems to have been led to use many new fictional devices as a way to pull all the "fear of isolation" strings at once while keeping mystical events to a minimum. Lovecraft's readers are asked to confront the image of waking up in another body or a mechanical body; waking in a distant time, completely out of touch with all that you ever knew; or waking up as an isolated head after being reanimated by scientific means. So potent is the peculiar vision of horror in these themes for Lovecraft that he cannot even wish them on his monsters without empathy. Indeed, the narrator of *At the Mountains of Madness* at one point is moved to pity the resurrected Antarctic starfish-vegetable creatures because of their anachronistic plight in modern times, where they are beset by men and dogs:

> Poor devils! After all, they were not evil things of their kind. . . . Nature had played a hellish jest on them—as it will on any others that human madness, callousness, or cruelty may hereafter dig up in that hideously dead or sleeping polar waste—and this was their tragic homecoming. . . . That awful awakening in the cold of an unknown epoch—perhaps an attack by the furry, frantically barking quadrupeds, and a dazed defense against them and the equally frantic white simians with the queer wrappings and paraphernalia. . . . [W]hat had they done that we would not have done in their place?[9]

What indeed? Perhaps that is Lovecraft's opinion in a nutshell— resurrecting someone (even some *thing*) into social isolation is "madness, callousness, or cruelty." His cryogenic vegetable-scientists pay a double penalty—the penalty of alienation for being cryogenically suspended and the penalty of death for creating life scientifically (playing God). Monsters in later movies may also come frozen in ice, but no one will stop to wonder how they feel about it. The prototype for these later movies is *The Thing* (1951; from a story by John W. Campbell, Jr., no credit to Lovecraft), in which the vegetable thing found in Arctic ice is mimed by a young James Arness. Other less memorable efforts include *The Deadly Mantis* (1957) and *The Navy vs. the Night Monsters* (1961), and there is even a cold-preserved Frankenstein's monster in *The Evil of Frankenstein* (1964). In these films, monsters are simply monsters, and they do not sin.

This is more than one can say for Lovecraft's physicians, to whom we turn again. Lovecraft, perhaps the first writer to consider the cold as a method of preserving horrific creatures, may also have been the first to portray "dead" humans who refuse to be done with life. In "Cool Air" (1928), which obviously owes a great debt to Poe's "Valdemar," he tells us of Dr. Muñoz, a physician-scientist who, because of a strange illness, must keep his rooms very cold. The narrator, who befriends the lonely doctor, eventually finds that his new acquaintance has not only begun to exhibit a strange odor but is requiring lower and lower temperatures as time goes on. Eventually the air-conditioning fails, and while the narrator goes off to get a replacement part, the doctor dissolves in the manner of Valdemar. It turns out that he has been clinically dead for eighteen years but has preserved himself by means of the cold.

Does Lovecraft now generally get credit for the cryonics idea? Perhaps he should. One of his stories ("The Whisperer in Darkness" [1931]) uses the device of having creatures from another planet remove human brains into mechanical containers for shipment across space, a treatment that makes them functionally immortal. The treatment is used to excellent effect as a device for horror. The earthlings find themselves kidnapped, removed from their bodies as naked brains kept alive by machinery, and taken away into space by fungoid creatures from Pluto—again, the Lovecraftian attempt at ultimate alienation. It may or may not be coincidence that much the same technical idea was used by the next identifiable cryonics writer, Neil R. Jones, who published "The Jameson Satellite" in *Amazing Stories* (July 1931). In the story, a frozen astronaut, Professor Jameson, is discovered in Earth orbit in the far future by a race of alien robots, who resuscitate him by implanting his brain in a mechanical body. The fundamental difference between this story and Lovecraft's is that Lovecraft is after horror and Jones is not: Jameson eventually adapts and comes to believe that his strange lot is better than death.

Would life in the far future be worse than death? In 1935 *Time* magazine featured the predictions of a chemist named Ralph S. Willard, who claimed that he could freeze and resuscitate monkeys. Like Dr. Cornish, Willard proposed to use the process on convicts to store them more cheaply, on jobless people (until times got better), on would-be suicides (until depression could be cured), and finally (of course), on those curious about the future. We now know that Willard was a humbug, but we see him one last time before he disappears into the mists of science fiction history—as technical consultant to a Karloff film, *The Man with Nine Lives* (1940).

This movie, co-written by the man who wrote *The Man They Could Not Hang* (former Billy Bitzer cameraman Karl Brown), shares some key plot elements with that film. Again we see a scientist conducting experiments in human suspended animation. Again the authorities visit his lab, see a frozen man, and decide that a murder has occurred. This time, however, the scientist takes revenge for his arrest: he locks himself and the authorities (the coroner, district attorney, and sheriff) in a freezer in the basement of his island laboratory, where all undergo cryonic suspension. Ten years later they are rediscovered and revived by another researcher.

Again, however, in the Brown script the experience of resuscitation from sleep/death has turned scientist into mad scientist (the mal-resurrection), and he begins to kill his fellow suspendees in a series of cryonics experiments. In the end the police arrive and put an end to him.

The history of the real practice of cryonics is less dramatic, at least at its beginning. Heedless of Karloff's fate, a young soldier took up the idea of cryonics again in the 1940s. While he was recovering from wounds sustained in World War II, Robert C. W. Ettinger read "The Jameson Satellite." Then, in 1948, he wrote a cryonics science fiction story ("The Penultimate Trump") in which he first suggested the idea of a man dying of old age deliberately being frozen to wait for advances in *human* rejuvenation technology. Ettinger became a college physics teacher, and in 1962, in *The Prospect of Immortality* (eventually republished by Doubleday in 1964), he argued formally for a cryonics program to begin in the real world.

Ettinger's philosophy of cryonics was an outgrowth of the materialism begun by Democritus, Epicurus, and others and formally restated beginning with La Mettrie in France in the eighteenth century. To materialists, life was simply a mechanical and chemical process properly defined not in terms of metabolism but in terms of structural information. As early as 1702, Leeuwenhoek had noted that small organisms called rotifers could be dried, stored, and then brought back to life by exposing them to a little moisture. By the early 1970s it was known that small crustaceans and worms, and even mammalian embryos, cooled in liquid nitrogen or helium to the temperature where all metabolism stops, can be stored indefinitely.[10] Here was structure but no function. Ettinger argued that because frozen organisms can be revived, "life" is not something that necessarily disappears when an organism's metabolic machinery stops running.

In Ettinger's view, organisms are like automobiles: a nonfunctioning organism may not be permanently "dead" if whatever caused the failure in function is repairable. The only criteria that matter in revival are the same ones a mechanic would use to learn whether a damaged automobile is repairable: What was the original structure? Does enough structure remain to infer what *was* from what *is*? Are the tools necessary to effect the repairs available?

Ettinger argued that we do not have such tools today, but we may have them tomorrow. Just as the man whose heart stopped three hundred years ago was "dead" then, but might be revivable today, today's "dead" people might be resuscitated in the future. Thus, we now conduct autopsies on people who may be, by future standards, only very sick. If we could *deliver* such people to the future reasonably intact (as by cryogenic preservation), and if future doctors could also repair the damage done by freezing, then it would make sense to freeze people who are now given up on (pronounced dead) in the hope that something might be done for them later. In 1965, a devotee of Ettinger's ideas suggested that the preservation process be called *cryonics*, and so it was. The word is now in most dictionaries.

This is an essay about science and mythology, so let us return briefly to the myth of the resurrected hero. On December 15, 1966, Walt Disney died of lung cancer. Some of the reporters who covered the death had earlier that day also happened to cover a press conference announcing the formation of the Cryonics Society of California (the first cryonics society on the West Coast). Somewhere in the melee, a story surfaced that Disney himself had been frozen.

It is almost certain that there was nothing to the rumor, though Disney did apparently once express interest in cryonics. What makes the story interesting is not so much the rumor's truth or falsehood but rather its astonishing *power*. It was a rumor of amazing vitality, a rumor that would not die despite repeated attempts by the Disney family to drive a stake through its heart. It insinuated itself as fact into at least one biography of Disney, although there is not a shred of physical evidence to support it. To this day, the notion that the great animator awaits "reanimation" somewhere in cold storage may still come up in conversation (as late as 1993, a comic strip featured the body of Disney in a huge block of ice, under the banner "Disney on Ice"). In fact, this factoid is the only thing that many people in this country "know" about cryonics: that Disney had it done to himself.

All this is curious and ironic. But must we believe that it is inexplicable as well—a result of unpredictable public appetite for a story? In mythologic terms, the answer is no. In the Disney story we see some essential elements for a particular archetypal pattern—possible resurrection and the attempt to beat death. But perhaps just as important is the fact that Disney was a hero to most Americans, a man who symbolized magic, wonder, imagination, kindness, daring, love of children, and (not incidentally) great wealth. Disney even ruled over his own Magic Kingdom. That a man with such power would try for immortality is a story that fits wonderfully well into the collective unconscious. There is simply something about the tale that makes it "go," as there also seems to be about modern myths that such public heroes as John F. Kennedy (King Arthur of his own Camelot) or Elvis Presley (the King of Rock and Roll) somehow managed to beat death and are off in the wings somewhere, waiting to return. As the *National Enquirer* would say: "It tickles the public's fancy," which is merely a common way of saying that an archetypal theme is operating.

In any case, cryonics received its maximum press coverage with Disney's death. When a nonfamous man made arrangements to be frozen at "death" and then followed through with the process in January 1967, the news was lost in the coverage of the fatal Apollo 1 fire. That first man frozen to cryogenic temperatures, Professor James Bedford, remains unchanged today, submerged in liquid nitrogen at 320 degrees below zero at the Alcor Life Extension Foundation (now in Scottsdale, Arizona). Since 1967, sixty-two people have followed his example.[11]

Because it is a frank attempt by the unheroic hoi polloi to gain immortality scientifically, without invoking deity, cryonics evokes various reactions. Some religious believers view cryonics with distaste, as a sort of Tower of Babel (trying to get to Heaven with engineering). Many socialists and humanists see cryonics as overly individualistic and selfish. Others (especially those who define themselves by family and social ties) view cryonics with horror, since it has the potential for destroying such social ties.

In film, the lot of cryonically preserved people is generally hard. Individuals who are *involuntarily* cryonically suspended may get away with only a severe case of alienation (*Caveman* [1984], *Late For Dinner* [1991]), but anyone who deliberately attempts to cheat death is in for the full Frankenstein treatment. A 1985 made-for-television movie called *Chiller* (directed by Wes Craven) features a cryogenically suspended man who is revived, after which it is discovered that (in the style of Lovecraft) the revenant is now without a soul and utterly evil. When the executive producer of *Chiller* was asked how the writers had come up with the plot for CBS (which wanted a horror movie with a cryonics slant), he said, "We just asked everybody we knew what bothered them most about the cryonics idea."[12] Mythically, cryonics seems to be the recipient of the backlash against life extension and resuscitation generated by the mal-resurrection horror films and stories of the last fifty years. Norman Spinrad's *Bug Jack Barron* (1969) and Clifford D. Simak's *Why Call Them Back from Heaven?* (1967) see the cryonics industries and those who operate them as evil, as does a non-SF thriller with a cryonics background, Thomas Noguchi's *Physical Evidence* (1990).

Some actual encounters between the authorities and cryonicists, who have a rather unique worldview, have played out as though scripted for a horror film. In late 1987, when an elderly woman in poor health died and was frozen at the Alcor laboratory, there was an investigation of her death. In 1930s B-movie fashion, police and coroners visited the laboratory looking for her body, which they considered dead but which cryonicists considered to be in suspension and possibly revivable. At that time no cryonicist was aware of *The Man with Nine Lives*, but all would have sympathized with that movie's protagonist. Several cryonicists briefly went to jail for failure to produce the woman's cryogenically preserved remains, which had been hidden by her son to prevent an autopsy. The action was in keeping with the fine old "mad scientist" genre: a crazy researcher sees something more in the dead body than do "proper" authorities. In this case, the authorities never did get the remains and finally closed the case.

The "Juliet problem" is inevitable, as my earlier discussion of fiction and history shows. To cryonicists, someone whose heart has stopped but who has not yet suffered brain decay is not necessarily permanently dead, only metabolically disadvantaged (or "flexionally disabled" or "thermally different"—make up your own politically correct term). Cryonicists do not consider fresh corpses "things" but rather sick people ("patients"). This view is bound to cause friction with (say) a coroner who wants a body to dissect; we have already seen such violence erupting over the body of the hanged man being dissected at Carlisle prison.

At present, cryonics remains legal in California, but only after several court battles between cryonics organizations and the state, culminating with a final appellate court decision in June 1992. The California Board of Public Health took the odd public position that cryonics was illegal because there was no "cryonics" box to check on the standard VS-9 form that the state of California uses to keep track of the disposition of human remains. It became clear, however, that more philosophical and visceral problems were worrying the state. In one appeal before the court, for example, the attorney acting for the California Department of Health Services asked:

> Should cryonically suspended people be considered dead, or should a separate category of suspended people be created? How should such people be registered in official records? What happens to the estate and the assets of the "decedent" after the decedent is put in cryonic suspension? What would happen to such estate and assets if and when cryonic suspension is successful and the decedent is restored to life? Whose identity is the person to assume or be assigned and what of the record of the person's death?[13]

We hear in this the anxious voice of the peasant, worried that the dead will come back to trouble the living and reclaim goods that properly should belong to younger people. Once upon a time, an agency of the state of California actually argued that cryonics was illegal, that it had to stop until such anxiety-provoking questions were answered. "Whose identity would the [restored] person assume?" asked the state attorney, as though the answer might be something other than the obvious—demons, perhaps, or soulless zombies. Just below the surface we sense something more than a frustrated bureaucrat who does not know which form to use. Just below the surface is horror.

From the beginning of the scientific revolution, the emerging technology of resuscitation suggested that the process by which human beings leave existence is as gradual and hard to define as the process by which they enter it. From the beginning of human culture, myths have helped humankind deal with threats like death, and some of these stories have been changed in the scientific age to help humans deal philosophically with limited resuscitation. Along the way, however, there have been plenty of nightmares.

In philosophical and religious matters, a fundamentalist is someone with no tolerance for ambiguity. Fundamentalists are often Aristotelians— binary thinkers who see only black and white in a world of continuous analog changes and shades of gray. In matters of death, the fundamentalist role is played by vitalists and the legal views of modern states (legal thinking is binary-Aristotelian in positing that all actions are either legal or illegal). Such people reject the ambiguity suggested by resuscitation or cryonics.

My thesis is that historically, many mal-resurrection stories have arisen as fundamentalist reactions to the ambiguities gradually introduced by science since the eighteenth century. Riots over dissections, fears of being buried alive, the hard-to-explain failure of resuscitation techniques to catch on in medicine for more than a century after they were invented, and California's attempts to suppress cryonics all show how the anxieties of vitalists have shaped society's ideas about resuscitation after a long period of clinical death.

In the literature of science fiction, from *Frankenstein* (our paradigm scientific resurrection story) to Poe, Lovecraft, and Stephen King's *Pet Sematary* (1983), scientific resurrection and resuscitation are rarely seen in a positive light. Nonhorror scientific resurrection stories (like *The Day the Earth Stood Still*) had to fight censorship because they failed to add enough of the *Frankenstein* voice. So strong has the literary tradition of horror become since *Frankenstein*, in fact, that even formerly positive stories of resurrection have been recast in darker terms: the walking mummy, for instance, reworks ancient Egyptian religious beliefs regarding technological resurrection, and in Nikos Kazantzakis's *The Last Temptation of*

Christ (1960) even the traditional Lazarus tale has mutated into a mal-resurrection.

Tales of "out-of-body" experiences now help us cope in mythic terms with short-term resuscitations. Most of these "just-so" stories involve having the soul jerked back and forth between the body and some kind of anteroom to Heaven (see, for instance, the movie *Flatliners* [1990]). Such stories work well enough to allow even vitalists to deal with the realities of everyday medicine. It is probable, however, that the mythic structure that helps us deal with such true-life situations is due shortly to come under more strain. Consider the following.

On June 10, 1988, a two-and-a-half-year-old girl fell into a mountain stream of snowmelt runoff near her home in Utah, was swept beneath the surface, and drowned. Her mother called the rescue squad. The rescue workers could not locate the body, but they managed to dam the flow to the stream where they were sure the body was located. The water level gradually fell, and an hour later one of the girl's arms emerged sixty feet downstream, where the body had wedged under a rock. The little girl had been underwater for sixty-six minutes. She was cold, her eyes were open, and there was no pulse, no heartbeat. After CPR, she was moved to a nearby medical center in Salt Lake City and resuscitated with the aid of a heart-lung machine. Although she had been clinically dead for over an hour, she recovered completely save for a slight residual tremor.[14]

There is no reason to believe that an hour represents the limit for resuscitation from hypothermic clinical death. One authoritative text says that the ultimate limit even "in the warm" may be as long as an hour,[15] long enough to put us in the realm of *The Day the Earth Stood Still*. Experimental dogs have been revived in good health after more than five hours at the temperature of ice. Only the future will show what the ultimate limit is. It is in the hope that the limits are wide that a few cryonicists are frozen every month in the United States.

Whatever the limit turns out to be, speculative fiction and myths must find a way to explain it at the emotional level; that is why we create them. Science fiction, in its ceaseless speculation about the boundaries of technology and human experience, will surely play a pivotal role in how we accept new resuscitation and life extension technologies, and how we live with them. Perhaps science fiction will escape from the fundamentalists and remain free to explore all the possible answers and questions. That may be difficult to do, given our human history of telling stories in one particular way, but we owe it to ourselves to try.

Notes

1. Paul Barber, *Vampires, Burial, and Death* (Binghamton, N.Y.: Vail-Ballou Press, 1988), 189–94.

2. Barber, *Vampires, Burial, and Death*, 102–19.

3. Richard S. Atkinson and Thomas V. Boulton, eds., *The History of Anaesthesia* (Park Ridge, N.J.: Parthenon Publishing Group, 1989).

4. Ruth Richardson, *Death, Dissection, and the Destitute* (New York: Viking Penguin, 1988), 75–76.

5. Mary Shelley, Introduction to *Frankenstein*, in *The Mary Shelley Reader*, ed. Betty T. Bennett and Charles R. Robinson (1831; New York: Oxford University Press, 1990), 170.

6. Benjamin Franklin, Letter to Barbeu Dubourg, April 15, 1773, in *Ben Franklin's Autobiographical Writings*, selected and edited by Carl Van Doren (New York: Viking Press, 1945), 290.

7. Edgar Allan Poe, "The Facts in the Case of M. Valdemar," in *Ten Great Mysteries by Edgar Allan Poe*, ed. Groff Conklin (New York: Scholastic Books, 1960), 96, 99.

8. Kenneth V. Gunden and Stuart H. Stock, *Twenty All-Time Great Science Fiction Films* (New York: Arlington House, 1982), 44.

9. H. P. Lovecraft, *At the Mountains of Madness*, in *At the Mountains of Madness and Other Tales of Terror* (New York: Ballantine Books, 1971), 99.

10. D. Whittingham, S. Leibo, and P. Mazur, "Survival of Mouse Embryos Frozen to -196°C and -269°C," *Science* 178 (1972): 411–14.

11. *Cryonics* 13 (July 1992): 8. *Cryonics* is published by Alcor Life Extension Foundation, 7895 E. Acoma Dr. #110, Scottsdale, AZ 85260.

12. *Cryonics* 6 (July 1985): 3–4.

13. California Court of Appeals, 2d Appellate District, Division 2, Case B055379; also see California Superior Court, County of Los Angeles, Case C697147.

14. *Journal of the American Medical Association* 260 (July 15, 1988): 377–79.

15. Peter Safar, "Dynamics of Brain Resuscitation after Ischemic Anoxia," *Hospital Practice* 16 (1981): 67.

A Roll of the Ice:
Cryonics as a Gamble

Sterling Blake

I regard science fiction as an entertaining game that aims to make us aware of the potentials we face. As fiction, it strives harder to entertain than to instruct. Still, I prefer to be more neat in writing about a huge problem like the pursuit of immortality. By this term—immortality is, strictly, an infinite lifetime, and thus impossible—I mean a significantly increased life span. Is there a more orderly way to discuss the range of the probable?

Such discussion is not scientific, because the results cannot be checked right now. This is not to say that predictions about the future are *un*scientific statements—that they were tested and failed. Rather, ideas of the future are *non*scientific; however systematically arrived at, they cannot be tested today. Someday they will be either disproved or not. But of course, like a tip about a horse race, they are most useful before one knows whether they are right.

Consider cryonics. The idea that properly freezing people immediately after they have crossed the threshold we call "death" may allow them to be later reanimated is an assertion about the future. It first figured in a Neil R. Jones science fiction story in 1931 and eventually inspired Dr. Robert Ettinger to propose the idea in detail in *The Prospect of Immortality* (1964).

Cryonics has since been explored in Clifford D. Simak's *Why Call Them Back from Heaven?* (1967), Frederik Pohl's *The Age of the Pussyfoot* (1969), and innumerable space flight stories (like *2001: A Space Odyssey* [1968]) that use cryonics for long-term storage of the crew. Pohl became an advocate of cryonics, even appearing on Johnny Carson's *To-*

night show to discuss it; Robert Heinlein used cryonics as part of a time-travel plot in *The Door into Summer* (1957); and Larry Niven coined the term *corpsicle* to describe such "deanimated" folk. But all these stories focus on the long term.

In my novel *Chiller* (1993) I treat cryonics as we know it today, in a more mainstream, suspenseful plot structure. *Chiller*'s armature is the adventures of a beleaguered band facing the present opposition to the idea. It is based on the three cryonics organizations that exist today and the considerable antagonism they face, much of it quite emotional. This fervent resistance suggests deep underlying uneasiness about death in our society. Imagine a scientist being rejected by a scientific society because he wants to present research relevant to long-term preservation of whole organisms, not necessarily humans. Yet this attitude continues today, along with widespread views that cryonics is either inherently wrong, greedy, or else the work of con men. (This last assumption is universal among physicians.)

Of course, cryonics is a huge gamble. Many thoughtful people discount cryonics because they simply consider it fantastically implausible—despite the fact that Canadian painted turtles and at least four species of frogs routinely make it through the winter by freezing and then reviving. The animals respond to low temperatures by making a cocktail of glucose, amino acids, and a kind of naturally produced antifreeze, glycerol. They move water out of their cells so that any ice crystals that form do so outside the delicate cell membranes. Although these animals have special adaptations, their body chemistries are not bizarre; their methods could be extended artificially to mammals like us. Based on such reasoning, cryonics has gathered momentum, although it has gone largely unnoticed by the world. The number of people investing in cryonics as a rational gamble is increasing exponentially. More than forty are now suspended in liquid nitrogen, and hundreds are signed up to be.

Many people regard cryonics as creepy and pointless. Even science fiction writers fascinated by its long-term aspects (like Simak and Heinlein) never made arrangements to be "suspended," as the cryonicists call it. I know of no science fiction writer who has publicly endorsed cryonics as a plausible possibility, except for Charles Platt, with the further marginal exception of a deposition Arthur C. Clarke made several years ago to support a court case.

The notion of suspension evokes images of the cold grave, zombies, and so on. Still, as eerie ideas go, being frozen strikes me as less horrific than turning into food for worms or being cremated. (When cremation first started out as a commercially available service, bodies of the departed were burned during a church service. The crematoria operators quickly added organ music because mourners wondered about the loud bang that often interrupted the funeral. It was the skull of the deceased, exploding.)

So even if suspension is not especially creepy, is it nonetheless pointless? That is, are cryonicists making a reasonable bet? That depends on many factors. Any vision of the future does. To analyze the variables in more than an arm-waving way, I will work out here a simple method for thinking quantitatively about future possibility—the essential signature of a hard science fiction approach, to my mind.

The simplest way to consider any proposed idea is to separate it into smaller, better-defined puzzles. Atomizing issues is crucial to science because it is easier to ponder one problem at a time. This approach has been applied to nonscientific questions as well, many closely allied to science. For example, the central goal of SETI (the Search for Extra-Terrestrial Intelligence) is calculating how many technological civilizations may exist in our galaxy. The estimate factors out such issues as how likely it is that a star has livable planets and how long a civilization lasts on average. Nobody expects a concrete result; it is only a way of discussing the elements that entered into the past, not the future, to yield the present density of radio-using aliens. The same techniques can be applied to future possibilities. This was first done for cryonics by engineer Dale Warren and then sharpened by UCLA physician Steven B. Harris.

I will have to use equations here, but they will be simple ones. So will my method. As long as every issue I raise is independent of the other issues, then we can multiply all the probability estimates together at the end to get the total likelihood of cryonics working. What kind of concerns enter here? I will break them down into three categories—metaphysical, social, and technical. Most science fiction deals with social aspects, because those generate the most interesting stories, but the other matters are equally vexing.

First, the metaphysical. To preserve people's minds, we naturally think of saving their brains. To begin with, what are the chances that the brain carries the mind? This is the materialistic worldview, and the chances that it is correct I will label with a probability M. I am a solid materialist, so I would say that $M = .99$; that is, there is a 99 percent chance that the vital soul does not leave the body when metabolism stops. There is evidence for this, actually. People cooled down to a state of clinical death on operating tables for brain surgery revive with their sense of self intact.

Next, what are the odds that the brain *structure* tells the whole story—that is, that the Self is not the product of continuing electrical activity in the brain? Here, too, although the brain rhythms cease when patients are cooled for brain surgery, the rhythms persist when the patients are revived. Further, some people have received jolts of heavy current that completely overloaded their delicate internal electrical circuits. This happens to the hundreds of people struck by lightning every year in the United States and was once part of routine shock treatments administered earlier in this century. Except for short-term recall, these people survived with their memories intact. Our minds, then, are something like hardwired, though rewritable, programs inscribed in the cells of our brains. So I will set the probability E that our Essence is in brain cells themselves, not momentary brain activity, at $E = .99$.

Finally we must calculate the chance that the Self can make it through the process of being frozen down to liquid nitrogen temperatures. The trick is to get to the brain quickly, before it degrades. Several years ago a boy drowned in a cold lake and was revived after an hour spent clinically dead. He survived. Even if one is cryonically suspended immediately—which means being perfused with a glycerol-type solution to minimize damage while being cooled—there lurk the huge unknowns of what this perfusion does to memories. Studies show that most of the damage occurs when the brain is rewarmed; neuronal membranes are ripped, pierced. Even so, experimental animals revive with memories intact, and the perfusion technology will certainly improve. So let us be optimistic and put the probability that the Self will persist through this Transition process, T, at $T = .9$.

Multiplying the metaphysical factors, MET, gives us $(.99)(.99)(.9)$, or just about $.9$.

Next, the social issues. First, what are the odds that the brain (and body—but the Self is in the brain, remember) will make it to some far-off revival time without accidental thawing out? Call this S, the chances for Survival of the brain. Many issues enter here. Presently, all cryonics patients are kept in carefully monitored steel containers. This has not always been so; financial failures doomed several to thawing in the two decades after Ettinger's pioneering book. But none has been lost in over a decade, and the first man frozen (named James Bedford, incidentally) is still coasting along at 77 degrees above absolute zero after twenty-six years. Given that cryonics is far sturdier now, let us set the brain Survival odds, S, at $.9$.

Sure, but what about the odds that society as a *whole* will make it through for, say, a century? Call this factor O, the Odds that civilization itself will have the resources to support cryonics over the long term. This includes the chances that society will turn irrational, break down (war, economic depression), or take a fervent dislike to cryonics. The economics of cryonics are modest. Liquid nitrogen is the third cheapest fluid, after water and crude oil, and is widely useful, so it would probably be available even in damaged economies. Of course, even democracies may decide to suppress those arrogant enough to spend their money on a chancy voyage across time into an unknown future. So I will set the Odds of social continuity allowing cryonics at $O = .8$.

Ah, but what if the cryonics organizations themselves do not last? This is a real worry. When Cryonic Interment, Inc., of California collapsed in the mid-1970s, all the suspended patients in the company's care were lost. The longest-lived institutions in human history have been religious, with the Catholic church arguably holding the record at nearly two thousand years. Cryonics has some of the aura of a religion: deeply persuaded people sustaining a long-range hope of personal salvation. Maybe that will help. Still, greedy corporate directors could someday simply find it more profitable to keep tapping the assets left behind by patients rather than reviving the patients. (See Simak's *Why Call Them Back from Heaven?* for a plausible argument that this would occur.) Or somebody could simply embezzle the funds: the more popular cryonics becomes, the bigger will be the spoils. Call the probability that Cryonics organizations will fail C, and my guess is that $C = .5$, a fifty-fifty chance the whole shebang will go under. After all, we are talking about a wait that could be a century. How many of today's corporations are that old? About 1 percent.

The social factors, then, I estimate at $SOC = (.9)(.8)(.5) = .36$, or a bit better than one-third.

I hear the tech types impatiently asking, "Can it be done at all?" And there's the rub. From the *MET*aphysical and *SOC*ial factors we come to the issues that blend the two. Is revival *TECH*nically possible, given the social and philosophical assumptions?

Cryonics began with no clear idea of how the revival part could be done. That led to a standard joke: How many cryonicists does it take to screw in a lightbulb? The answer is none—they just sit in the dark and wait for the technology to improve. The rise of nanotechnology at the hands of Eric Drexler in the late 1980s and early 1990s has made him the patron saint of cryonics. Drexler envisions self-replicating machines of molecular size that have been programmed with orders to repair freezing damage, bind up torn membranes, and generally knit together the sundered house of a frozen brain. There seems to be no fundamental reason why such machines cannot be made on the scale of a billionth (nano-) of a meter. The rewards of developing such handy devices would be immense, a revolution in society (which is why *SOC* issues intertwine with *TECH* ones, as I will discuss below). Not only must this marvelous technology appear, however, but we must survive its flowering. This is tricky; runaway use of nanotechnology could produce virulent diseases or everything-eaters to wipe us out. Modern Promethean technology, like nuclear physics, shares this daunting property. I suspect it will take at least fifty years, more plausibly a century, to develop nanotechnology capable of repairing freeze damage. The good thing about being frozen is that you are not going anywhere; you can afford to wait. Given these immense uncertainties, I put T, the chances that the Technology will arrive and we will survive it, at $T = .5$.

But, of course, a future society must have the *desire* to apply the technology to cryonics. If we do not yield to a kind of temporocentric insulation and lose our curiosity about representatives from a century before, I suspect we will have the cultural Energy to work out nanotechnology for cryonics purposes. (After all, much of it will be useful in curing and repairing ordinary living people.) I put this cultural Energy probability, E, at $E = .9$.

Still, will our descendants pay the bill? The first revived cryonicists will probably be on the twenty-second century's talk shows—as will famous suspended people. (Wouldn't you pay a few bucks to talk to Benjamin Franklin? He was the first American to speculate on means for preserving people for later revival. And philosopher Francis Bacon died of pneumonia caught as he was experimenting with suspension of animals.) But if ten thousand cryonicists are waiting to be thawed . . . This is a major imponderable problem. Humanitarians will argue that spending money on the living is always morally superior to spending it on the dead but salvageable. Will this argument win the day? Or, in the fullness of time, will nanotechnology make revival so cheap that the Cost factor, C, becomes a nonissue? You can argue it either way—and science fiction writers already have. Given such uncertainties, I will guess that the Cost probability factor $C = .5$.

Finally, there is the truly unknowable factor, H, which stands for the contrariness of Humans. Some powerful social force may emerge and make cryonics reprehensible. After all, many people already think it is creepy, a Stephen King kind of idea. Maybe people will utterly lose interest in the past. I doubt this, noting the world's fascination with the frozen man found in the Alps in 1991. Considerable expense is going into careful examination of this remarkably preserved inhabitant of four thousand years ago, and his clothing and belongings will tell us much about his era. But still, he cannot speak, as a revived cryonicist could. Or perhaps some other grand issue will captivate human society, making cryonics and the whole problem of death irrelevant. Maybe we will lose interest in technology itself. Factor in also the Second Coming of Christ or the arrival of aliens who will spirit us all away. The choices are endless, but all rather unlikely, I suspect. I am rather optimistic about Humanity, so I will take the odds that we will still care about suspended cryonicists to be fairly large, perhaps $H = .9$.

This means that the *TECH* issues multiply out to $(.5)(.9)(.5)(.9) = .2$.

With all this homework done, we can now savor our final result. The probability that cryonics will work, delivering you from suspension to a high-tech future, blinking in astonishment, is: $MET \times SOC \times TECH = (.9)(.36)(.2) = .07$, or a 7 percent chance.

Do I "believe" this number? Of course not. It is very rough. Calculations such as these are worthwhile only to sharpen thinking, not as infallible guides. Some people decry numerical estimates as hopelessly deceptive, too exact in matters that are slippery and qualitative. True, for some, but the goal here is to use simple arithmetic means of assessing to aid us in planning. This does not rule out emotional issues; it merely places them in perspective.

Still, to wax numerical a bit more, suppose you regard cryonics purely as an investment. Does it yield a good return? Well, what is a person worth? Most Americans will work about fifty years at a salary in the range of $20,000 to $30,000 per year—the national average today. In other words, they will make somewhere between $1 and $2 million in their lifetimes. One crude way to size up an investment is to multiply the probability of success (7 percent here) times the expected return (a million dollars), then compare it with the amount you must invest to achieve your aim. This operation yields $70,000, which is in the range of what cryonics costs today. (Cryonicists buy a life insurance policy that pays off the cryonics organization when they die; they do not finance it all at once.)

The goal of cryonics is not money but time—a future life. Another way to decide whether cryonics is a rational gamble is to take a person's expected life span (75 years) and divide it by the expected gain in years after revival. This would be at least another 75 years, although if the technology for revival exists, people may quite possibly live for centuries. Then the ratio of gained years to present life span is, say, 150 years divided by 75 years, or a factor of 2. It could be higher, of course. Then even if the probability of success is 1 percent, the probable yield from the investment of your time would be 2 x 1 percent = 2 percent. It would make sense to invest 2 percent of your time in this gamble. Two percent of your lifetime earnings ($1 million) would be abut $20,000, which you could use to pay your cryonics fees. Or you could invest 2 percent of your time—half an hour a day—working for cryonics. Make it a hobby. You would meet interesting people and you might enjoy it; most people spend more time in the bathroom.

Take another angle. Probability estimates should tell us the range of outcomes, not just an average like 7 percent. If I wanted to be a flagrant optimist, I could go back and make the loosely technical issues much more probable, so that $TECH = .9$, say. That would give us a 29 percent probability. This is about the upper end of the plausible range for me. Or I could be a gloomy pessimist with equal justification and take the social issues to be $SOC = .05$, say. Then my original 7 percent estimate becomes less than 1 percent. So the realm of plausible probabilities, to me, is between 1 percent and about 30 percent. Low odds like 1 percent emerge because we consider many factors, each of which is fairly probable, but the remorseless act of multiplying them yields a low estimate. Gambling is entirely natural to us. Studies show that most people of even temperament, considering chains of events, are invariably optimistic; we do not atomize issues, we look for obliging conditions. This seems built into us. We humans will always lose cash in crap games; it is a habit of the species.

I have dwelled on using this simple probability estimate to show some properties of the method. The deeper question is whether it truly makes sense to break up any future possibility into a set of mutually independent possibilities.

This comes powerfully into play in the SOC factors. Once the $TECH$ issues look good, people will begin to change their minds about cryonics. The prospect of longer life may make society more stable, so O becomes larger. Cryonics organizations will fare better, so C improves. The slicing up into factors assumes that the general fate of humankind is the same for the folk of the freezers, and this may not be so. Cryonicists are a hard-nosed, practical lot, in my experience. They have many technical skills. Society might crash badly, but they would manage to keep patients suspended through extraordinary effort. They have already done so. Police raided a cryonics company in the late 1980s (Alcor of Riverside, California—

where Heinlein put his cryonics firm in *The Door into Summer*) and demanded that a recently frozen patient be handed over for autopsy. Someone hid the patient until Alcor got the police and district attorney called off, but not before the police hauled five staff members off to jail and ransacked the facility.

Perhaps a better way to analyze this is to note that the biggest uncertainties lie in intertwined *SOC* and *TECH* factors. A techno-optimist might say that cryonics will probably work on technical grounds, but social factors lessen the odds, maybe to the fifty-fifty range. Of course, numbers do not tell the whole tale. Ray Bradbury has related that he once was interested in any chance of seeing the future, but thinking about cryonics made him realize that he would be torn away from everything he loved. What would the future be worth without his wife, his children, his friends? No, he would not take that option at any price.

Still, he came into this world without those associations. And why assume that nobody else would go with him? This is an example of the "neighborhood" argument, which says that mature people are so entwined with their surroundings, people, and habits of mind, that to yank them out is a trauma worse than death. One is fond of one's own era, certainly. But ordinary immigrants often face similar challenges and manage to come through. If you truly feel this way, no mathematical argument will dissuade you. For many, I suspect, the future is not open to rational gambles, because it is too deeply embedded in emotional issues.

So it must be with any way of thinking quantitatively about the future. We cannot see the range of possibilities without imposing our own values and views, mired in our time, culture, and place. Often, these are the things we value most—our idiosyncratic angles on the world. The best literature can do is cast an oblique, austere light upon them.

Living Forever or Dying in the Attempt: Mortality and Immortality in Science and Science Fiction

Joseph D. Miller

Do not go gentle into that good night. Rage, rage
against the dying of the light.
—Dylan Thomas

One of the true cultural universals is the desire for eternal life. It is a desire tapped by many religions, which, unable to demonstrate physical immortality, nonetheless offer immortality in the abstract: in promises of paradise or reincarnation. Intimations of physical immortality may coexist with organized religion, but the immortal becomes conveniently invisible—Pharaoh continuing existence with his retinue but locked forever in a pyramidal tomb—or legendary—the myth of the Wandering Jew, an archetypal example of the Faustian price of immortality: for his sin the Wandering Jew gains earthly immortality (at least until Judgment Day) but is denied entry into the Kingdom of Heaven. Of course, the Catholic subtext is that physical, secular immortality is a poor substitute for the joys of Christian Paradise. In spite of such religious propaganda, the desire for secular immortality has continued through the ages—manifested in such projects as Ponce de Leon's obsessive search for the Fountain of Youth. The underlying motive of medical science, from ancient times, could likewise be considered the secular abolition of mortality, although stopgap measures aimed at disease and injury have historically been its primary focus.

In fantastic literature, immortality is often the result of a kind of implicit Faustian bargain. Frankenstein's monster, while potentially immortal, is still doomed to wander the polar wastes without hope of redemption or even the punctuation of some future Judgment Day—to which, at least, the Wandering Jew is entitled. Dracula possesses secular immortality, but the price is blood and any human notion of morality. Perhaps these prototypical characters indicate our unconscious realization that the sheer weight of eternal life must result in the complete transformation of humanity, as defined by the short-lived.

Yet, in modern, technologically optimistic science fiction there is a prevalent notion that immortality is obtainable with "business as usual." That is, immortals are fairly ordinary human beings who will simply maintain their ordinariness forever. Time allows for some honing of skills, perhaps some philosophical insight, but the protagonists are still generic *Homo sapiens*. Examples of such characters are rife in the literature: Roger Zelazny's Conrad in *This Immortal* (1966), the citizens of the Culture in Iain M. Banks's *The Player of Games* (1988), and Poul Anderson's immortals in *The Boat of a Million Years* (1989).

Undoubtedly, the ultimate example of the pedestrian immortal is Robert A. Heinlein's Lazarus Long. Long is as skilled, strong, virtuous, heroic, and long-winded as any of Heinlein's characters, but he is also quintessentially human. In *Methuselah's Children* (1958), however, he encounters two different variants of the immortal. He loses a compatriot, Mary Sperling, to the seduction of immortality through telepathic communion. The Little People share a group mind, and to them the loss of an individual body is as unimportant as losing a sock. Marriage into this group mind is irresistible to the aging Sperling. This theme of seductive communion has often been examined in science fiction, most notably in Theodore Sturgeon's *More Than Human* (1953) and George R. R. Martin's *Dying of the Light* (1977). But it is not the only form of immortality that Long and his fellow immortals confront. Earlier in the novel, one of their leaders, Slayton Ford, lost his mind after encountering the gods of another alien race, the Jockaira. Apparently, to even look upon the faces of such entities is a prescription for insanity. At the end of *Methuselah's Children*, Long says,

> The last two and a half centuries have just been my adolescence, so to speak. Long as I've hung around, I don't know more about the final answers, the *important* answers, than Peggy Weatheral does. Men—*our* kind of men—Earth men—never have had enough time to tackle the important questions. Lots of

capacity and not time enough to use it properly. When it came to the important questions we might as well have still been monkeys.

And later:

> "Take those Jockaira gods—"
> "They weren't gods, Lazarus. . . ."
> "Of course they weren't—I think. My guess is that they are creatures who have had time enough to do a little hard thinking. Someday, about a thousand years from now, I intend to march straight into the temple of Kreel, look him in the eye, and say 'Howdy, bub—what do you know that I don't know?'"[1]

This is the wonderfully pugnacious, curiously humble Lazarus Long of Heinlein's youth. Unfortunately, when Long resurfaces years later in *Time Enough for Love* (1973), pomposity has largely replaced pugnacity (consider *The Notebooks of Lazarus Long* [1978]). Long revisits the Little People before indulging in adolescent wish fulfillment in the remainder of the novel, but nowhere in *Time Enough for Love* is there any mention of the Jockaira gods. Apparently Long, and probably Heinlein himself, never did have enough time for the "important" answers. Thus, Long remains a developmentally retarded, completely pedestrian immortal monkey. Confrontations between upstart monkeys and potential deities can be resolved in two ways: either the monkey reveals the "Wizard" as the product of smoke and mirrors, or the deity thoroughly humiliates the monkey in a necessarily unknowable fashion (the mechanics of humiliation must remain opaque to avoid undermining the generation of religious awe). Eating that particular Fruit is too much of a threat to the plausibility of the Gardener. Of course, it was an impossible problem for Heinlein: the Jockaira were simply too powerful to be finally revealed as patent medicine salesmen from Kansas; on the other hand, it was psychologically impossible for Heinlein to allow any force to trash his alter ego. So he ignored the issue.

Cosmetic changes in the human condition occur in other novels of pedestrian immortality, but the heroes remain largely recognizable as human. In Zelazny's *Lord of Light* (1967), longevity per se ultimately produces the appropriate physical aspects and attributes of godly power, previously generated by technological fixes, in the poseurs who took the identities of gods in the Hindu pantheon. But most of these characters remain corrupt and venal examples of humanity. Here, technological reincarnation is commonplace: before each death the conscious mind is imprinted as an electromagnetic pattern on the brains of an unending series of clones. The critical step is that the transfer must precede death, at least for the majority of characters. As Gregory Benford has suggested, it is difficult to imagine accepting immediate, personal death on the mere promise of subsequent transfer of consciousness into a host body.[2] Credible technological reincarnation requires that continuity of consciousness be preserved.

In that regard it is interesting that the precise moment of sleep (or the exact moment of anesthesia) can never be recalled.[3] The recollection, no matter how imperfect, of that moment of nonbeing might, in its terrible similarity to the apprehension of death, destroy the continuity of subjective experience. The terror here, as in Parkinson's or Alzheimer's disease, is conscious experience of the deterioration of consciousness itself. Our amnesia for the little death we die each night preserves our sanity. If this is so, modern strategies for cryonic preservation should be initiated before brain death, else the eventual resurrectee, having seen something of the physiognomy of Death, may be revived insane with that memory.[4]

In *Lord of Light*, Yama, the death god, is an exception who *has* seen his own death (and perhaps suffered a degree of brain damage in the process), but his mutant brain, and good electronics, allowed him to survive. He cannot die because his consciousness is automatically transmitted to a clone at the moment of death. But the price of Yama's immortality is eternal identification and obsession with death. The other exception to the rule of unpunctuated consciousness is Sam, the ersatz Buddha, who survives two deaths in Zelazny's novel because of spiritual strengthening granted by the Rakasha energy demons, and because of his own mutant powers. After his first death, Sam simply takes over an appropriate body; he experiences no terror in death, possibly because his conscious mind, strengthened by the Rakasha—and unlike that of the young Yama—is impervious to the body's deterioration. Sam's second death involves being injected into the magnetic cloud surrounding his planet, a kind of electromagnetic Nirvana. So the Lord of Light one-ups the god of death; Sam has seen death but has also known the infinite ground of being. But he too pays a heavy price for immortality, particularly after his return from the Nirvana of the Golden Cloud. The Faustian price Sam pays is loss of self (in contrast with Yama, who cleaves to a self that is paradoxically the active antithesis of self). Sam must bind himself again to life; only by gambling for his soul does he finally regain it. The sly psychology here is that the reflexive act of gambling reifies the value of that which is gambled for. In any event, it is not surprising that the only characters in this novel who are assured the avoidance of "true death" are those who pay the heaviest price for immortality.

In Robert Silverberg's *The Book of Skulls* (1971), the price of immortality is the human sacrifice of close friends. In Mark Clifton and Frank Riley's *The Forever Machine* (1958; as *They'd Rather Be Right* [1953]), immortality is attained by a computer-controlled psychosomatic cleansing at the cellular level of "mistakes, repressions, frustrations, disappointments, tensions."[5] Individuals willing or able to surrender their wrongheadedness are transformed into telepathic innocents, in a fashion reminiscent of the best meanderings of L. Ron Hubbard. In Larry Niven's *A World Out of Time* (1976), the common road to immortality requires a developmental regression to a physically prepubescent, permanently neuter state. But the Boys and Girls, though extremely intelligent and perceptive, are still recognizably human. A second form of immortality is achieved once again through cellular cleansing, this time via a very selective teleportation device.

But science fiction has its high-priced immortality also. In Frank Herbert's *Dune* (1965), the price of immortality is life as a hybrid sandworm. In Greg Bear's *Blood Music* (1985), the price is incorporation into a community of intelligent lymphocytes. In *The Annals of the Heechee* (1987), by Frederik Pohl, "vastening" is eternal existence as a program running on sophisticated hardware in virtual reality. Rudy Rucker's *Software* (1982) similarly treats the mind as a program that can run indefinitely on arbitrary hardware. In Martin's *Dying of the Light*, Arthur C. Clarke's *Childhood's End* (1953), and Sturgeon's *More Than Human*, immortality means the abandonment of individuality. Sturgeon tries to have it both ways in *The Cosmic Rape* (1958), in which he posits a group mind that is compatible with personal identity. The point in these examples is that immortality *must be* a Faustian bargain—not "business as usual" but a radical transformation in the human condition.

The means by which immortality is achieved helps determine its Faustian price. To examine this issue, we must review what little is known of the biology of aging and death.[6] One of the most relevant observations in this regard is that normal cells do not continue to divide indefinitely in culture; in fact, after about fifty divisions, further division ceases and the cells subsequently die. This is called Hayflick's limit.[7] But cancer cells divide indefinitely. It is possible to transform normal cells into indefinitely dividing cells by the transfection of oncogenes, cancer-causing genes, into the nucleus of the cell. Oncogenes are molecular switches for cell division. They are normally inhibited by repressor genes, except during the processes of division, growth, and differentiation. When repressor genes are lost or inactivated in adult differentiated tissue, the tissue often dedifferentiates to a state not terribly dissimilar from fetal tissue, and rapid cell division ensues. The selective control of oncogenes and their associated repressor genes would allow the production of indefinite numbers of any cell type. Further, controlled dedifferentiation could regress any body tissue back to an undifferentiated state. Activating another set of oncogenes in that undifferentiated tissue could then theoretically differentiate that tissue into any arbitrary body tissue. Such a technique would mean the end of tissue rejection and ethical difficulties with transplantation of fetal tissue. In the future, it may suffice for any young adult to donate skin tissue to a tissue bank. Later, when that person needs an organ transplant—due to heart failure, for example—the tissue bank would simply take some donated tissue through these steps of dedifferentiation and redifferentiation. Voilà! Your own autotransplanted heart, with no possibility of immunological rejection. Organ-legging—à la Larry Niven—would be bereft of any rationale.

The Hayflick limit and oncogene concept have led biologists to suggest the existence of programmed "death genes" that limit cell division and, ultimately, longevity. Of course, it is just as likely for a "life gene" to be deactivated as for a "death gene" to be turned on at a particular age.[8] In any event, it appears that aging is under a considerable degree of genetic control. So a chance mutation leading to Zelazny's Conrad or Heinlein's Long is a definite possibility. In fact, selective breeding for longevity—what produced the Howard Families of *Methuselah's Children*—has been accomplished in fruit flies. By mating long-lived flies, experimenters can create a strain that lives twice as long as wild-type flies.[9] Genetic analysis of long-lived flies has shown that they make much more of a particular gene product than normal flies. This gene product is an antioxidant functionally similar to vitamin C or E. Antioxidants scavenge free radicals, toxic byproducts of cellular activity that accumulate in cells and ultimately poison them. This observation lends support to a very old theory of aging—that it represents the buildup of toxic cellular metabolites that finally overcome the body's intrinsic housekeeping apparatus. If this mechanism of toxicity is important in the aging process, then any behavior that slows metabolism should increase longevity.

Indeed, hibernation, which produces a drastic lowering of basal metabolic rate, is also associated with longer life spans.[10] Artificial hibernation, or "cold sleep," is a chestnut in science fiction. It is employed for long-distance space travel at nonrelativistic velocities or simply as a form of one-way time travel to the future (as in Niven's *A World Out of Time*). If hibernation could indeed be pharmacologically or genetically induced in humans, it would be an alternative to life extension by cryonic suspension. But even at the near-freezing temperatures of hibernation, cellular metabolites do accumulate, requiring periodic arousals from hibernation for "cellular housekeeping," which would not be necessary in cryonic suspension. On the other hand, artificial hibernation may be more technologically feasible. Many mammals are capable of arousing after hibernating at near-freezing temperatures; there are no examples of mammals reviving following immersion in liquid nitrogen. Of course, cold sleep and cryonic suspension are examples of unconscious life extension, not the usual notion of immortality as both objective and subjective extensions of experience. If the "moment of hibernation" is as opaque to memory as the "moment of sleep," the subjective experience of periodic hibernation and arousal (or periodic cryonic suspension and arousal) may be as seamless and quotidian as the ordinary progression of our days, but punctuated by "sleeps" of far greater objective duration.

Unlike hibernation, ordinary sleep is restorative. Sleep's low metabolic requirements allow the body to catch up with cellular housekeeping.[11] One potent naturally occurring sleep-inducing factor is another antioxidant, surely not a coincidence.[12] In any event, stories about immortality attained through deep cellular cleaning (*The Forever Machine*) or diktat immortality (*A World Out of Time*) may be truly prescient. Of course, the cellular tuneups of the future will more likely involve antioxidant-spraying nanomachines than computerized psychosomatic medicine or cell-cleaning teleporters!

A World Out of Time, as noted, offers another form of immortality in the eternally prepubescent Boys. Again, this makes considerable sense because the capacity for regeneration is maximal in children, whose tissues have not yet fully differentiated. Presumably, appropriate repressor genes are kept inactivated and growth beyond the capacity of skeletal support is hormonally inhibited. But the protagonist, Corbell, also had a supply of age-retarding hormones on his ship. That endocrine factors may be involved in the aging process is another old idea in biology.[13] Destruction of the pituitary, source of many hormones, actually *increases* the life span in rodents. Interestingly, an even larger increase in life span is seen with severe caloric restriction.[14] In both cases there is a pronounced decrease in a variety of circulating hormones, decreased metabolism, and, at least in food-restricted rodents, an increase in antioxidant activity. On the other hand, chronic administration of at least one hormone, growth hormone, increases the life span in mice.[15] It may be that a growth hormone–inhibiting factor produced by the pituitary is the true "death factor." This would explain the prolonged life span resulting from pituitary removal, since growth hormone can still be made in brain regions outside the pituitary. Clinical trials of growth hormone in aged humans are currently under way. Preliminary results suggest a big increase in lean muscle and bone mass in hormone-treated subjects.

So far, it seems that immortality may depend on a combination of genetic control of growth and cell division/differentiation, endocrine manipulation, and/or improvements in general cellular housekeeping. To that list many biologists would add a mechanism for maintaining the fidelity of DNA replication. Random genetic errors are as likely to activate oncogenes as any hypothetical death factor. Further, highly efficient liver detoxification enzymes and an eternally competent immune system are prerequisites for handling environmental toxins, viruses, and bacteria. These mechanisms all depend on accurate genetic control of cellular function, including regeneration. But what of cells that do not normally grow, divide, or regenerate? Unfortunately, the brain is a collection of just such cells. Actually, brain cells can be made to divide when appropriate growth factors are applied to them,[16] but that would be of little help if the cells involved were part of the substrate of personality, consciousness, and memory, whose functions seem to depend on a particular differentiated and interconnected network of neurons. An autobrain transplant using dedifferentiated and redifferentiated tissue could not hope to duplicate this wiring diagram. Such transplants would be more valuable for repairing brain regions that do not seem to have such a strong functional dependency on precise wiring, like the regions affected in Parkinson's disease or Huntington's chorea. In these cases autotransplants should be tremendously valuable.

But what of the prospective immortal? For the reasons just stated, banks of autocultured brain cells would be of little value for preserving continuity in consciousness over the millennia if the immortal unluckily sustained damage to brain regions vital to the preservation of personality. And even with the best possible cerebral housekeeping nanomachines, brain cells would still die. I think this is where the radical solutions come into play. If we knew how memory is laid down in the brain, perhaps we could "read out" the program onto some other medium, as in the "vastening" of the Heechee, the transcriptions of human mind into hardware in *Software*, or the personality transfer machines of *Lord of Light*. Unfortunately, current notions of how the consciousness software is mapped onto the cerebral hardware are nebulous, to say the least.

Are there other options? One possibility is longevity by extending the subjective sense of time (the opposite of the cold sleep paradigm). Mammals exhibit an innate temporal organization of behavior with a period of about twenty-four hours—the circadian rhythm.[17] Normally this rhythm is entrained to the daily light-dark cycle, but near twenty-four-hour rhythmicity persists under constant stimulus conditions in all species, excepting some humans. When humans were isolated from all temporal cues in deep caves, most of their physiological rhythms persisted with a period of twenty-four hours. In 30 percent of the humans, however, the sleep-wake rhythm went to forty hours or more. These individuals lived forty-hour days. Even their motor reaction time slowed to a rate consistent with altered temporal perception. When they left the cave they could not believe how much time had passed until shown the date on a newspaper.

It has been conclusively demonstrated that circadian timekeeping depends on the integrity of a small nucleus in the hypothalamus. This suprachiasmatic nucleus, or SCN, is necessary and sufficient to maintain biological timekeeping in mammals.[18] Constant jet lag–like disruption of circadian rhythmicity greatly reduces life span in fruit flies.[19] Similarly, hamsters with a critical mutation in this mechanism have shorter life spans.[20] Experimental destruction of the SCN severely disrupts the temporal organization of behavior, including sleep and hibernation. Aging seems to cause cell loss in this nucleus, with concomitant changes in the nocturnal consolidation of sleep. Such findings suggest that this biological clock affects subjective estimation of temporal duration, perhaps even objective longevity. Understanding the neurochemical nature of the biological clock could lead to drugs that directly alter subjective temporal duration. Objective longevity may still be limited to threescore and ten, but who cares, if the subjective life span could be extended to a thousand years or so by making the biological clock run faster? (Joe Haldeman, in *Buying Time* [1989], suggests a variant of this idea: longevity automatically entails control of subjective temporal perception.) Furthermore, drugs that make the clock run more slowly would also be useful. Thus could one control subjective duration: speed up perception of the workday and slow down perception of vacation. Better living through chronochemistry!

Whether or not subjective or objective immortality is attainable, and independent of its Faustian price, some questions remain. What does an immortal do? We can answer this question for the pedestrian Lazarus Long, but for a true change in the human condition, we can only guess. Perhaps the pursuit of knowledge is the only enterprise that would not ultimately become boring. But where does one store the new memories and knowledge? There are probably limits to the human brain's capacity for information storage, and immortals would finally run up against them. Does one engage in selective memory wiping and imposed forgetting? Or does one simply let matters take their ordinary biological course? In that case, perhaps only a hundred years or so of the most recent memory would be retained. Perhaps immortals would hold experience in a kind of random-access memory, consciously deciding what to "write" in long-term storage. In that scenario much stuff of existence would be like the most evanescent of dreams. Alternatively, once we break the cerebral code of memory, it might be possible to store memory externally, in a different medium. One could literally relive one's own past lives at will by opening the appropriate stored file. Another approach would be artificially enhancing internal cerebral storage.

Will the quest for knowledge finally pall? Will eternal life always end with boredom-induced suicide (consider Banks's Culture), or will the sheer weight of many years make life more precious? More mundane considerations include the effects of immortality on the global ecology and human gene pool. Technologically driven, widely disseminated biological immortality, attained in nearly any way, would maintain variability in the gene pool, our hedge against ecological calamity, but the result would be a Malthusian catastrophe of heroic proportions unless we pay the Faustian price of imposed sterility. (Or forced interplanetary expatriation?)

On the other hand, the immortality technique might not be widely disseminated. It is more likely that immortality would be a privilege of the elite class (diktat immortality, in Niven's words). In a world ruled by an immortal elite, what would prevent cultural stagnation and the most rigid age-related caste system ever conceived? It is hard to see how such a world could avoid stultifying conservatism. Imagine a society dominated by the likes of the Lazarus Long of *Time Enough for Love*. On the other hand, a society of Lazarus Longs from *Methuselah's Children* might still be capable of risk taking and adventure. Even so, selection theory predicts that, in the absence of imposed sterilization, the genes of the immortals would eventually dominate the gene pool, effectively ending genetic variation and thus making the species more vulnerable to any number of ecological cataclysms. An alternative might be to artificially induce genetic heterogeneity in the gene pool through molecular genetic engineering. In the case of reincarnation technology, maintaining genetic variability in the cloned host bodies would prevent the problem. But stagnant caste societies and Malthusian collapse remain probable outcomes for such scenarios. Would a naturally occurring rare mutation for longevity (like Lazarus Long's) be preferable? In this case, too, however, a genotype predisposed to long life with continuous fertility will eventually dominate the gene pool. Only if fertility is limited can this outcome be avoided.

The only biological forms of immortality that might avoid catastrophic effects on the gene pool, human society, and global ecology are those that either extend the subjective perception of temporal duration or effectively remove potentially long-lived individuals from the gene pool and society (e.g., cryonic suspension). Alternatively, virtual immortality or storage of personality in a nonbiological medium might avoid social and ecological disruption (though a society dominated by Ancestors on hard disk is a possible outcome).

Would immortality improve the human condition? To answer that question it would help to have a test case of an immortal organism more complex than a protozoan. What about human society itself? By analogy, human society is an organism perhaps ten thousand years old. Has it improved with age? Certainly it is *different* from the prototypical societies of Sumer and the Indus Valley. In the same way, I believe the Faustian price of immortality, defined in terms of eventual qualitative deviation from the human status quo, will be a function of the duration of existence. Of course, these are my idiosyncratic speculations, subject to the normal fallibility of human predictions. For better answers, I might say, like Lazarus Long in *Methuselah's Children*, "Ask me again in about five hundred years."

Notes

1. Robert A. Heinlein, *Methuselah's Children* (New York: New American Library, 1958), 160.
2. This may represent a Western cultural bias, however, since both Hinduism and Buddhism posit reincarnation subsequent to death.
3. Entry into deep sleep or anesthesia requires passage through various stages of slow-wave sleep. The mechanisms needed for recall may be inhibited in this hypometabolic state. But the recollection of experience in deepest dream sleep and a generalized increase in neural activity are commonplace. Interpretation

of dreams, perhaps because it can reestablish the continuity of consciousness, is a human cultural universal. For a discussion of these issues, see M. H. Kryger, T. Roth, and W. C. Dement, eds., *Principles and Practice of Sleep Medicine* (Philadelphia: Saunders, 1989).

4. This view is in sharp distinction to almost euphoric reports of near-death experience, as in Elisabeth Kübler-Ross, *On Death and Dying* (New York: Macmillan, 1969). Perhaps these experiences (like seeing a light at the end of the tunnel) are posttraumatic epiphenomena, as Carl Sagan argues in *Broca's Brain* (New York: Random House, 1979).

5. Mark Clifton and Frank Riley, *The Forever Machine* (New York: Galaxy, 1958), 53.

6. For a review, see Robin Holliday, "The Ancient Origins and Causes of Aging," *News in Physiological Sciences* 7 (1992): 38–40.

7. D. A. Juckett, "Cellular Aging (the Hayflick Limit) and Species Longevity: A Unification Model Based on Clonal Succession," *Mechanisms of Ageing and Development* 38 (1987): 49–71; see also L. Hayflick, "The Origins of Longevity," in *Modern Biological Theories of Aging*, vol. 32, ed. H. Warner, R. Butler, R. Spratt, and E. Schneider (New York: Raven Press, 1987), 21–34.

8. M. Ciriolo, K. Fiskin, A. De Martino, M. Corasaniti, G. Nistico, and G. Rotilio, "Age-Related Changes in Cu, Zn Superoxide Dismutase, Se-Dependent-and-Independent Glutathione Peroxidase anad Catalase Activities in Specific Areas of Rat Brain," *Mechanisms of Ageing and Development* 61 (1991): 287–97.

9. E. Hutchinson and M. Rose, "Quantitative Genetics of Postponed Aging in *Drosophila melanogaster*. I. Analysis of Outbred Populations," *Genetics* 127 (1991): 719–27.

10. Based on a comparison of hibernating and nonhibernating organisms of the same species; see C. Lyman, R. O'Brien, G. Greene, and E. Papafrangos, "Hibernation and Longevity in the Turkish Hamster *Mesocricetus brandti*," *Science* 212 (1981): 668–71.

11. Animals arouse from hibernation to sleep, apparently because such cellular restoration is impeded at low temperatures. See L. Trachsel, D. Edgar, and H. Heller, "Are Ground Squirrels Sleep Deprived during Hibernation?" *American Journal of Physiology* 260 (1991): R1123–29.

12. Y. Komoda, H. Kazuki, and S. Inoue, "SPS-B, a Physiological Sleep Regulator from the Brainstems of Sleep-Deprived Rats, Identified as Oxidized Glutathione," *Chemical and Pharmaceutical Bulletin* 38 (1990): 2057–59.

13. A. Everitt and J. Meites, "Aging and Anti-aging Effects of Hormones," *Journal of Gerontology* 44 (1989): B139–47.

14. A. Everitt, B. Porter, and J. Wyndham, "Effects of Caloric Intake and Dietary Composition on the Development of Proteinuria, Age-Associated Renal Disease, and Longevity in the Male Rat," *Gerontology* 28 (1982): 168–75.

15. D. Khansari and T. Gustad, "Effects of Long-Term, Low-Dose Growth Hormone Therapy on Immune Function and Life Expectancy of Mice," *Mechanisms of Ageing and Development* 57 (1991): 87–100.

16. B. Reynolds and S. Weiss, "Generation of Neurons and Astrocytes from Isolated Cells of the Adult Mammalian Central Nervous System," *Science* 255 (1992): 1707–10.

17. M. Moore-Ede, F. Sulzman, and C. Fuller, *The Clocks That Time Us* (Cambridge: Harvard University Press, 1982).

18. For reviews, see J. Meijer and W. Rietveld, "Neurophysiology of the Suprachiasmatic Pacemaker in Rodents," *Physiological Reviews* 69 (1989): 671–707; and J. Miller, "On the Nature of the Circadian Clock in Mammals," *American Journal of Physiology* 264 (1993): R821–32.

19. C. Pittendrigh and D. Minis, "Circadian Systems: Longevity as a Function of Circadian Resonance in *Drosophila melanogaster*," *Proceedings of National Academy of Sciences* 69 (1972): 1537–39.

20. M. Ralph, unpublished data, 1992.

The Biopoetics of Immortality:
A Darwinist Perspective on Science Fiction

Brett Cooke

Richard Dawkins begins *The Selfish Gene* by saying, "This book should be read almost as if it were science fiction."[1] Such is the strangeness of the new perspective he casts on a scientifically demonstrable *reality*, his vision of how things *actually are*, that he often resorts to science fiction for examples, either actual classics or unwritten novels of his own fancy. Evidently Dawkins is no stranger to science fiction, especially its use of unusual perspectives brought to bear on familiar phenomena. Cognitive estrangement is an antidote to taking things for granted, a way to subject them to rational analysis. Thus Dawkins maintains that the gene—not the species, group, or organism—is the unit of selection. There is a science fiction cast to his deduction that "we are survival machines—robot vehicles blindly programmed to preserve the selfish molecules known as genes" (*SG* v).

In this view, biological immortality, once assumed to be impossible, enters the realm of possibility. Along with its successors, *The Extended Phenotype* and *The Blind Watchmaker*, Dawkins's book remarkably asserts that an urge for immortality, not necessarily expressed as intention, at the level of the gene is the basis for all behavior. Understandably, we take behavior to include science fiction and accept Dawkins's implicit invitation to read his books as science fiction *theory*; in this case, for the common science fiction theme of the immortality of the human race.

The catch, as Dawkins points out, is that immortality takes the form of replication of information, not maintenance of the same protoplasmic material or whatever. As individual organisms, we are barely even temporary. Like all life-forms, we exist in a state of continual flux, whether this in-

90

volves our opinions, our psyche (which is hardly a monolith), or even our cells and the atoms that constitute them. On the other hand, our "genes are forever," since they have the potential to be immortal, already being "denizens of geological time"; their life expectancy can be measured in millions of years (SG 35, 34). Nor is this some sort of pie in the sky. Our genes have done pretty well; if they were not on a winning streak of more than two billion years, we would not be here. Of course, many genes do not make it past a single generation, and those that survive do so in spite of intense competition from other "gene machines." As Dawkins notes, all of your forebears survived at least to the point of reproduction: "Ancestors just don't die young!" (SG 40). Though a genome has been pretty well diluted after three generations, and specific combinations of genes are unlikely to survive beyond that, there is a good chance that you share at least one gene with your ancient predecessors or even with prehuman hominids (SG 30).

An even more ancient common heritage seems evident in the fact that all life-forms utilize the same twenty amino acids, and the same four nucleotide building blocks, some four billion years after the original replicators came into existence (SG 20). Graham Cairns-Smith traces the common pattern of replication even further—to preorganic chemistry, whereby molecular compounds attract the same or opposite constituent elements and create replicates of crystals and minerals, perhaps even of a few fistfuls of clay![2] Dawkins speculates about future consequences of this common quality when he wonders if greater advanced computers will someday ponder

> their own lost origins? Will one of them tumble to the heretical truth, that they have sprung from a remote, earlier form of life, rooted in organic, carbon chemistry, rather than the silicon-based electronic principles of their own bodies? . . . Will he rediscover the electronic equivalent of the metaphor of the arch, and realize that computers could not have sprung spontaneously into existence but must have originated from some earlier process of cumulative selection? Will he go into detail and reconstruct DNA as a plausible early replicator, victim of electronic usurpation? And will he be far-sighted enough to guess that even DNA may itself have been the usurper of yet more remote and primitive replicators, crystals of inorganic silicates? If he is of a poetic turn of mind, will he even see a kind of justice in the eventual return to silicon-based life, with DNA no more than an interlude, albeit one that lasted longer than three aeons?

"That is science fiction," Dawkins concludes, "and it probably sounds far-fetched" (BW 158). Fortunately, he abandons his imitation of Isaac Asimov at this point. His outline of the history of life on Earth serves a larger purpose: namely, it illustrates his argument that such developments are entirely plausible and may reflect the natural inclination of the universe for replication—for matter, especially living matter, to make copies of itself. Indeed, he posits *"the survival of the stable"* as a general law of the universe (*SG* 12).

This urge to replicate, as opposed to self-preservation, is especially evident in people up against the inescapable fact of their own annihilation. Typically such people behave as if they are aware of their informational heritage and feel the need to preserve it for another generation. Consider a few science fiction classics that illustrate this point. At the end of Olaf Stapledon's *Last and First Men* (1930), our final descendants, living on Neptune two billion years from now, learn that their world will be incinerated as part of the Sun's death cycle. They could have spent their last days hedonistically, but the response of the Last Men is so characteristic that I suspect most of us would try to do the same: they develop "an artificial human dust" capable of seeding other planets with "the potential of life and of spiritual development."[3] After it is manufactured in huge quantities, this "seminal matter" will be "disseminated" at various points in the planet's orbit. True, this matter does not involve actual human gamete, but since it conveys a vestige of a human image, some of our information, it is better than doing nothing or having a party. These last humans also strive to recall all their history, including that of each individual. This they communicate telepathically, two eons backward in time, to one of our contemporaries. The felt need is that great. What need could be greater?

Two decades after Stapledon's requiem to our kind, his admirer James Blish envisioned a smaller cataclysm in "Surface Tension" (1952), later part of *The Seedling Stars* (1957). Crash-landed on a planet of mud puddles, survivors of a seeding expedition, knowing this will be their grave, alter their genes to create a microscopic variant of their race, one that can live in the muddy water. The crew members also wish to leave a trace of their individual heritage behind, and they go to great trouble to microengrave their history on corrosion-proof metal leaves, which their distant progeny will be unable to read for generations.

In Arthur C. Clarke's *The Songs of Distant Earth* (1986), Earth responds to the impending explosion of the Sun by sending off seed ships. At first these ships carry frozen embryos and automatic equipment to revive and rear them in unknown environments, along with plants, animals, insects, and even microorganisms. Though D-Day is still centuries off, this enterprise is the only "long-term goal—the *last* long-term goal—that could now give some meaning to life, even after Earth had been destroyed."[4] As they improve the efficiency of the process, the scientists dispense with organic matter and encode genetic information in computers, so one ship may carry a million genotypes, an "entire unborn nation, with all the replicating equipment needed to set up a new civilization" (*SDE* 24). Notably, rather than carrying only genotypes, much space is reserved for *cultural* information in the form of gigantic libraries. Even when new technological developments allow some of Earth's humans to escape the holocaust, room is still reserved for art treasures such as Tutankhamen's golden funeral mask. Why a new civilization requires a cultural heritage is not made clear; as with much that we take for granted, a biological basis should be considered. It should be remembered that Clarke's novel, per the author's note, is meant to be a "wholly *realistic* piece of fiction" on the theme (*SDE* xiv), just as Stapledon hoped he had written "a possible, or least not wholly impossible" future history of our species (*LFM* 11).

This effort to preserve works of art is consistent with Dawkins's observation that "when we die there are two things we can leave behind us: genes and memes" (*SG* 199; memes are units of information that I discuss in more detail below). From the viewpoint of the gene, whose survival vehicles we are, successful replication alone will suffice; indeed, that is the entirety of the gene's ambitions, if you pardon the intentionalist fallacy. For in replication there is renewal. Though genes continually exchange identical parts, they remain forever young as long as they are replicated (*SG* 34). And that is the sole aim of the influence they exert on us, the disposable "gene machines" that they inhabit. What really constitutes a gene is not those constantly changing parts but the informational pattern the parts preserve.

The potential for immortality lies (to gallicize Dawkins) in the genes' penchant for longevity, fecundity, and fidelity. Longevity requires survival only to the point of replication, with added time in many species for postpartum care. But as Dawkins reminds us, eventual death is necessary for reproduction.[5] While death provides a great incentive for biological and intellectual replication, humans do not resist it as much as one might expect, especially when we have passed the point of reproduction. The Last Men, for example, know how to make themselves immortal, but they limit their lives to only about a quarter of a million years because "our policy is to produce new individuals of higher type than ourselves, for we are very far from biologically perfect"; indeed, this is the only reason they permit themselves to have children (*LFM* 291–92). Later, when the Sun's nova makes the potential for individual immortality moot, they cease all procreation, much as inhabitants in *The Songs of Distant Earth* control birth rates and encourage dangerous sports, including play wars, so Earth's population will shrink to a million at the time of the catastrophe. Though the Last Men despair at their fate, their death will be "permissible" once their seed is sown (*LFM* 325). When the automated Ship of Pamela Sargent's *Earthseed* (1983) produces offspring prematurely and must offer these children a childless existence, with no hope of building anything lasting, many take the significant risk of undergoing suspended animation until the ship reaches a habitable planet, saying that suicide is "better than a pointless life."[6]

There are ten trillion copies of the same DNA in a normal body, all produced with amazing fidelity. Immortality exists in the form of copies, and the fidelity yields lasting power. Dawkins describes one gene remarkably shared by cows and peas. Though their common ancestor lived about a billion and a half years ago, peas and cows are identical in 304 of the 306 characters this gene's DNA contains, so there have been only two changes or copying errors in roughly 20 billion replications (*BW* 123). Yet, if the fidelity of most genes approached this case, there would not have been enough mutations for *Homo sapiens* to have come into existence.

Finally, there is fecundity, the urge to disseminate a carefully judged balance of the highest quantity and/or quality of one's offspring. In this the parents' resources and the costs involved play a role. One wonders what Dr. Cecil Jacobsen was thinking as he artificially inseminated seventy-five of his fertility patients with his own sperm—truly a remarkable procreative urge, without the joy of sex. Could it have been merely reasons of economy that led him to defraud so many women? Dawkins advises that any motivation will do, however, so long as the replication is accomplished; "motivation is irrelevant for molecules" (*BW* 134). Indeed, the urge to replicate one's genes is enforced by other powerful urges to the point that, until the advent of modern technology, it was hard to prevent reproduction, and we had no control over the genes we passed on, only some choice of partners. In humanistic terms, nature is not proud. Rather, it is content to get by, generation after generation, without a plan for a glowing or a merely lasting future, for that is how replication has been accomplished over all but the last hundred thousand years (*EP* 45). Voilà! The only immortality we know of, other than possible afterlives, is in the information we transmit to the next generation. And it is little more than information that we *can* transmit over the large stretches of time meaningful for immortality.

What indications can we cite that this replication behavior depicted in literature—for our purposes, science fiction—derives from actual biological influences? A surprising clue is the relative blindness of the life force. Like the nature Dawkins depicts, flowing down the path of least resistance, genetic replication from the gene's point of view is an inexorable process that goes on willy-nilly, not necessarily requiring conscious motivation other than the urge to maximize one's contribution to the next gene pool (*EP* 14, 46). Generally, humans do not share this perspective. Life seems permanent; only our nails and hair remind us that time does not stand still. As insurance salesmen know well, we do not like to look far ahead, let alone into a future history beyond our demise. Whether humans plan for future family members or look back to their ancestors, the usual limit is in the range of three generations, the point at which Dawkins says our personal contribution of genetic *combinations* is diluted beyond the point of significance. This applies to inhabitants of doomed planets who cannot be stirred to action when there is plenty of time remaining. In *The Songs of Distant Earth*, humanity reacts to early news of a solar nova with

> a stunned silence—then a shrug of the shoulders and the resumption of normal, everyday business.
>
> Few governments had ever looked more than an election ahead, few individuals beyond the lifetimes of their grandchildren. And anyway, the astronomers might be wrong. Even if humanity was under sentence of death, the date of execution was still indefinite. The Sun would not blow up for at least a thousand years; and who would weep for the fortieth generation? (*SDE* 17)

Only as extinction approaches do they accelerate the seeding program. Are science fiction readers and environmentalists the only citizens who think about the far distant future?

Despite the popularity of future histories, the question persists: Do we care enough about immortality to really want it? Notably, the form of biological immortality found in science fiction usually involves the colonization or insemination of space. What else could provide the motivation for taking on the staggering costs of such a program? Significantly, frontier planets are peopled not with adventurers but rather with seeding projects or forced colonization. Robert Silverberg's *The Seed of Earth* (1962) depicts a future version of the draft that randomly selects space pioneers on a week's notice with no appeal; in fact, guards are assigned so that those chosen do not opt for suicide.[7] But there can be no choice if the policy of sending off sixty thousand conscripts a day is to be executed. When the call is made "for the good of the species," the all-too-typical response is, "Let the other guy colonize the stars. Me, I'll stay here and read about it" (*SE* 17)—a sentiment that closely parallels Dawkins's antinomy of gene and group selection (*SG* 10). It is different for single organisms faced with certain extinction, as in Blish's *All the Stars a Stage* (1971). When there is literally nothing left to lose, people will fight to get a place on the spaceships; witness instances of wartime refugees fighting for space on evacuation ships. The same goes for pilgrims fleeing from persecution, whether the settlers at Plymouth Rock or the long-lifers of Robert A. Heinlein's *Methuselah's Children* (1958). In the absence of such external pressure to immigrate, planetary colonies may be populated with convicts, as was the case with Georgia and Australia. Heinlein (*The Moon Is a Harsh Mistress* [1966]) and Robert Sheckley (*The Status Civilization* [1960]), for example, may know that our own country initially was colonized by damn few volunteers. If the gene is the unit of selection, as Dawkins says, it is also the locus of self-interest. All other things being equal, a gene would certainly prefer to send off copies of itself—something it is uniquely equipped to do. Indeed, this is what happens not only in *The Songs of Distant Earth* but also in *Earthseed*, in which a ship is sent off with combinations of sperm and ova so that the parents of the future colonists can stay on Earth.

Following the notion of the extended phenotype, genes work to promote the futures of their copies in other organisms; after all, a copy of a gene is the same gene. Dawkins cites evidence that likenesses do attract, that genes can show a spontaneous preference for unknown relatives (*EP* 150). Yet, science fiction suggests that likenesses can be taken too far. Depictions of clones, people with identical genomes, emphasize the unhealthiness of oversimilarity. Of course, this pertains to identical twins, too; though they are often presented in narrative as having an advantage in being genetic "teammates," twins, at least, did not come into being as the result of someone trying to "cheat" in the game of normal reproduction. Not so the enterprise of Aldous Huxley's *Brave New World* (1932), in which large "Bokanized" sets of Gamma and Delta clones are produced in factories, the very image of an inhumane eugenics, if not an ego gone out of control. Ira Levin's *The Boys from Brazil* (1976), with its clones of Adolf Hitler, also comes to mind. As members of a gendered species we know that reproduction is meant to be shared, even though in the process our chromosomes are split and reshuffled and then combined with someone else's; we want it that way. As much as we want a child to resemble ourselves, we also want it to resemble the one we love. Our selection of mates may reflect a preference for certain genes; attraction works by phenotypes. Consider the quiet triumph at the end of Joe Haldeman's *The Forever War* (1974): after being separated during centuries of interstellar conflict, the lovers reunite and have a baby almost twelve hundred years after leaving Earth. The contribution we want to make to the future is a partial one, not a whole one. Dawkins seems to contradict what he said about the self-interested gene when he states, "There is no obvious reason why any thinking entity should be motivated to make copies of itself" (*BW* 134). Perhaps he is heeding a subconscious aversion to clones, for the statement is easily refuted by self-portraits, diaries, and other forms of partial self-replication.

Far better, then, is the coincident urge for diversity, the inevitable consequence of sexual reproduction. Not only is variety the spice of life, it is a hedge against extinction. One of the joys of space stories, like travel itself, is that they allow us to wander about the universe and see the different forms humans have taken. In Brian W. Aldiss's *Starswarm* (1964), the huge interstellar distances—prohibitive obstacles to meaningful communication—have caused further speciation. The human genome is significantly reshaped here and in *The Seedling Stars* to suit humankind to exotic and inhospitable environments. In "Surface Tension," the crew hardly prefer microscopic progeny, but they have no choice: microorganisms are their only path to genetic immortality. While differentiation can inspire bias and xenophobia, the wider perspective shows that all people are human and in theory should cooperate in furthering each other's genetic posterity. After all, a species shares much genetic information. Narrative interest invariably requires potential kin altruism: we prefer to read about our own kind, no matter how distant in space or time, no matter how they are reshaped. In contrast, would anyone wish to read *The White Cloud*, Dawkins's novel about replicating clouds? Never fear, he didn't write it (*BW* 50). There is a great sense of gratification at the end of *The Seedling Stars* when distant descendants of the seeding program, one of them seal-like, return to repopulate the devastated Earth. Humanity has been saved, at least for a while. Only such thinking could justify the creation of the Ninth Men, some of them subhuman types adapted to the harsh conditions of Neptune, including "certain grazers which in times of hardship would meet together and give tongue in cacophonous ululation; or, sitting on their haunches with fore-limbs pressed together, they would listen by the hour to the howls of some leader" (*LFM* 277–78). They are, nevertheless, our distant relatives.

As Blish's noncorroding metal plates and Stapledon's book-long mental transmission sent back in time suggest, genes alone do not suffice to create what we recognize as human: there must be an intellectual heritage as well. The point is well made in Asimov's "Nightfall" (1941), in which attacks of mass insanity every two thousand years destroy all vestiges of human culture and make the victory of genetic survival a pyrrhic one. A small group tries to stave off the next catastrophe by going into hiding with weapons, food, water, and, most important, their records, which "will mean everything to the next cycle, and *that's* what must survive. The rest can go hang."[8] This anxiety does much to account for the popularity of Dark Ages themes in science fiction: we are still dispossessed by the burning of the library in Alexandria. The rise and fall of civilization is a repeated pattern in *Last and First Men*; the fictional motivation for the book is the Last Men's attempt to recapture and preserve lost knowledge. At an early stage in the chronicle, when a worldwide conflagration has killed all but a score of the First Men, the tiny band, though struggling to keep the species going on the north coast of Siberia, endures great hardships to engrave what they can remember of the recently destroyed civilization on stone slabs. They bury them in a cave with an ingenious pictorial dictionary and grammar so future generations will be able to decipher them. These prove to be invaluable, for the slabs are discovered by the Second Men almost ten million years later (*LFM* 126, 149–50). Before leaving Earth, travelers to Thalassa in *The Songs of Distant Earth* fill their rocket's computer banks with as much information as can be crammed in. Though the advanced systems of memory storage available in the thirty-sixth century permit them to accommodate roughly 10 percent of the ten billion books that have been written, no room can be found for Beethoven's Second and Fourth Symphonies, Sibelius's Third through Sixth Symphonies, or the first thirty-eight symphonies of Mozart's canon (*LFM* 147, 143–44); imagine, if you can, a future without the Haffner Symphony—like Heaven without Lowenbrau. Similar care to express our cultural heritage—less tastefully—was seen in the Voyager program when we sent our first nonelectronic message to the stars; much of the gold-plated record featured greetings expressed in most of Earth's languages.

Dawkins's theory of the selfish gene might suffice if libraries like Clarke's were limited to manuals and reference books; but if art squeezes other information or people off the ship, another element is required: the *meme*, the unit of mental—cultural—information. Memes resemble genes in that they form parts of larger bodies—here, texts—but memes can be broken into smaller sets, like the first notes of the Fifth Symphony. Though they recombine with other memes to create new ideas, their parentage may be traceable. After all, did I have to specify Beethoven? People can behave as if they own certain memes as intellectual progeny, treating memes like genes.

The "new replicators" are potentially immortal if they survive a new variant of "the survival of the fittest"; a few will prove to be *seminal*, while most will fall on *fallow ground*. Like genes, memes convey no absolute value; that depends on their environment (Ernst Mayr, in *EP* 245). Although generally useless as far as immediately promoting survival goes, artistic memes must be adept at attracting interest; successful ones gain an extraordinary privilege because they, like the Parthenon or Tutankhamen's mask, may represent an entire civilization. Unlike other memes, artistic memes can grow in value with age. Notably, Clarke mentions no *non*-artistic works preserved in the memory banks of the *Magellan*.

No one has argued an organic basis for Dawkins's memes; still, they offer an elegant and flexible device to help us understand cultural phenomena in new ways. If they exist, they replicate more quickly than genes, spreading in microseconds from brain to brain, brain to book, and so on (*SG* 192). Memes can mutate in transmission by recombination with an "allele" already present in the mind of the host. When liberated from organisms and lodged in, say, books or paintings, memes enjoy a sort of cryogenic suspension from which they can leap back into influential behavior and invade our nervous systems to take temporary ideological control over us (*SG* 199).

Indeed, people may treat memes as living things, as if they were genes. The confusion is understandable when we consider that, like culture, memes evolved as a way to accelerate adaptation. Memes were co-opted into the enterprise of biological immortality, but they outstripped their genetic predecessors. Horace boasted that he had built himself a monument made of words that would outlast the stone monuments erected by the caesars. Alexander Pushkin grafted his memes onto Horace's with a poem that borrowed his title, but he added a variation that betrays a particulate basis: his immortality will not be contingent on the preservation of his name, but as long as the Russian language he so conditioned lives, he will be there. Names are not the sine qua non of memeic immortality. Given a choice, the poet most wants to promote his or her productive thoughts, sometimes at great personal cost. Crew members in "Surface Tension" ask to retain a vestige of their personalities on the metal plates but relent in the interests of their mutual cause. Despite the efforts of the Last Men to recover every past personality, Stapledon's book has no personal names. It does not matter if our individual memeic contributions blend into our common intellectual posterity; they still give meaning to our existence.

So, memes may stand in for genes. Dawkins says, "We can lead fulfilling lives by reproducing ideas instead of offspring."[9] More than "gene machines," we are also meme machines, subservient to our "selfish memes" (SG 330, v). In *The Songs of Distant Earth*, Sergei Di Petro sees how his symphony will outstrip his earthly frame. The composer with a name that suggests he is made of stone says in a record, "Now, the *Lamentation* exists quite apart from me; it has taken on a life of its own. Even when Earth is gone, it will be speeding out toward the Andromeda Galaxy, driven by fifty thousand megawatts from the Deep Space transmitter" (SDE 290). Here is no self-pity, only deep satisfaction in the face of inevitable death. After all, reproductive success is achieved not by longevity alone but when one's genes, separate from oneself, make it on their own; when, to the parent's joy, children walk, catch a pass, or begin the replication process themselves. And memes can play this role. Dawkins told *Omni* that he is "interested in the possibility of ideas taking on a life of their own" ("Interview," 84), an experience familiar to readers and probably the chief excitement of literature. Such is happening for the meme, which is about to be accepted by the *Oxford English Dictionary*—if it can be shown to exist independently of Dawkins's name. The replicator senses that even if his name is lost, he still will have made a contribution, will have built himself a monument. This sort of memeic immortality is often sufficient for us. It may be all we have.

Notes

1. Richard Dawkins, *The Selfish Gene* (New York: Oxford University Press, 1976), v. Page references preceded by *SG* are to this edition.
2. Richard Dawkins, *The Blind Watchmaker: Why the Evidence of Evolution Reveals a Universe Without Design* (New York: Norton, 1987), 148. Page references preceded by *BW* are to this edition.
3. Olaf Stapledon, *Last and First Men* (1930; Harmondsworth: Penguin, 1963), 322. Later page references preceded by *LFM* are to this edition.
4. Arthur C. Clarke, *The Songs of Distant Earth* (New York: Ballantine Books, 1986), 22, 23. Later page references preceded by *SDE* are to this edition.
5. Richard Dawkins, *The Extended Phenotype: The Gene as the Unit of Selection* (Oxford: W. H. Freeman, 1982), 84, 263. Page references preceded by *EP* are to this edition.
6. Pamela Sargent, *Earthseed* (New York: Harper and Row, 1983), 131–32.
7. Robert Silverberg, *The Seed of Earth* (New York: Ace Books, 1962), 8. A later page reference preceded by *SE* is to this edition.
8. Isaac Asimov, "Nightfall," in *The Science Fiction Hall of Fame,* vol. 1, ed. Robert Silverberg (New York: Avon Books, 1970), 150.
9. "Interview with Richard Dawkins," *Omni* 12 (January 1990): 84.

IBMortality: Putting the Ghost in the Machine

Stephen Potts

When Marvin Minsky, the noted expert on robotics and artificial intelligence (AI), addressed the Eighth Annual Eaton Conference in 1986, his most striking assertion was that humanity would eventually—indeed, inevitably—create machine minds and bodies efficient enough that individuals could transfer into them when their natural bodies grew decrepit through age or disease. Thus technology—in the form of hard engineering—offers the promise of personal immortality. The main obstacle Minsky identified as standing between us and this consummation is the objection of humanists that people are not and never can be machines. Minsky observed, though, that this obstacle would someday be removed: once machine immortality becomes possible, humanists will refuse it and die out, in a form of cybernetic Darwinism. And good riddance, as far as he was concerned.

Minsky can dismiss humanists as irrelevant because his real battle has always been with others in the AI community. Minsky represents only one school of AI research, one that sees artificial intelligence primarily as a software problem: how to create programming that will perfectly imitate human intelligence. On the other side are the neural networkers, holists, or "connectionists," who focus on making the hardware as analogous as possible to biological brains so that machines will evolve intelligence on their own.

Holists Hubert and Stuart Dreyfus delineate the two schools, which have been wrestling since the 1950s, in this way:

One faction saw computers as a system for manipulating mental symbols; the other, as a medium for modeling the brain. One sought to use computers to instantiate a formal representation of the world; the other, to simulate the interactions of neurons. One took problem solving as its paradigm of intelligence; the other, learning. One utilized logic; the other, statistics. One school was the heir to the rationalist, reductionist tradition in philosophy; the other viewed itself as idealized, holistic neuroscience.[1]

Each method has drawbacks. Although computer hardware has advanced manyfold since Minsky and his collaborator Seymour Papert devastated the holistic school in their 1969 work *Perceptrons*, they and others continue to make the case that neural networks and the learning method are time-consuming, inefficient, and unpredictable. Counterarguments from holists, such as Dreyfus and Dreyfus, focus on the impossible task that the rationalists set for themselves—the same impossible task that earlier generations of scientific determinists stumbled over—namely, encoding in concrete form everything that a mind, whether natural or artificial, must have to react to the world.

In their attack on Minsky's determinism, Dreyfus and Dreyfus summarize the history of logical positivism, which ended when Russell and Whitehead gave way to Gödel, Husserl to Heidegger, and the early Wittgenstein of the *Tractatus* to the later Wittgenstein of *Philosophical Investigations*. Dreyfus and Dreyfus observe that not only has Minsky met the same barriers to a comprehensive phenomenology, he was guilty of philosophical naïveté when he complained, in his "A Framework for Representing Knowledge," that "we still know far too little about the contents and structure of common-sense knowledge," and that "we need a serious epistemological research effort in this area," an effort Minsky himself later attempted in his 1986 book *The Society of Mind*. "Husserl's phenomenology *was* just such a research effort," Dreyfus and Dreyfus point out. "Indeed, philosophers from Socrates through Leibniz to early Wittgenstein carried on serious epistemological research in this area for two thousand years without notable success."[2]

Perhaps for this reason, along with the quantum hardware leaps of the silicon era, neural networking has enjoyed a resurgence since the early 1980s; hardly a month goes by without the publication of some new development along this line, such as the December 1991 announcement of a chip that displays the same electrical potentials as a biological cell. Most of the many books on AI published in the 1980s and early 1990s take this approach, which prompted Minsky and Papert, with some alarm, to re-issue *Perceptrons* virtually unchanged.

Despite Minsky's advocacy of cybernetic immortality the subject comes up only rarely and in passing in his writings on machine intelligence. In the 1985 book *Robotics*, he asks, "Should we roboticize ourselves and stop dying?"[3] He advances his argument mainly in science fiction terms, alluding to Arthur C. Clarke's *The City and the Stars* (1956) and stories by Philip K. Dick. And he brings up one objection from the humanist camp: Would a machine that copied our mental patterns actually have our consciousness? Minsky offers no answer here but observes that similar questions about the relationship of consciousness and the individual organism have been around for centuries and provides relevant quotations from Goethe and Percy Shelley. Elsewhere, as in *The Society of Mind*, Minsky dismisses consciousness as simply another function of the mechanism: "What we call 'consciousness' consists of little more than menu lists that flash, from time to time, on mental screen displays that other systems use."[4] Indeed, consciousness is little more than registering, in short-term memory, acts we have already performed more or less autonomically—like turning a corner—with a degree of self-modeling, like that needed by a robot to understand its physical shape within determinate space. We mystify consciousness because we do not understand how it works.

Another objection to mechanizing human intelligence concerns the question of free will, an issue brought against Minsky by both humanist and religious thinkers. Minsky logically takes the positivist view: everything that happens in our universe is either completely determined by what has already happened in the past or else depends in part on random chance. Everything, including what happens in our brains, depends on these and only on these: *A set of fixed, deterministic laws. A purely random set of accidents.*[5] Human beings invented free will both as a "strong primitive defense mechanism" against the notion that we are being controlled by forces beyond our control, and, as with consciousness, as an unnecessary mystification of the brain's processes.[6] Ascribing a decision to "free will" means "*my decision was determined by internal forces I do not understand.*"[7] A determinist objection to free will is suggested by Minsky's complaint that "there is no structure to this part [of the mind]; one can say nothing meaningful about it, because whenever a regularity is observed, its representation is transferred to the deterministic rule region."[8] For Minsky's objectives, of course, this is a good thing; the more the brain becomes mechanically and logically deterministic, the more completely a technological mechanism can imitate its functions.

In fact, for Minsky—as for earlier positivists—the entire concept of "mind" is itself meaningless because the mind does not exist independently of the brain as a physically quantifiable unit. In his words, "*Minds are simply what brains do.*" And, he adds, "there is not the slightest reason to doubt that brains are anything other than machines with enormous numbers of parts that work in perfect accord with physical laws. As far as anyone can tell, our minds are merely complex processes." With "mind" the result of purely physical, if admittedly complex, processes, psychology becomes, in Minsky's terms, simply a more complicated order of physics or engineering, the main difference being the larger number of basic principles involved. Learn to understand these principles and you can create a machine that can reproduce them as well as a human brain. It follows that such a machine could assume the functions of a human brain: "If that new machine had a suitable body and were placed in a similar environment, its sequence of thoughts would be essentially the same as yours—since its mental states would be equivalent to yours."[9]

Science fiction, even the science fiction cited by Minsky as providing good examples of cybernetic immortality, has been at best ambivalent on the desirability of implanting human minds in machine bodies. In *The City and the Stars*, the computerized city of Diaspar lacks not only aging and death but basic drives like love and curiosity; its human inhabitants must regain their natural biological heritage by rejoining the Edenic Lys before they can be complete again. We are familiar with Dick's androids. Despite technically superior bodies they fall short of full humanity; those in *Do Androids Dream of Electric Sheep?* not only suffer from planned obsolescence but are also set apart by their lack of empathy for other life-forms, even other androids. Garson Poole in "The Electric Ant" is haunted by the fear that he lacks free will; he finally asserts it only by severing the tape operating his consciousness.

Recently, of course, the SF contemplation of the overlap of human and machine has been shaped by cyberpunk. A standard element of the sub-genre, ultimately a cliché, is the computerized personality of a dead character, as seen, for example, in Dixie Flatline in William Gibson's *Neuromancer* (1984), and Reno in Walter Jon Williams's *Hardwired* (1986). Independently, Samuel R. Delany came up with a similar entity in *Stars in My Pocket Like Grains of Sand* (1984): Mother Dyeth, who like Dixie Flatline begs to be erased, presumably because what is left of her consciousness and free will feels, like the electric ant's, less than human. Another form of computerized immortality appears in Greg Bear's *Eon* (1985) and its sequel, *Eternity* (1988), the books that got Bear branded (erroneously) a cyberpunk. Here humans spend most of their theoretically eternal lives downloaded into a communal network, granted a few mobile lives in bodies of their own choice, some not recognizably human.

The most focused discussion of cybernetic immortality comes from a writer who has also been lumped in with the cyberpunks, though his work has its origins in the 1970s. Rudy Rucker's *Software* was published in 1982, two years before *Neuromancer*, before the *c*-word was even a gleam in Bruce Sterling's mirrorshades. Like Minsky, Rucker comes to the subject from a background in mathematics and computer science, with the same inevitable drift toward cognitive science. And also like Minsky, Rucker has wrestled in nonfiction writings with the philosophical questions wracking AI research. But Rucker's conclusions are significantly different from Minsky's, so that Rucker would have to be placed at the holist end of the spectrum, even somewhat beyond it.

Software posits a somewhat "phildickian" near future with well-developed robot technology; indeed, robots are so advanced that they have evolved objectives of their own and have rebelled against human control. They have taken over the human colony on the Moon, whose airless and frigid environment suits their supercooled mechanisms. The independence of their thought processes was made possible by inventor Cobb Anderson, who freed robots from the strictures of Isaac Asimov's Three Laws of Robotics and thus gave them free will—in effect, releasing them from slavery; robots still chained to human control, we learn later, are called "asimovs," robot versions of Uncle Toms.

Freedom, in fact, is built into Anderson's very creation of these machines, called "boppers"; instead of preprogramming all of their functions and thought processes, he let the boppers evolve in quasi-Darwinian fashion—a notion, Rucker reminds us, that was suggested by John von Neumann in the 1950s and accords with the evolutionary learning approach of holist neural networkers. In this version of AI evolution, machines engage in a pseudo-sexual sharing during which they exchange bits of software; they build other robots using this software and hard-to-come-by spare parts from those who have been terminated, as all robots must be on a set schedule. So both death and competition exist in the robot realm. Every bopper is programmed to hook up periodically with a master computer that generates random bits of computer code, scrambling small units of their programming and making mutations possible; the computer also retains bits of all the robots' software in a state many boppers regard as immortality within the godhead.

Although this behavior is part of their programming, they are free in that the results are not predetermined. Indeed, despite the apparent centralization of bopper software in the master computer, individual boppers can operate independently. As a bopper named Misty tells human protagonist Sta-Hi, she can oppose the mental commands being beamed to her by a senior computer because she has free will: "It's part of the brain-tape. I can do what I like." Free will is the most important attribute that distinguishes the humanly intelligent machines from their purely mechanical ancestors; it evolved as a survival trait under Anderson's program. This is not just the *illusion* of free will that Minsky views as a human defense mechanism, but genuine freedom. And though boppers are at odds with humanity, they remain eager to move on to a new stage of reunification. This they attempt to accomplish by kidnapping human minds—recording the software of brains—and translating them into androids of their own construction; Misty is one such being. About to go public with this endeavor, they offer their creator, ailing in a retirement community in Florida, a new immortal body. Anderson, despite his faith in artificial intelligence, has the usual doubts about whether or not his consciousness will continue along with his software. It turns out that he shares such doubts with his prototypical bopper, Ralph Numbers. At a crucial moment on the verge of his transfer from one metallic housing to another, Ralph muses that he "would again be equipped with a self symbol and a feeling of personal consciousness. But would the consciousness really be the same?" The general bopper attitude toward hardware exchanges is summed up by Misty, however: "The software is what counts, the habits and the memories. The brain and the body are just meat." She further claims, "The soul *is* the software."[10]

Rucker's ideas are more carefully detailed in his nonfiction works on higher mathematics, cognitive science, and the metaphysical ramifications of these fields. At one level his arguments match Minsky's; Rucker believes that a cybernetic immortality is not only feasible but inevitable. He uses the same language of mechanical analogy: if a machine could mimic all our behavior, both internal and external, then it would seem that there is nothing left to be added. Body and brain fall under the heading of *hardware*. Habits, knowledge, self-image, and the like can be classed as *software*.[11]

But Rucker adds a third quality to the complete mind, encompassing consciousness and free will, two elements that Minsky dismisses as humanist fantasies. For Rucker, this part of the mind is not quantifiable, or even subject to intentional creation, but inheres in all beings. And he argues that this consciousness continues unaltered even if the hardware or software is replaced.

Consciousness, for Rucker, has a transcendental existence. Of the three chief parts of the mind, it is the one that embodies "the sense of self or personal identity, pure awareness, the spark of life, or even the soul." Consciousness is rooted in a simple assertion, "*I am. I am me. I exist.*"[12] Rucker echoes this view in *Software* when Ralph Numbers contemplates moving to his next machine body and settles his doubts about the continuity of consciousness by repeating, "*I am. I am me.*"[13] But Rucker goes even further: consciousness, he asserts, is independent of the individual mind; it inheres in everything that exists, even a rock or a piece of paper. Thus there is no reason to deny it to a thinking machine.

To back up this transholist approach, Rucker appeals to the work of Kurt Gödel, whose holographic form appears in a bopper museum in *Software*; indeed, in challenging the axioms of linear thought, Rucker may be to Minsky's determinism what Gödel was to the logical positivism of Russell and Whitehead. Reviewing the work of Gödel along with that of Türing and Church in *Mind Tools*, Rucker concludes emphatically, "Our highest goals are not to be exhausted by the logical working out of any single system. . . . [T]he old dream of capturing all truth in a finite logical net can be seen to be thoroughly bankrupt."[14] This, you recall, is the charge leveled by Dreyfus and Dreyfus against Minsky's pursuit.

Rucker actually spoke to Gödel a few times in the last years of the mathematician's life, and he asserts that the two had common views of cognition and the evolutionary model for machine intelligence. He also calls on the authority of Gödel with regard to the question of the transcendental existence of Mind. When Rucker says that "the Mind exists independently of its individual properties"—independently of hardware, software, and even individual beings—he avers anecdotally that Gödel approved of this classically mystical stance on the ubiquity of consciousness. Rucker, in fact, divides thinkers on the artificial intelligence question into three schools: "*Mechanism*: Neither men nor robots are anything but machines, and there is no reason why man-like machines cannot exist. *Humanism*: Men have souls and machines do not, therefore no robot can be quite like a man. *Mysticism*: Everything, whether man or machine, participates in the Absolute, therefore it should be possible for man-like machines to exist."[15] Minsky belongs in the first category, while Rucker cheerfully enlists in the last. The humanists, once more, seem irrelevant.

We glimpse Rucker's mysticism, cast in the language of nonlinear science, in *Wetware*, his 1988 sequel to *Software*—which he dedicated, significantly, to Philip K. Dick. In *Wetware*, the humanoid bopper Berenice contrasts the narrow human notion of Self with the boppers' more comprehensive view: human uniqueness is illusory because all individuals are fractal cellular automata of the One, thus part of the One's consciousness. We see Anderson experiencing this greater fractal awareness in *Wetware* as he lingers in the master computer between bodies, a condition he simply calls "heaven." Having explained it as an existence on several dimensional levels at once, independent of the particular body he is in, he receives support from Berenice, who, true to her particular sisterhood, speaks in a patois borrowed from Edgar Allen Poe: "I am heartened by your suggestion that flesher and bopper bodies are in every way of a rude and democratic equivalence and that we boppers do indeed have claim on an eternal resting place in the precincts of that misty *heaven* whence emanates the One. I believe this to be true."[16]

Unfortunately, it is no easier for the skeptical humanist to accept Rucker's axiomatic leap of faith (everything that exists has consciousness and a soul, therefore cybernetic immortality is possible) than Minsky's (consciousness and the soul do not exist, therefore cybernetic immortality is possible). Indeed, Rucker only muddies his case for human-machine equivalence in *Wetware*. There, boppers take the next evolutionary leap by actually producing organic humans with bits of machine programming in their DNA, implanting them as embryos in human women in an imitation of divine conception. But even the best of these wetware boppers still have problems in common with Dick's androids—notably, a lack of empathy. One eats the family dog, and another a man living at a trash dump. It does not help to assert, like one of the sympathetic human characters, that the man "was a zero and a jerk" and thus worthless;[17] doing so only makes the human characters seem less human. If everything that exists has consciousness and a soul, is not everything, certainly a human, worth preserving as something more than meat? Or is this just an irrelevant humanist objection?

In terms of the AI debate, however, Rucker's brand of holistic fuzzy logic is clearly and wholly opposed to Minsky's strict, if phenomenologically doomed, logical positivism. No opposition could better demonstrate the maelstrom where AI studies and the promise of cybernetic immortality find themselves today. If the determinist Minsky leaves us only with the unsubstantiated promise that methodical research into finite technology will eventually result in completely humanoid machines, the idealist Rucker offers us a mystical faith in the unrestricted freedom of the transfinite: "Our world is endlessly more complicated than any finite program or any finite set of rules. You're free, and you're really alive, and there's no telling what you'll think of next, nor is there any reason you shouldn't kick over the traces and start a new life at any time."[18] But if that new life turns out to be in an android body, the evidence suggests it will not come any time soon.

Notes

1. Hubert L. Dreyfus and Stuart E. Dreyfus, "Making a Mind versus Modeling the Brain," in *The Artificial Intelligence Debate*, ed. Stephen R. Graubard (Cambridge: MIT Press, 1988), 15–16.

2. Dreyfus and Dreyfus, "Making a Mind," 30–31.

3. Marvin Minsky, ed., *Robotics* (Garden City, N.Y.: Doubleday, 1985), 304.

4. Marvin Minsky, *The Society of Mind* (New York: Simon and Schuster, 1986), 57.

5. Minsky, *The Society of Mind*, 306.

6. Marvin Minsky, ed., *Semantic Information Processing* (Cambridge: MIT Press, 1968), 431.

7. Minsky, *The Society of Mind*, 306.

8. Minsky, *Semantic Information Processing*, 431.

9. Minsky, *The Society of Mind*, 287, 288, 289.

10. Rudy Rucker, *Software* (New York: Ace Books, 1982), 34, 82, 83.

11. Rudy Rucker, *Infinity and the Mind: The Science and Philosophy of the Infinite* (Boston: Birkhauser, 1982), 170.

12. Rucker, *Infinity and the Mind*, 183.

13. Rucker, *Software*, 35.

14. Rudy Rucker, *Mind Tools: The Five Levels of Mathematical Reality* (Boston: Houghton Mifflin, 1987), 247.

15. Rucker, *Infinity and the Mind*, 170, 185.

16. Rucker, *Wetware* (New York: Avon Books, 1988), 69.

17. Rucker, *Wetware*, 172.

18. Rucker, *Mind Tools*, 247.

How Cyberspace Signifies:
Taking Immortality Literally

N. Katherine Hayles

Through their individual imaginations, writers can evoke a world that differs in significant respects from the society in which they live. But in the very act of creating difference authors necessarily reinscribe similarity, for presuppositions eluding their artistic or linguistic grasp always far outnumber the few they can consciously modify. Most science fiction stories that imagine immortality fall into this category. Treating mortality as an independent variable that can be altered to show the effects on society, they create narratives whose thematics deal with immortality but whose underlying processes of signification remain unchanged. As comedy and tragedy testify, the fact of mortality is central to literary form and signification. Because deep assumptions about mortality are encoded in the signifiers that constitute narratives of immortality, what is given with one hand is taken away with the other.

How might narratives change if mortality were not a fact but an option, an option summoned not merely by a writer's imagination but by pervasive social and material conditions? The possibility of an immortality that seems almost within our technological grasp shimmers in Hans Moravec's dream of downloading consciousness into a computer.[1] Moravec believes that once the transfer is complete, the body will be dispensable, a mortal coil as obsolete as it is potentially deadly. Summarizing the attitude, Ed Regis writes, "Tired of the ills of the flesh? Then get rid of the flesh. We can do that now!"[2] Although these dreams remain fantasies, they point to larger social and economic changes that make the transformation of material structures into informational patterns everyday events. As the practices of everyday life change, the substrate of cultural assumptions shifts accordingly, precipitating further changes in life experiences. Among the many cultural sites involved in these feedback loops are contemporary fictions, as information technologies change not merely the subjects represented but the codes used to represent them. Thus the possibility exists for a writer to bring computerized immortality as a thematic together with processes of signification changed by computer technology, setting up complex reverberations between the signifiers that produce meaning and the meanings they produce.

In William Gibson's Sprawl trilogy—*Neuromancer, Count Zero,* and *Mona Lisa Overdrive*—this explosive combination catches fire.[3] The catalyst is the deceptively simple premise that a landscape of computerized information can literally become a space through which consciousness can move. It is no secret to literary critics that the creation of a new kind of space can profoundly alter the stories written within and about it. The virgin forests of James Fenimore Cooper and Nathaniel Hawthorne and the oceanic expanses of Herman Melville led to narratives different in kind, not merely in degree, from those that emerged from the stuffy drawing rooms of English society. So too the novels spun out of cyberspace differ in important ways even from their close cousins within science fiction. What are the catalytic properties of cyberspace, and how do these properties interact with changing codes of representation?

Underlying the idea of cyberspace is a fundamental shift in the premises of what constitutes reality. Reality is considered to be formed not primarily from matter or energy but from information. Although information can be carried by matter or energy, it remains distinct from them. Properly speaking, it is a pattern rather than a presence. Deconstruction has taught us that presence is never self-evident by itself; to come into being, it must always already be joined with absence in a generative dialectic that produces both simultaneously. In the same way, pattern does not come into being by itself; rather, it is always already joined by randomness in a generative dialectic that produces both simultaneously.[4] The cultural context for cyberspace is a wide-ranging displacement of presence and absence by pattern and randomness as the generative dialectic producing representations. The displacement of presence/absence by pattern/randomness is visually evident in new scientific imaging technologies that interface humans and computers, such as positron emission tomography, or PET.[5] In PET, naturally occurring biological substrates are synthesized in mildly radioactive forms and injected into the patient. To reveal brain function, a glucose isotope is used as the substrate. The emission intensity correlates with glucose metabolism, which in turn correlates with different kinds of perceptual and cognitive activity. Detecting and mapping the radioactive particles yields a data array indicating the signal strength at various points across a plane through the patient's brain. The data are analyzed tomographically by a computer using Fourier transform techniques, from which a two-dimensional image "slice" is constructed with colors to indicate signal intensity. If the patient is talking to himself during the scan, verbal centers will be colored hot in the resulting image; if she is performing motor tasks, the hot areas will be the appropriate motor centers.

New software can stack these two-dimensional images to create a projected three-dimensional simulation, which can be spatially manipulated by the computer to yield images from many perspectives. Moreover, the 3-D simulation can be overlaid back onto the patient by means of an electronic wand passed over the patient's head. The wand allows the simulation to be precisely correlated with the topography of the patient's head. Say the patient has a brain tumor. By moving the wand to the tumor's location in the simulation, the technician knows where to mark the patient's head to indicate the exact point where the surgeon should make the incision. Thus the technique creates a space in which patient and simulation come together in real time, as if the patient had moved inside the screen or the simulation had moved out into the world.

The transformations involved in this technology illustrate how presence/absence is interpenetrated and displaced by pattern/randomness. During PET scans the living body is turned into a data array, an image is constructed from the array, then the image is overlaid back onto the living body to form body-plus-simulation. We can visualize the transformation as a keyhole shape, appropriate to the *Alice in Wonderland* flavor of having gone through the computer screen and come out the other side. The large upper end is an embodied actuality, which is reduced through the scanning technique to the wasp waist of the data array; this disembodied array becomes a visually rich image again through tomographic simulation techniques. When the bottom end of the keyhole is folded back onto the top end, the result may seem to be a fuller, richer version of the patient, whose interior cranial terrain is now as visually accessible and medically significant to the technicians as external physiognomy was to nineteenth-century practitioners. But make no mistake: these transformations do not simply yield back the original subject. The reconstituted body-plus-simulation is neither flesh and blood alone nor computer image, but a new kind of entity that, following Xerox PARC's Mark Wieser, I call an *embodied virtuality*.

Embodied virtuality differs from traditional embodiment because in it, presence is understood to be always already penetrated by the virtuality of information.

The systematic transformations that create embodied virtuality are not limited to scientific visualization; they occur in a variety of sites and diverse media, including modern fiction. To show how they work in printed texts, I return to Gibson's cyberspace. The question I want to pose is not *What does cyberspace mean?* but *How it is constituted as a verbal entity?* Like the body transformed into a data array, representations referencing embodied actualities in Gibson's text are presumed to be reduced to data-like abstractions as they enter cyberspace. From these abstractions the text generates new representations through the trope of literalization; this phase corresponds to the creation of the simulation in a PET scan. It may seem as if the reconstituted representations can simply stand in for the old, like the simulation overlaid onto the patient's body, but the move through abstraction has caused them to be riddled with the virtuality of simulation. Like the body-plus-simulation, the verbally constituted entities of cyberspace refer to presence interpenetrated by the immateriality of information. As the trilogy progresses, there is increasing pressure for pattern to usurp presence, information to displace materiality.

To see these transformations at work, consider how movement is constituted in cyberspace. Representations referencing a body—descriptions of Case, for example—are displaced by a signifier written as *pov*. More than an acronym, pov is literalized into a substantive noun that signifies the body's abstraction into a point of view. The pov does not, however, merely signify the character's position; rather, increasingly it signifies the character himself. Movement is achieved when the pov flies, the mode of transportation that comes closest to reducing the friction of distance to zero. Movement takes place in relation to the fixed data structures that form the landscape, generating a distinction between free and occupied space that also operates as a public/private division. The distinction is enforced not by social prohibitions such as laws against trespassing but by privately owned *ice* (intrusion countermeasures electronics) that are lethal to a pov violating the space. The field of movement is constituted through descriptions that rely primarily on visual sense (as distinct from aural, kinesthetic, or tactile senses). The horizontal dimension is usually the axis along which movement takes place, whereas the vertical dimension is used primarily to signify complexity and size of data structures—another abstraction that has been literalized into a spatial dimension. In contrast with the endless empty landscapes of the New World or the empty expanses of outer space, this frontier is always already crowded. Exploration takes place under the trope of violation and transgression of the already owned and already occupied rather than under the imperialist fiction of the discovery of a dark continent or a new world. Consequently, in this world innocence is hardly possible, even as a self-delusion.

Underlying these spatial qualities is a presupposition that I have underscored in my description: cyberspace is constituted through signifiers that literalize abstractions, particularly the abstractions characteristic of postmodernity. We learn in *Count Zero*, for example, that only underdeveloped Third World countries still have governments. In the First World, government functions have been taken over by multinational corporations. This abstract proposition is represented in cyberspace by the proliferation of corporate structures in the landscape and the transfer of police authority from laws to ice. Laws can be written down, but they are not themselves physical objects. By contrast, ice is represented in cyberspace as having the sensory properties one associates with materiality. It glows white or blue, has an intricate physical geometry, and can move through space in pursuit of a trespasser. The abstraction it represents has been literalized into a virtual presence that has as much physical reality as anything else in this virtual space. The largest sense in which literalization occurs is, of course, cyberspace itself, a space constituted by literalizing data fields into actual physical localities.

Literalizing abstractions, cyberspace creates a level playing field where abstract entities, data constructs, and physically embodied consciousnesses interact on an equal basis. All forms are equivalent in this space; none is more physically real or immediate than any other. The signifiers representing an actually existing person cannot claim more materiality than those representing the shape of a data bank or construct generated by a computer program, because all signifiers within this space—include those generating the space itself—operate according to a logic of literalization.

Case, the protagonist of *Neuromancer*, tries to maintain the distinction between life that exists literally outside cyberspace and life that exists as a literality only because of cyberspace. When he sees Linda Lee in cyberspace after she has been killed, he insists she cannot be real because she is not alive. Neuromancer, the artificial intelligence who has created the simulacrum, claims that the distinction is not valid. "To live here [in cyberspace] is to live. There is no difference," he tells Case (*N* 305). The claim is central to all three books, although they take different stances toward it. As the arc of the trilogy progresses, the preponderance of evidence shifts to support the claim, however much Case resists it initially. There are deeper reasons for this progression than authorial preference or a need to generate new plots. In this literalized space, life is indeed life, for literalization flattens differential relations between signifiers that could constitute a distinction between life that is literally alive and life that is simulated metaphorically. Immortality thus happens not only at the level of thematics, as when Bobby, Angie, and 3 Jane cast off their bodies and decide to live in the aleph's biosoft memory, but at the level of signification as well.

If signifiers in cyberspace cannot constitute the life/death difference, what differences can they bring into play? In this system of signification, the distinction corresponding to life/death is on/off, or, more precisely, continuity/discontinuity. When one is alive, consciousness and memory continue to exist after the plug is pulled. After Case jacks out of cyberspace, he remembers who he is and what happened; but Dixie Flatline, a cyberspace jockey who died after something in cyberspace made him "flatline" (cease brain activity), now lives only as a computer construct whose memory terminates when the on/off switch is flipped:

> "What's the last thing you remember before I spoke to you, Dix?" [Case asks the Flatline.]
>
> "Nothin'."
>
> "Hang on." He disconnected the construct. The presence was gone. He reconnected it. "Dix? Who am I?"
>
> "You got me, Jack. Who the fuck are you?" (N 78).

Mortality and termination, already synonyms in popular culture, here are constructed as functions of an electrical circuit. The pun, as Scott Bukatman convincingly argues in *Terminal Identity*, is central to the construction of subjectivity in postmodern science fiction.[6]

In this passage it seems as though the vulnerability to on/off can reliably distinguish between artificial and natural life-forms. As the trilogy proceeds, however, the boundaries separating cyberspace from the real world become progressively more permeable, until finally there is scarcely any space that cannot be literalized. As a consequence, even the on/off distinction is undermined. In a continuation of the passage cited above, for example, Case temporarily overcomes the problem of Dixie's on/off consciousness by jacking the construct into the data bank he is using, giving it "sequential, real-time memory" (N 79). The distinction between on and off continues to erode in the next volumes of the trilogy. Isolated in a small hand unit, Colin (a computer construct built as a companion to Kumi in *Mona Lisa Overdrive*) cannot maintain consciousness when the machine is off. Released into the aleph's cyberspace, however, he immediately achieves continuity, taunting 3Jane that he is just as real as she is despite the fact that she once had a material body and he did not. The progression reaches its logical end in *Mona Lisa Overdrive* when continuity itself becomes a machine function, personified in Sense/Net's sentient computer consciousness called Continuity. Once computer consciousness finds a way to overcome the on/off problem and maintain continuity, it has effectively achieved real immortality, not the spurious kind that makes Dixie Flatline ask to be permanently disconnected.

As computer simulacra evolve toward memory continuity, humans seem to devolve toward memory discontinuity. Literalized into a space, memory becomes an area available for expropriation, discipline, and punishment. Slick had his memory "colonized" while he was in prison so that he could remember nothing other than the routine information he needed to perform forced labor. The effects of the colonization continue after he is released. The stigmata of his suffering take the form of Korsakov's Syndrome, which makes him lose the ability to remember under stress. In an unintentional parody of the conversation between Case and Dixie Flatline in the first volume, Slick in the final volume repeatedly gives Candy the same answers to the same questions without remembering how he has just responded (*MLO* 136–37). Human and computer simulacrum have changed places: now the human, not the construct, is shackled to the on/off button of mnemonic continuity.

The literalization that drives this progression is inscribed into pov, deepening the reach of immortality beyond thematics and into processes of signification. In all three books Gibson uses point of view to construct narratives in ways that would be familiar to Henry James. In *Neuromancer* the third-person narrator has access primarily to Case's consciousness, and the story is told mostly from his point of view. Because Case can share the sensorium of other characters, the text reads like multiple narratives spliced together. *Count Zero* also uses third-person narration, but now the narrative explicitly splits into parallel stories of Mitchell's "extraction" from Maas Biolabs and Bobby Newmark's adventures in and around cyberspace. *Mona Lisa Overdrive* continues to proliferate points of view, bifurcating between the four viewpoints of Kumi, Mona, Angie, and Slick, with the fifth implicit viewpoint of Count Zero emerging only at the end, and only within cyberspace.

Beyond this conventional use of point of view lies a more innovative mode of construction that can be described as a literalization of point of view. In its Jamesian sense, point of view presumes the fiction of a person who observes the action from a particular angle and tells what he or she sees. In the preface to *The Portrait of a Lady*, James imagines a "house of fiction" with a "million windows" formed by "the need of the individual vision and by the pressure of the individual will." At each "stands a figure with a pair of eyes, or at least with a field glass, which forms, again and again, for observation, a unique instrument, insuring to the person making use of it an impression distinct from every other."[7] For James, the observer is an embodied creature, and the specificity of his location determines what he can see as he looks out at a scene that is itself physically specific. When an omniscient viewpoint is used, the limitations of the narrator's corporeality begin to fall away, but the suggestion of embodiment lingers in the idea of focus, the "scene" created by the eye's movement.

Even for James, vision is not unmediated technologically. Significantly, he imagines the viewer's field glass as no less constitutive of vision than the angle of vision or eyes. Cyberspace makes a quantum leap forward into the technological mediation of vision. Instead of an embodied consciousness looking through the window, the pov moves through the screen, leaving the body behind as an unoccupied shell. In cyberspace, point of view does not describe the character; it creates him. Lacking a body and reduced to his consciousness, the character literally *is* his point of view. If his point of view is annihilated he also disappears, ceasing to exist as a consciousness both in and out of cyberspace. In cyberspace the realist fiction of a narrator who observes but does not create is unmasked; the effect of unmasking is not metafictional, however, but in a literal sense metaphysical, above and beyond physicality. The key difference between the Jamesian and cyberspace points of view is that the former implies physical presence while the latter does not.

In several passages Gibson plays with these conventions, conflating Jamesian fiction with the cyberspace construction. When Case "rides" with Molly by hitting the simstim switch that connects them, the narrative jumps to her point of view at the time that Case's consciousness is joined with hers by cyberspace technology. When her leg is broken, she feels excruciating pain that jolts Case when he shares her sensorium. The difference is that she cannot escape her body, while he can elude the screaming nerves by flipping a switch. For her, pain is as inevitable as mortality; for him, it is an option. Nor is it coincidence that the character immersed in her physicality is a woman and the character who can escape it is a man. Though both males and females can enter cyberspace, pervasive gender encodings throughout the trilogy cast immersion in the body as female, alienation and escape from it as male.

Central to these encodings is the manipulation of point of view. In all three books there are recognition scenes in which a male character sees his body from the outside, at first fails to recognize it, and then is shocked and disgusted at his vulnerability when he does. The first such scene occurred when Case hit the simstim switch and found himself staring down, through Molly's good eye, at a "white-faced, wasted figure, afloat in a loose fetal crouch, a cyberspace deck between its thighs, a band of silver trodes over closed, shadowed eyes. The man's cheeks were hollowed with a day's growth of dark beard, his face slick with sweat. He was looking at himself" (N 256). The regressive behavior of the fetal position, the wasted body seen only as "it," and the implications of disease and mortality are in stark contrast with the consciousness who just played a heroic role in a perilous adventure in cyberspace. This dramatizes the split between Jamesian and cyberspace pov, representing both a body whose physicality is described by pov and a consciousness that exists only because it has been literalized through pov.

In *Count Zero* the alienation between physical presence and literalized pov deepens when Bobby perceives himself flattened against the ceiling, "staring straight down at a blood-stained white doll that had no head at all. . . . There were pink and blue dermadisks stuck to the skin on either side of the doll's neck. The edges of the wound seemed to have been painted with something that looked like chocolate syrup. . . . Then Bobby got the picture, and the universe reversed itself sickeningly. The lamp was suspended from the ceiling, the ceiling was mirrored, and he was the doll" (CZ 53–54). By *Mona Lisa Overdrive*, alienation is so extreme that it is not possible to recover any exterior view of the body from a subject's perspective. The only descriptions we have of Count Zero (aka Bobby) are through the eyes of others as they look at the wasted, tube-fed body so obviously superfluous that its death is scarcely noticed. By then his subjectivity does not inhere in the flesh at all, having been "decremented" by a count to zero. As his name implies, Count Zero has gone through the boundary point and exists only as a literalized pov in cyberspace.

In contrast with this male alienation from one's physical self is the immersion of the female characters in their bodies. Molly delights in using her cyborg body as a physical weapon; Mona has cosmetic surgery to make her a near double of her idol, Angie Mitchell; Angie's father performs extensive neurosurgery on her brain, impregnating it with biosoft circuitry. Although men can also be simstim stars, like Robin Lanier (the name a bow to the father of virtual reality, Jaron Lanier), it is only with female characters that the narrative pov representing the simstim viewer moves inside the body. The construction suggests that the gendered language of electrical circuits is inscribed within and through the signifiers that constitute the bodies of these texts. While men jack in, an expression alluding both to the phallus and to a male electrical fitting, women become receptacles for biocybernetic intrusions. With male characters the connection is exterior, as the alienated cyberspace pov suggests; with female characters it is interior, enmeshed within their physicality.

The two sides of this gendered dichotomy become entangled in the fecund and phallic ambiguities of the matrix—meaning both a mathematical array, an abstract arrangement of data unfolded according to logical rules, and the female ground of creation, the unformed materia that for Renaissance science was female matter before male spirit gave it form and shape. Bobby jacks into the aleph that provides the abstract space he and Angie will inhabit, but Angie accesses it directly through the biosoft interior of her brain that her father reconfigured into the necessary patterns. In a more than figurative sense, her father gives her away. To consummate marriage with the cyberspace pov Bobby has become, Angie must bring her cybernetic receptacle into physical proximity with the aleph's exterior form. Though both Angie and Bobby leave their bodies to live in the aleph's abstraction of cyberspace, they do so through different, and differently gendered, topologies.

If the female is identified with immersion in physicality and the male with abstraction from it, the arc of the trilogy is overwhelmingly male. The logic moves progressively, relentlessly toward abstraction. Cyberspace, a literalized abstraction of the world, is fully occupied the first time we see it. In later volumes it becomes progressively more crowded, until Bobby seeks a new frontier in the aleph, a space described as an abstraction of cyberspace. With abstraction piled on abstraction, consciousness becomes more remote from physicality and the smell of mortality. Working in tandem with the abstractions are the literalizations that make them into spaces that can be occupied as if they were physical locations. Once, immortality was represented through metaphor: people were immortal when they were like gods. It is a measure of how far immortality has permeated into the processes of signification that now it is constituted through the opposite trope of literalization: people are immortal when they are literalized into pov and placed in abstract arrays literalized into spaces.

Oddly, as the spaces become more literalized and abstract, they become more domestic. All we see in cyberspace are geometric forms; it's a nice place to visit, but who would want to live there? By contrast, the aleph has houses, fields, and horses. But perhaps it is not so odd, for having the spaces become more habitable as they move further into abstraction makes them as cozy as the spaces of the world—with a crucial difference. In the aleph there is no omega, no necessary end, no inevitable mortality. Ironically, as immortality penetrates deeper into the textures of the texts and as physicality is apparently left behind, gender becomes if anything more rather than less important. Fleeing physicality, Angie, Bobby, and other characters inhabit cyberspace and have its gendered topologies reinscribed in the electrical circuitry that now serves as their bodies. Thus is immateriality made in the image of the physicality that it displaces and preempts. The reinscription can serve as a reminder that even though immortality now reaches beyond thematics into the signifiers themselves, the ground for life remains rooted in the matrix of physicality. Literalized abstractions can never be wholeness.

Notes

1. Moravec discusses these possibilities in the significantly titled *Mind Children: The Future of Robot and Human Intelligence* (Cambridge: Harvard University Press, 1989).

2. Ed Regis, *Great Mambo Chicken and the Transhuman Condition: Science Slightly over the Edge* (Reading, Mass.: Addison-Wesley, 1990), 7.

3. William Gibson, *Neuromancer* (1984; London: Grafton Books, 1986); *Count Zero* (New York: Ace Books, 1987); *Mona Lisa Overdrive* (New York: Bantam Books, 1988). All future page references in the text are to these editions, abbreviated, respectively, as N, CZ, and *MLO*.

4. The pattern/randomness dialectic and information/noise interplay are connected in information theory. For a discussion of how these pairs are complementary, see Hayles, *Chaos Bound: Orderly Disorder in Contemporary Literature and Science* (Ithaca: Cornell University Press, 1990), 1–60.

5. PET scans are discussed in Richard Mark Friedhoff and William Benzon, *Visualization: The Second Computer Revolution* (New York: Abrams, 1989), 64–66, 81. An overview is in *Brain Imaging*, a project proposal by Robert N. Beck, Oscar H. Kapp, and Chin-Tu Chen (Chicago: ANL Center for Imaging Science, no date).

6. Scott Bukatman, *Terminal Identity: The Virtual Subject in Postmodern Science Fiction* (Durham: Duke University Press, 1993).

7. Henry James, *The Art of the Novel* (New York: Scribner's, 1937), 46.

Part III

Literature and Immortality

Alienation as the Price of Immortality: The Tithonus Syndrome in Science Fiction and Fantasy

S. L. Rosen

It has been observed that immortality does not receive sympathetic treatment in English-language science fiction. Brian Stableford in *The Encyclopedia of Science Fiction* summarizes the negative views of immortality both inside science fiction and in novels outside the genre. Joseph Francavilla echoes this as he contrasts the treatment of immortality in the works of Roger Zelazny: "Immortality has not fared well in science fiction. The typical immortal or race of immortals in a science fiction story is plagued with infinite ennui, listless decadence, agonizing aging, or a combination of these. The immortal sees no reason to live any longer, but he can't die, or else his spirit continues to exist in limbo after the death of his body."[1]

The recurring motif that the search for or achievement of immortality is neither desirable nor possible, except at terrible cost, certainly seems out of keeping with the steady increase in the projected human life span. Immortality is widely represented, Stableford reports, as "the ultimate stagnation and the end of innovation and change."[2] Since the motif of futility and punishment resulting from a search for immortality appears in various guises in folklore, mythology, and literature, it warrants a descriptive name: I will call it the Tithonus Syndrome. In the Tithonus myth, futility and punishment result from partial granting of the desired outcome: instead of eternal life as a blessing, Tithonus is cursed with the suffering that comes with advancing age. Certain aspects of the syndrome, such as alienation, change of physical state, and degeneration, are inherent in its manifestations.

When folk legends or classical myths present the quest for immortality, there are three general modes for its achievement. First, immortality may be a direct grant from the gods, usually as a reward for meritorious service or the result of the intervention of some deity. Examples of this mode include the myths of Herakles, Ganymede, Orpheus, and Tithonus.[3] Herakles and Ganymede obtain translation to the immortality of the gods, the latter by the good fortune of being attractive, the former by hard work in correcting the world's ills. In neither case is the achievement of apotheosis the result of a conscious desire or quest. The agency of the gods is unsolicited; no hubris can be attributed to the recipient, thus no punishment is inflicted on the recipient. In these cases, the immortality is always accompanied by a translation of state as well.

When immortality is consciously sought, the results, as in the cases of Orpheus and Tithonus, fall short of success. The Orpheus legend belongs to the failed test archetype. In such a situation, similar to that of Pandora or Psyche, the human condition ensures failure. The failure of Tithonus's wife, Eos, to request eternal youth (renewal) as well as immortality is more complex. On the surface, this myth is easily confused with a "just-so" story that explains the genesis of a species, in this case the grasshopper. Despite the resemblance, however, the two types are different. The myth does not suggest that the aged though undying man is the archetype of grasshoppers; rather, a comparison is drawn between the dried skin and rasping voice of the unrenewed Tithonus and the chitinous exoskeleton and drone of the insect. The transformation is similar to that in the Callisto myth. Callisto is not the *ur*-mother of the ursines. Her transformation, like that of Tithonus, is an aspect of divine punishment.

Attempting to wrest immortality from the deities by storming their home or stealing some food or drink is the second method. It is a widespread folk theme, although its expression varies from culture to culture. Unlike the familiar theme of the trickster fooling the gods into accepting the least attractive portions of animals sacrificed or bargaining with the deity for the salvation of Sodom and Gomorrah, the conscious attempt to circumvent death without change of state rarely meets with success. The gods are jealous of the gift of eternal life and are inclined to pose insurmountable obstacles to its proliferation. Deliberate attempts to achieve immortality by conquest or other conscious means are usually accompanied by savage punishment. It should be noted, however, that the punishment results not from the attempt but from failure.

A third mode for achieving immortality is to be or become a member of a species or group for which immortality or an extremely long life is natural. The centaurs, the teachers of humanity in Greek myth, are extremely long-lived. The association of longevity with the teaching profession is an idea that continues with little justification today (save, perhaps, in the dissipated lives academics lead, which makes them all appear much older than they actually are). In folklore and, more recently, the novel, the wisdom of the West, the Orient, Africa, the mountains, and so on is traditionally imparted by an aged figure, one of a select group that enjoys longevity or immortality. In most examples, no punishment is associated with this form of longevity, and it is sometimes possible for humans to join the select group by training or enlightenment (Luke Skywalker comes to mind). If the wise old one belongs to another species, that transition is more honorary than real, though a few exceptions exist. One form involves the melding of minds by telepathy or technological means. A product of the Howard Foundation's experiment in eugenics in Robert A. Heinlein's *Methuselah's Children* becomes obsessed with the possibility that her life is drawing to a close and joins a group mind: "Mary Sperling, moved by conviction of her own impending death, saw in the deathless group egos a way out. Faced with the eternal problem of life and death, she had escaped the problem by choosing neither . . . selflessness. She had found a group willing to receive her, she had crossed over."[4]

In summary, this motif, as found in Greek myth and Homeric epic, presents death as neither a necessary nor desirable outcome of a series of well-ordered actions. The implication even in the classical Tithonus myth is that Eos might have requested renewal in addition to immortality. Most protagonists of the *Iliad* survive the end of the epic, and it is the chief antagonist, Hektor, who is afforded a heroic death. Odysseus expels the suitors and retires with Penelope. The Homeric epic has no final dragon battle as in *Beowulf*, no defense of a pass as in *Song of Roland*, or tragic squabbles of succession as in the Arthurian cycle. Francavilla tries to make a case for the classical rejection of immortality: "The dispirited dead in the *Odyssey* are trapped in their undesirable immortality and are beyond the barrier—exhausted, insubstantial shades of humanity, untouchable by the living like Odysseus who can never be immortal gods."[5] It is more likely, however, that the ghost of Achilles is miserable precisely because he is dead, and not immortal. It is the state of death that is rejected by Homer's Achilles, not the state of immortality.

In the European or Christian epic, in contrast with the Homeric epic, to die the "good" death, either in the aura of holiness or honor, after a heroic life, or in defense of a narrow place against impossible odds, is a common, natural, and desired culmination to life. Some European folk legends and mythology, particularly Celtic and Scandinavian myths, lend themselves to the Christian notion of redemption by the self-sacrifice of a deity or hero. It is interesting to note the strong influence of the European and Christian epic and medieval romance on contemporary fantasy.[6]

In the European and Christian epic and romance tradition, immortality is a less-than-positive value because it means separation from the joys of heaven and the afterlife. In fact, only those irretrievably damned to suffer punishment after death would desire immortality. Thus, any human who ignores the biblical limit of life is bound to be an evil creature. The appearance of the Tithonus Syndrome, therefore, would be expected to be pervasive in fantasy, a genre more strongly influenced by the Christian epic and romance traditions, than in science fiction. The majority of the immortal figures in fantasy have been reduced to malignant shades clinging to existence until they are dissipated by magical means. The barrow wight, the Ringwraiths, and Sauron himself in J. R. R. Tolkien's *The Lord of the Rings* are examples. Except for the immortal gods dwelling in the West and the demigod Tom Bombadil, Tolkien's wizards and elves, as well as Bilbo and Frodo Baggins, have long life spans, but they are not immortal. Whether because of world-weariness, as in the case of the elves, or as a relief from the pain associated with old age, they are destined to undergo a change of state in a passage to the West. The normal life span of a species is extended only at a high cost, ranging from alienation and physical pain in the case of Frodo, to the loss of the personality in the case of the Ringwraiths. In the words of Tolkien's hobbits complaining about the longevity of Bilbo Baggins, "'It will have to be paid for,' they said. 'It isn't natural, and trouble will come of it!'"[7]

In contemporary fantasy, the alienation concomitant with immortality is illustrated by the figure of the King in Yellow in Lawrence Watt-Evans's series *The Lords of Dûs*.[8] Although the entire series revolves around varieties of alienation, the King's alienation is the direct result of his immortality and relationship with death. A predominantly passive figure in the first three novels in the series, the King becomes a major actor in *The Book of Silence*. In the earlier novels, the King had provided the non-human protagonist Garth with avenues for the achievement of the immortality of fame. Though Garth becomes aware of the hollowness of this particular quest, he continues to depend on the King for advice and direction. The King, it is revealed, is "the one true high priest of the god of death. . . . As such, the King could not die; he had lived through several ages and now desired nothing but the death that was denied him."[9] Watt-Evans places the King solidly in the Tithonus tradition; his immortality was originally sought, not accidental, and so results in suffering. The one thing that the King desires is the oblivion of death, but he is to experience this only symbolically. Instead of dying, he becomes Death itself. The King's existence continues, albeit on a different plane, and he is cheated of the release he seeks.

The merging of the King in Yellow with the quality of death is akin to the personification of death that has become a popular fantasy theme in recent years. Even more than showing that death may be preferable to immortality, equating the absence of life with a developed character is an indication of cultural bias. The personification has radically changed in the contemporary novel, harking back to the imagery of the medieval "Dance of Death." Personifying death is a means of humanizing it and reducing its impersonality. Death personified is a major figure in Piers Anthony's *On a Pale Horse* (1983), and it also appears in the other sections of the Intimations of Immortality series. Anthony's Thanatos conceals an attempt to come to grips with the concept of mortality in a comic opera plot. Continuations of the series build an increasingly indefinite and timeless universe as the playing field for a multisided game among personifications. As one of the most sympathetic of them, the existence and office of Death are an accepted and acceptable part of the Intimations universe.

An anthropomorphic Death is a constant character in the works of Terry Pratchett, a modern fantasy writer who revels in the conjunction of fantasy and science. Like Anthony, Pratchett tries to justify the place of death in nature while his personification ironically shows more range and depth of human emotional responses than most of his other characters. Death is even susceptible to a certain amount of slapstick. But there is nothing humorous about Death's perception of his role in the universe:

"'And he goes around killing people?' said Mort. He shook his head. 'There's no justice.' Death sighed. 'NO,' he said, handing his drink to a page who was surprised to find he was suddenly holding an empty glass, 'THERE'S JUST ME.'"[10] Such humor establishes the impossibility of immortality, and in the face of the "humanity" of death, leads us to accept this impossibility.

Pratchett's Death, the only immortal character developed at length, suffers the alienation of the Tithonus Syndrome. In *Mort* (1987), he is portrayed as a somewhat overworked executive and doting stepfather. In

Reaper Man (1991), he is the protagonist. Relieved of his post by three overzealous demiurges, Death learns what it is to be human and mortal. Returned to his position, he rejects isolation during the process of recalling the various submanifestations that his loss of position had engendered, refusing to face eternity alone, as does Azrael, the prime mover.

As opposed to fantasy, in which alienation is a suspended sentence earned by the most worthy of immortal characters in place of harsher punishments, in science fiction, alienation from society is the standard cost of immortality or extended youth, even if they are not consciously sought, and the most frequently observed modern symptom of the Tithonus Syndrome.

In modern science fiction, the theme of alienation is central to Clifford D. Simak's *Way Station* (1963). Like the Wandering Jew, Enoch Wallace is an innkeeper, but, ironically, it is necessary for him to reject all human affiliations to accept this role. The subplots of the theft of an alien artifact, the occult powers of the mute girl he saves from a brutal family, and his rejection of the kind gift of the simulacra of human relationships are arranged so that Simak's innkeeper is shown to be furthering his own alienation. Only when this is complete can he accept the status of immortal.

Occasionally in science fiction, alienation, ennui, and enmity are not considered sufficient payment for immortality, and instability and madness are added to the cost. Even more terrible threats, such as the futility of all human activity, as in Aldous Huxley's *After Many a Summer Dies the Swan*, are sometimes promised. Huxley's novel begins as a satirical view of the extravagances of the Hollywood lifestyle as seen through the eyes of the narrator, who is not himself immune to a bit of satire, as in Mr. Propter's initial characterization of Jeremy: "'Take a decayed Christian,' he said at last in a meditative tone, 'and the remains of a Stoic; mix thoroughly with good manners, a bit of money and an old-fashioned education; simmer for several years in a university. Result: a scholar and a gentleman. Well, there were worse types of human being.' He uttered a little laugh. 'I might almost claim to have been one myself, once, long ago.'"[11] The theme of the search for longevity, orchestrated by the corrupting Dr. Obispo, runs along with the gradually darkening satire of social and intellectual institutions. As the novel progresses, love, religion, art, music, and the political idealism of the International Brigade come under attack. The result is a movement from the initial perception of the boorishness of contemporary taste to the hollowness and futility of human aspiration, against which the search for longevity is scarcely worth the trouble. In spite of the increasing revelation of hollowness, the positive characters retain their hope in the

meaningfulness of an extended life. With the murder of Pete, the structure
of the affluent society collapses, leaving Jeremy Pordage, the narrator, to
witness the final unfolding of a worldview that is, if anything, darker than
that of George Orwell's *1984* (1949). Here, longevity, if not immortality,
is shown to be obtainable, but at the cost of the intellect. The final images,
juxtaposing the sash of the Order of the Garter and the nakedness of the
ape, the music of Mozart with the brutal coupling of the remains of the
Fifth Earl of Gonister and his housekeeper, are ultimate condemnation
of the human condition, rendered even more shocking by Mr. Stoyte's
whimpering: "'How long do you figure it would take before a person went
like that?' he said in a slow hesitating voice. 'I mean, it wouldn't happen at
once . . . there'd be a long time while a person . . . well, you know; while he
wouldn't change any. And once you get over the first shock—well, they
look like they were having a pretty good time. I mean in their own way, of
course. Don't you think so, Obispo?' he insisted."[12]

In fantasy, the Tithonus Syndrome usually manifests itself in harsher
terms than alienation. As I stated earlier, alienation in fantasy is usually a
sort of suspended sentence reserved for characters who have lived an ex-
emplary life or who did not directly seek the prolongation of life.

The similarities in the treatment of suspended animation in the two
genres further support the notion of a cultural bias against immortality.
The sleeping, frozen, or otherwise preserved hero or heroine, awaiting resuscitation at some later period of need, is a commonplace. Akin to the hibernating hero of fantasy is the preserved character of science fiction. In
intentional preservation, the purpose is to extend the span of life to accomplish a purpose such as interstellar travel. Unintentional preservation
is a popular mechanism for inserting a contemporary character into an
imagined future. In general, the Tithonus Syndrome does not manifest itself strongly in cases of suspended animation, either in fantasy or science
fiction, probably because it is considered a mechanism of neither immortality nor longevity. Although not without attendant dangers, preservation
by suspended animation is usually not accompanied by lasting negative effects. Evidently, suspended animation in the fantasy or science fiction
novel is not considered to be as serious a breach of the natural order as
other forms of seeking immortality. An exception is Lou Fisher's *The
Blue Ice Pilot* (1986), in which the mechanism of preservation itself becomes a cause of the protagonist's alienation.

The character inserted into the future after a period of suspended animation is very common. The awakened principal is usually a positive
character who can call on some sort of primitive value, whether strength,

as in the case of Buck Rogers, or sexual adventurousness, as in the case of Woody Allen's *Sleeper* (1973). Richard A. Lupoff's Parker, the quick-frozen aviator in *One Million Centuries* (1967), benefits from the cultural relativism that his historical perspective produces. In general, any sort of suspended animation permits a character to avoid the Tithonus Syndrome.

The science fiction novel offers another method of avoiding the Tithonus Syndrome: the nonorganic survival of the personality. Mechanical or biomechanical prosthetics of ever-increasing complexity in science fiction, like the complex magical means of rejuvenation in fantasy, are rarely found to be sufficient. Discussing James Gunn's *The Immortals* (1962), Michael R. Collings notes that prosthetics of any sort, as opposed to the development of natural longevity, do not seem to work in most novels: "The difference between destructive artificial immortality and positive natural immortality lies in the will to live, not in an elixir, a machine, drugs, or surgery. Even in his guarded optimism, Gunn confirms the conclusions of most science fiction writers. Immortality based on scientifically observable, mechanical processes demands a higher price than humanity can pay."[13]

Two other modes of obtaining immortality in science fiction that have fantasy analogues are the "recording" of an individual electromechanically and the production of shared-consciousness clones. Advances in the technology of data storage, artificial intelligence, and experiments in neuron simulation have produced works that portray immortality achieved by means of changing from the human state to an electrical state or computer program. This "recording" of an individual—not the creation of human or superhuman intelligence via computer programming—is occasionally encountered either as an aside, as in K. W. Jeter's *Farewell Horizontal*,[14] or as a central theme, as in Rudy Rucker's *Software* (1982). As in the case of cybernetic mechanisms, the recording of personality and its fantasy analogues are rarely found to be adequate means of achieving immortality. The creation of clones, whole individuals grown from samples of body tissue, had a brief vogue as a method for obtaining immortality. Both Jack Chalker's Four Lords of the Diamond series and A. E. van Vogt's Null-A series use cloning as a way of ensuring continuation in the face of physical threats, but the mechanism of keeping a unified consciousness among the clones has not been mastered.[15]

Compared with the manifestations of such themes as travel to strange worlds in science fiction and the cleansing of the land in fantasy, the theme of obtaining immortality or longevity is less frequently found than one might expect. Further evidence does not bear out Joseph Sanders's implication that there is a difference between views of immortality in fantasy and science fiction;[16] instead, the evidence points to similar attitudes in both genres. Similarities in the treatment of certain themes in literary works can result from cultural bias and stock responses. Instances of this may cut across the genre divisions of literature. (The association of "natural nobility" with separation from urban civilization in the adventure novel, the romance, and the modern western is an example of such a bias.)

I have found, then, that immortality is treated in a negative manner with a good degree of consistency in both science fiction and fantasy, at least in the English-language novels I surveyed. The implication is that there is a basic cultural rejection of the idea of immortality and longevity. It may be true that every individual has no doubt about his or her own immortality, but the prevalence of the Tithonus Syndrome indicates that each of us has serious reservations.

Notes

1. Joseph V. Francavilla, "These Immortals: An Alternate View of Immortality in Roger Zelazny's Science Fiction," *Extrapolation* 25 (Spring 1984): 22.

2. Brian Stableford, "Immortality," in *The Encyclopedia of Science Fiction*, ed. John Clute and Peter Nicholls (New York: St. Martin's Press, 1993), 616.

3. It is interesting to note that the Tithonus Syndrome seems to have evoked an abreaction in the lexicographers of *The American Heritage Dictionary*, 2d college ed. (Boston: Houghton Mifflin, 1985), who, I was surprised to find, include references to Laodemon, Tithonus's father; Priam, his brother; Eos, his wife; and Memnon, his son, but omit any reference to Tithonus himself.

4. Robert A. Heinlein, *Methuselah's Children* (1958; Riverdale, N.Y.: Baen Books, 1986), 238.

5. Francavilla, "These Immortals," 21.

6. Late-nineteenth- and early-twentieth-century fantasy was more eclectic than contemporary fantasy, with its influences from Near East and Far East legend and materials. Along with obvious examples, consider Lafcadio Hearn, *Some Chinese Ghosts* (New York: Modern Library, 1927); James Branch Cabell, *Jurgen: A Comedy of Justice* (New York: R. M. McBride, 1928); and Edward Bulwer Lytton, *Leila, or the Siege of Grenada* (Boston: Dana Estes, n.d.).

7. J. R. R. Tolkien, *The Fellowship of the Ring*, 2d ed. (Boston: Houghton Mifflin, 1965), 29. Such a payment exacted is implied in Oscar Wilde's *The Picture of Dorian Gray* (1897). The relationship between Gray and his portrait is

a traditional manifestation of sympathetic magic. Thus the story is a fantasy in which the gifts of potential immortality and protection from the warning effects of immorality bring the increased dissolution and self-revulsion that lead to Gray's "suicide." Effectively, the relationship between Gray and the painting leads to his death. Fantasy novels like Charles Maturin's *Melmoth the Wanderer* (1820) and Eugène Sue's *Le Juif Errant* (1844–45) picture the immortal individual as a shadowy figure, cursed to pass along the periphery of normal life. Indeed, the immortality of the Wandering Jew is the punishment for his lack of compassion and involvement in the lives of those around him. His salvation and return to mortality are possible only if he develops human relationships.

8. The series consists of *The Lure of the Basilisk* (1980), *The Seven Altars of Du-Saara* (1981), *The Sword of the Bheleu* (1982), and *The Book of Silence* (1984).

9. Lawrence Watt-Evans, *The Book of Silence* (New York: Ballantine Books, 1984), 7–8.

10. Terry Pratchett, *Mort* (London: Gollancz, 1987), 41.

11. Aldous Huxley, *After Many a Summer Dies the Swan* (London: Chatto and Windus, 1959), 17.

12. Huxley, *After Many a Summer Dies the Swan*, 314.

13. Michael R. Collings, "The Mechanics of Immortality," in *Death and the Serpent: Immortality in Science Fiction and Fantasy*, ed. Carl B. Yoke and Donald M. Hassler (Westport, Conn.: Greenwood Press, 1985), 34.

14. K. W. Jeter, *Farewell Horizontal* (New York: Penguin, 1989). Axxter's encounter with the curious female image that may be the manifestation of an artificial intelligence is not pursued (56–57), though Felony, a sort of electronic vampire, is considered at greater length (235).

15. Novels in Chalker's series are *Lilith: A Snake in the Grass* (1981), *Cerberus: A Wolf in the Fold* (1982), *Charon: A Dragon at the Gate* (1982), and *Medusa: A Tiger by the Tale* (1983). Novels in van Vogt's series are *The World of Null-A* (1948; rev. 1970), *The Players of Null-A* (1956; rev. 1966), and *Null-A Three* (1985).

16. Joseph Sanders, "Dancing on the Tightrope: Immortality in Roger Zelazny," in *Death and the Serpent*, 135–43: "Because it presupposes human inability to understand or control individual lives or the general environment, fantasy depicts immortality as an ultimately undesirable condition. . . . The outlook of science fiction is different. Presupposing that people are able to understand and control their lives and surroundings, science fiction eagerly looks forward to immortality as a way to acquire more knowledge and power" (135).

"No Woman Born": Immortality and Gender in Feminist Science Fiction

Robin Roberts

It all comes back to man who goes through a woman
to reach immortality.
—Catherine Clement

If, as some feminist critics suggest, women have a different relationship to immortality because of their reproductive capacity, we would expect science fiction written by women to reflect that difference.[1] Immortality as it is portrayed in science fiction reveals a masculine view that emphasizes the anxieties and stagnation of immortality, and an alternative feminist perspective that defines immortality as a condition that allows change and flexibility. In feminist science fiction, depictions of immortality fall into three categories: the cyborg or machine woman, whose immortality is created by technology; the regenerate, whose immortality stems from biology or reproduction; and the clone, who draws on biology and technology. Each type of immortality is connected to ideas about femininity and the relationship of technology to gender. Bearing tremendous powers, of which immortality may be the most terrifying, these female characters are alien to mankind and have the potential to dominate man and rule his world.[2] In this essay I will focus on the works of three modern male science fiction writers and four feminist science fiction writers to illustrate my point.

Isaac Asimov, Gregory Benford, and Bruce Sterling are award-winning science fiction writers who, respectively, represent classic, hard, and cyberpunk science fiction. The women writers whose works I examine are also Hugo and Nebula Award winners: Alice Sheldon (who wrote as James Tiptree, Jr.), Octavia Butler, C. J. Cherryh, and Joan D. Vinge. Their novels— *Up the Walls of the World*, *Wild Seed*, *Cyteen*, and *The Snow Queen*, respectively—reflect the range of immortality represented in feminist science fiction. Studying these women's depictions of immortality illuminates the central themes of this feminist literature and reveals that, as in many other areas, gender affects both the conceptualization and the interpretation of a theme.

Male science fiction writers such as Asimov, Benford, and Sterling present immortality as either "limitless opportunity" or "the ultimate stagnation," which Brian Stableford claims are the two definitions of immortality in science fiction.[3] In Asimov's "The Bicentennial Man," for example, a robot wrestles with unwelcome immortality. Andrew, the Bicentennial Man of the title, is a unique robot who is also a superb artist and scientist. Immortality is depicted in this work as the primary separation between human and machine—and indeed, between human and corporation. "A corporation does not die any more than a robot does," the narrator observes. But unlike corporations, Andrew renounces its tremendous powers. While the corporation "had its directions and it followed them soullessly" (again the narrator's words), Andrew is troubled by his orders and his isolation from humanity. Despite his purported masculinity, Andrew is really asexual. (Earlier in the story he discusses the necessity of an orifice for elimination and the possibility of obtaining genitalia, but the latter possibility is never realized.) At the end of the story he announces, "The truth is I want to be a man. I have wanted it through six generations of human beings."[4] He succeeds in lengthening the human life span through prosthetics, but this merely extends people's lives; it does not make them truly immortal. Since they cannot achieve his status as an immortal, Andrew undergoes an operation to connect his positronic brain to organic nerves so that he will eventually die. Like his predecessor, Uncle Tom from Harriet Beecher Stowe's *Uncle Tom's Cabin*, Andrew is acceptable because of his saintliness. He appears to have no sexual desires, only a pure platonic love for his "Little Miss," whose name is the last words on his lips before his apotheosis. Immortality and humanity are depicted as incompatible: only soulless, inhuman corporations can be immortal.

On the surface, Benford's "Time's Rub" can be read as a humorous invocation of immortality. In the story, three aliens repeat lines from Matthew Arnold's "Dover Beach." Two aliens are on a battlefield facing death when they are suddenly approached by a third alien who speaks enigmatically in the words of the poem and various other literary sources, including Andrew Marvell's "To His Coy Mistress," in which the poet uses the idea of immortality to attempt a seduction. This immortal alien offers the others rejuvenation and immortality, but in the form of a game—they must choose between two boxes. The game involves probability and logic, and its very aridity suggests the sterility and boredom attendant on immortality. One alien chooses immortality and the other opts for a mortal life so he can return to his mate, whom he loves. Eventually, this latter character becomes human in a world in which the human race has ceased to exist. Benford depicts the choice of joining a loved one as more desirable than a solitary immortal existence. The alien who chooses immortality realizes that his mortal self must die. "*Nothing* could be sure it was the original," he muses. From the narrator's point of view, immortality is "a monument of unaging intellect, gathered into the artifice of eternity."[5] While this picture is not entirely unappealing, it has the characteristics of loneliness and inhumanity represented by Asimov.

This perspective on immortality is partially echoed by Sterling in *Schismatrix*. Like Asimov's humans, Sterling's characters can lengthen their lives with prosthetics. The enhanced life span changes their outlook on life; they do not experience an extended youth but rather are "very old for a long time. The feeling changed things."[6] The Schismatrix of the title is "a posthuman solar system, diverse yet unified, where tolerance would rule and every faction would have a share" (S 133). This new point of view is made possible in part by the alien Investors—an interesting parallel to Asimov's depiction of corporations as immortal.

The Investors, who are immensely ancient and long-lived, take a different view of time. They speak of "a matter of mere centuries" (S 209). Yet, in comparison with humans the Investors seem aloof, remote, and passionless. Like the creature who offers immortality to Benford's characters, the Investors are an unattractive alternative to the human hero's vibrant and passionate personality. Feeling "the sting of mortality" (S 153), the human hero is seized by energy and passion for action. Yet, all humans seem to desire immortality, even the protagonist. Its lure is irresistible, and there is a "black-market scramble for immortality" when the Investor-maintained peace collapses. When the protagonist examines the first animal made immortal by humans, he realizes the dangers and weaknesses attendant on achieving immortality. "'Don't be afraid,' he told the rat seriously. 'There's a whole new world out there'" (S 259). In response, the rat viciously attacks him. "Its capacity to learn completely exhausted by age, [it] had been reduced to absolute rote behaviour" (S 258). This is the specter of a wasted and worthless immortality that faces humanity. Yet, while other humans become aquatic posthumans as an alternative to immortality, the protagonist chooses an immortal life with a creature far more advanced than the Investors, a creature so godlike in its powers that it is described only as a Presence who is taking him "somewhere wonderful" (S 288). The novel ends with this glowing vision of an absolutely vague future. It is as though true, perfect immortality is undescribable because the transformation from humanity is so complete and total. Through the help of an alien, the protagonist becomes immortal, but inhuman.

In feminist science fiction, however, the life that is generated by machinery does not depend on immensely powerful aliens or on men. Instead, the mingling of woman and machine provides one means of immortality. Through the figure of the cyborg, women writers combine a human personality with the potentially immortal and infinitely repairable capacity of a machine. The association of woman with machine confuses traditional categorizations of technology as masculine and biology as feminine and provides women characters with another source of immortality for themselves. At the same time, the figure of the cyborg collapses categories and enables feminists to question the status quo. As Donna Haraway writes in her "A Manifesto for Cyborgs," "there are also great riches for feminists in explicitly embracing the possibilities inherent in the breakdown of clean distinctions between organism and machine and similar distinctions structuring the Western self."[7] One of the breakdowns is the questioning of the construction of gender and the concomitant exposure of misogyny. While Haraway stresses the postmodern quality of the breakdown of categories, the association of woman and machine is actually a long and venerable one, as C. L. Moore notes: "Ships and guns and planes are 'she' to men who operate them and depend on them for their lives. It is as if machinery with complicated moving parts almost simulates life, and does acquire from the men who used it—well, not exactly life, of course—but a personality."[8]

Feminist science fiction writers expand this stereotype and give feminized machines not only life but immortality. Tiptree (Sheldon) uses the figure of the cyborg to challenge traditional dichotomies between male and female, human and machine, magic and science. In *Up the Walls of the World*, she creates an immortal goddess of unparalleled powers who is part computer, part woman, and part alien. Before her transformation, protagonist Margaret Omali is the consummate computer scientist who relishes the cool impersonality of her work and seems to despise humans. Like Asimov's Susan Calvin, she prefers computers to human beings. Tiptree does not make fun of or belittle this character, however, but gives her a personal history of physical and psychological trauma, including a clitoridectomy and racist mistreatment, that explains her coldness. Tiptree joins hard and soft science in Margaret, for she is not only a superb scientist but also an accomplished practitioner of psionics. Using her psi powers, she contacts and merges with her computer system and a powerful entity described as "Star Destroyer," an alien capable of destroying worlds. Together the three become "LIFE PRESERVERS." But while all-powerful now, Margaret still appears in human form occasionally, and she is described as the "goddess of the night."[9] Margaret/LIFE PRESERVER is immortal and has the power to destroy and resuscitate races and worlds. To misogynists, the final words of the novel ominously hint at this goddess's power and next target: her "POWERS MAY ONE DAY FOCUS WITHOUT WARNING UPON THE TINY LIVES OF ANY NESCIENT EARTH" (*WW* 319).

For the immortal female goddess, tremendous powers and even immortality are to be shared. The transformed woman draws humans, aliens, and even a dog to her. Her new form includes the human, but her larger self is described in terms that evoke a womb. From the perspective of a human male, her shape is at first threatening. "Reach, stretch, get in! . . . [H]e is crawling through a perilously frail dark tube, a frightened astronaut squirming through an umbilicus to the haven of some capsule. Get on, crawl, squeeze, go" (*WW* 271). Immortality involves confronting and finally embracing the other. Margaret acknowledges her computer's life and that of the alien. Being immortal provides her with a new perspective, and those she draws to her become similarly imbued with a vision of eternity and benevolence, "an eternity of unimaginable projects" (*WW* 298). What will characterize their lives is no grand or specious philosophy but "the old necessity of kindness" (*WW* 299) and love. The male character, Daniel, who has followed Margaret, realizes that "no matter how long the future stretches, or what it holds, he will carry into it his love" (*WW* 300). This emphasis on community, tenderness, and love is typical of feminist science fiction, as critics have noted.[10] What is different about this cyborg and her immortality is that she uses her powers to promote feminist values of community. While immortal cyborgs cannot provide role models for real human women, they can be used to criticize patriarchal society and to provide an alternative vision of a world based on feminist principles. And if immortality or linkage to a machine may sometimes be seen as a curse, here Tiptree suggests that with a feminist value system, immortality could be a blessing. Haraway concludes her essay by declaring, "I would rather be a cyborg than a goddess" (MC 223), but Tiptree provides us with a character who is both.

While the cyborg provides feminist writers with a means of immortality via technology, immortality is also available to women especially through regeneration or biology. Octavia Butler's *Wild Seed* depicts a woman ruler who is immortal through her regenerative powers. Anyawu, or Sun Woman, a character based on mythic goddesses, is 300 years old when the novel begins, and the book follows her and her male counterpart, Doro, who is almost 4,000 years old, across 150 years and two continents, Africa and America. The struggle between the two immortals embodies the conflict between gendered worldviews, which is reflected in their differing forms of immortality.

Doro provides a negative exemplar of evil and corrupting immortality based on hierarchy, domination, and control. He practices a predatory immortality, living eternally by taking over the bodies of other human beings. He began thousands of years ago when he accidentally leapt into his parents' bodies, killing them. Within a brief period he destroyed his village by taking over the bodies of the inhabitants one by one. He eventually regained control of himself, but he can only sustain his immortality by killing—which he enjoys. He has begun a breeding program to produce people like himself, but he has had no permanent success when by chance he encounters Anyawu, who will feature prominently in his breeding program. Even from her, his equal in power, he demands fear and respect. He terrorizes her and others by killing in anger. While Anyawu is depicted as attractive and is loved by her family of genetic descendants and other misfits, Doro is feared and hated by his offspring. Butler emphasizes the inutility of Doro's masculinist approach to genetics by having Anyawu do a better job of preserving witchlike traits in her offspring; she accomplishes in decades what Doro failed to do in thousands of years. While Anyawu cares for her family, Doro is alienated from his; he has almost become a thing rather than a human. Anyawu sees his alienation: "A thing looked at her, and that feral and cold-spirit thing that spoke softly."[11] His son pleads with Anyawu to stay with Doro, saying, "He's warped because he can't die, but he's still a man" (WS 300). Doro exemplifies the dangers of a masculinity run amok because it has immortality.

In contrast with Doro's appropriation of other bodies, Anyawu is immortal because she can regenerate and alter her physical form. She can become an animal, a man, a woman, white, black, old, young—whatever she chooses. She is a healer who uses her powers to identify illnesses and microbes in her own body and those of others. In her African village she is revered and feared as an oracle and witch, and she has spent generations preserving and watching over her extended family. Abhorring violence, she kills only in self-defense. Her immortal body shows her the unity of all life and allows her to identify intelligent life in all its forms, including dolphins. Because of her powers, she provides a feminist role model through her concerns for others, her emphasis on equality, and her trenchant comments about racism and sexism. For example, she adopts a European-American male body to protect women and African-American slaves in antebellum Louisiana. Her intimate self-knowledge allows her to cure herself and others in ways unknown to doctors and scientists. Through Anyawu, Butler suggests that the key to a productive and energizing immortality is self-knowledge and self-awareness.

Anyawu finally tames Doro—partially. Because they are the only immortals they know, Anyawu and Doro eventually come to terms with each other. Because she represents feminine values, and perhaps also because she is so much younger, Anyawu has not lost her humanity, and through intimate mental contact with Doro she persuades him to stop killing so callously and capriciously. She also demands and receives respect as his equal. Their rapprochement thus signals an uneasy balance between values identified as feminine and masculine. What each gains is companionship and love—values Doro thought that he despised but which, by the end of the novel, he finds that he cannot live without. As in Tiptree's novel, immortality is presented in *Wild Seed* as undesirable unless accompanied by love and companionship. All Doro's powers—and Anyawu's too, for that matter—are a curse without the domesticity conventionally considered feminine. Their immortality makes of them a new, transformed Adam and Eve, who hope to breed a race of humans who can also live forever. The only blot on their reconciliation is the fact that "people are temporary. So temporary" (WS 237). Like science fiction readers, and those who sign up for cryonic suspension, the two immortals cling to the hope that "someday, we'll have others who won't die" (WS 252).

This altruistic hope based on biology is challenged by the elitism of a third means of achieving immortality by combining technology and biology—cloning. In C. J. Cherryh's *Cyteen*, cloning provides a way for "Specials," scientific and political geniuses, to reproduce themselves. Most "azi," lab-born humans, are fed tapes that program them from birth, but

Ariane Emory, the Special who clones herself, grows up in familial circumstances designed to imitate her original upbringing. Her Security team, a
couple with whom she is extremely intimate, are also replicated, and she
has computer records that detail every aspect of her first life. The novel details the end of Emory's first life, then follows her rebirth and the merging
of her old and new selves. In the world of the novel, Emory's duplication is
considered experimental because the previous attempts to clone a Special
failed spectacularly. Emory's cloning, though, is successful, and she extends her life well beyond the 140 years made available by rejuvenation
treatments.

Cloning as a means of immortality raises issues of identity and ethics
in the same way that Doro's body leaping does in *Wild Seed*. While Butler
seems to present identity as psychologically constant despite new bodies,
Cherryh plays with the complications produced by duplication. Ari Emory
explains, "It's spooky to know that you're an experiment, and to watch
yourself work."[12] She herself is an expert in psychogenesis, or "mind-
origination. Mind-cloning" (C 252). The novel focuses on Emory's synthesis of her selves—a synthesis that lets her gain a position of power with
over a hundred years to expand where the old Ari left off. More important
than the time she has gained, however, is the addition of benevolence to her
personality. Given the chance to live her childhood over, Emory avoids a
critical and damaging sexual exploitation by her guardian and so never develops the sadism that marred the original Ari. Cloning, then, provides the
possibility of improving on the original. The daughter clone has the chance
to reject the harsh and dominating qualities her mother developed.

This vision of the clone as a creature with choices and the possibility of
improvement appears also in Joan Vinge's *The Snow Queen*,[13] in which a
powerful ruler clones herself as a means of immortality. At first, the Snow
Queen artificially extends her life, as Emory does, through rejuvenation
treatments. But while Emory's treatments are synthesized, the Snow
Queen must imbibe the blood of sentient beings called "mers" to prolong
her life. Ingesting the blood of other beings is immortality at its most ex-
ploitative, and it produces in the Snow Queen a ruler callous and cruel.
Eventually, she too turns to cloning as an alternate means of immortality.
But as in Emory's case, Moon, the Snow Queen's clone, develops a benevolence unseen in the parent. With its flexibility and the possibility of
change, cloning as a combination of technology and biology brings together the best of both means of immortality.

This unexpected offshoot of cloning suggests that feminist science fiction writers depict cloning as more positive and less controlled than male

writers generally do. The clone is not an exact replica of its parent: it develops free will. The immortality is thus compromised in a way that implies that the original woman's desire for immortality was unjust and greedy, and finally that it is unattainable. Cloning does provide a way for women to reproduce without men. Emory grows in a lab while Moon develops in a foster mother, but in both cases the mother's power is uncompromised by alliance. Like the cyborg, the clone represents a way for the feminine power of reproduction to be intensified rather than diminished by technology. Cloning thus enables women to be less controlled by a patriarchal system that tries to oppress them—in the case of Emory, by the men of the Council who oppose her reproduction of lab humans; and in the case of the Snow Queen, by the male-dominated Hegemony that denies her colonized planet the technology its inhabitants want and need.

Immortality provides female characters with a way to fight the oppression that they face from misogyny and patriarchal societies. For Tiptree's Omali, immortality produces an escape from a world that contains racism and sexism. For Butler's Anyawu, immortality provides commentary on the need for equality in male-female relationships and an end to hierarchy and domination in social structures. And through Cherryh's Emory and Vinge's Snow Queen, immortality is shown to be practically unattainable, for their clones are both them and not them. While the daughter clones continue their mother's work and are genetically identical, the daughters are significantly more benevolent—new and improved versions of their earlier selves. In all instances, immortality creates a chance for the woman ruler to extend or consolidate her reign—a reign that is depicted as more benevolent than the patriarchal structures she replaces or resists.

In this sense, the need for immortality should be regarded as a sign of how stringent and overwhelming sexism can be: only through immortality can women characters promote alternative feminine values. The theme of immortality in feminist fiction, then, emphasizes that women may see immortality not as a means of extending an otherwise perfect existence but as a way to challenge the strictures placed on women in a sexist society. Like other features of science fiction, immortality provides feminist writers with an opportunity to defamiliarize the real world and comment on what an ideal feminist person or society would look like.

Notes

1. The epigraph is from Helene Cixous and Catherine Clement, *The Newly Born Woman*, trans. Betsy Wing (Minneapolis: University of Minnesota Press, 1986), 56.

2. There are numerous examples of immortal female aliens, going back to the murdered mate for Frankenstein's creature and through pulp science fiction magazines, which are peopled by strong, powerful female aliens. See my *A New Species: Gender and Science in Science Fiction* (Urbana: University of Illinois Press, 1993).

3. Brian Stableford, "Immortality," in *The Encyclopedia of Science Fiction*, ed. John Clute and Peter Nicholls (New York: St. Martin's Press, 1993), 616.

4. Isaac Asimov, "The Bicentennial Man," in *The Bicentennial Man and Other Stories* (New York: Doubleday, 1976), 160, 161, 166.

5. Gregory Benford, "Time's Rub," *Isaac Asimov's Science Fiction Magazine* 90 (1985): 60.

6. Bruce Sterling, *Schismatrix* (New York: Arbor House, 1985), 29. Page references in the text preceded by *S* are to this edition.

7. Donna Haraway, "A Manifesto for Cyborgs: Science, Technology, and Socialist Feminism for the 1980s," in *Feminism/Postmodernism* (New York: Routledge, 1990), 216. A page reference in the text preceded by MC is to this edition.

8. C. L. Moore, *The Best of C. L. Moore* (New York: Ballantine Books, 1975), 249–50.

9. James Tiptree, Jr., *Up the Walls of the World* (1978; New York: Ace Books, 1984), 271. Page references in the text preceded by WW are to this edition.

10. In her study of Utopias, for example, Carol Farley Kessler discovers that "typically, women [writers] make issues of family, sexuality, and marriage more central than do men" (*Daring to Dream* [New York: Routledge, 1979], 7). See also Carol Gilligan, *In a Different Voice* (Cambridge: Harvard University Press, 1982), 149.

11. Octavia Butler, *Wild Seed* (New York: Bantam Books, 1978), 270. Page references in the text preceded by WS are to this edition.

12. C. J. Cherryh, *Cyteen* (New York: Warner Books, 1988), 11. Page references in the text preceded by C are to this edition.

13. Joan D. Vinge, *The Snow Queen* (New York: Dial Press, 1980).

The Science Fiction of the House of Saul: From Frankenstein's Monster to Lazarus Long

Barry Crawford

In the oldest work of literature, Gilgamesh goes in search of immortality but is told by the one man granted that gift that he cannot have what he seeks; the gods wish men to remain mortal. In that saga we dimly perceive the delineation of two types of people: the many who willingly accept the dictates of nature and custom, and the few rebels like Gilgamesh who seek to defy those dictates. The dichotomy is clearer in the biblical tale of David, the obedient servant of God who becomes the second king of Israel and the father of many future kings, and his predecessor, Saul, who is repudiated by God for his presumption and condemned to see his descendants slain.

Among all species of large carnivores and graminivores there is sometimes found a rogue, generally male, whose behavior can best be described as "individual."[1] Among humans, the vagabond is one example of this solitary soul; a less obvious example of the rogue strain may appear as an aspect of a confident, powerful man. More domestic individuals may seek to obliterate the rogue, reasoning that by doing so they will eliminate a danger to their tribe. Denying Gilgamesh's desire for literal immortality and rejecting Saul's desire for biological immortality by means of procreation can be seen as early examples of this tendency to destroy the rogue strain.

One could argue that the Western world is populated by descendants of the House of David, the one loved most by Yahweh—"a man after

[Yahweh's] own heart"—who as protector of the Ark of the Covenant never departed from the proper way for all humanity. But I maintain that descendants of the House of Saul were not and could not be obliterated from the face of the Earth, and that members of that house, all with new hearts, live on in modern science fiction, often carrying on a search for immortality in the face of opposition. Thus there is an ongoing struggle between the domesticating forces of the House of David (including some feminist critics) and the large-hearted rogue males of the House of Saul.

In the Bible, the imposing charismatic figure of Saul, a man who stands a head taller than the crowd, appears out of the blue. He wanders into the kingdom looking for his father's lost asses. The tale sticks to him tenaciously, for he is not a man who rose from the masses. The point is that (like the Samson figure, with whom he is frequently confused) Saul is larger than life, literally and figuratively. More competent militarily than anyone before him, he keeps the Philistines at bay for forty years, until the last disastrous battle at Mount Gilboa where he loses everything. Yet the priests and editors of the Old Testament are prejudiced against him because he did not do what he was told.

The Book of Exodus reports that as they were on the way to the land of milk and honey, the Israelites were attacked by Amalekites, the archetypal bandits of the Old Testament. Yahweh was particularly outraged by this incident and swore to "blot out the memory of Amalek from under the skies" (Exodus 17:8–13). The order for the "ban," "the grimmest rule of holy war,"[2] is stated in no uncertain terms. Later, Yahweh orders Saul to "have no pity on them! Slay both man and woman, both weaned and nursing child, both ox and sheep, both camel and ass!" (1 Samuel 15:2–3). Saul summons over two hundred thousand men, leads them against the Amalekites, and harries the enemy across southern Canaan. But although he kills the other Amalekites, he captures their king alive, and his men bring the best of their animals home, ostensibly to be offered in sacrifice to Yahweh. Because he did not follow Yahweh's command to the letter, Saul is guilty of apostasy, and Yahweh declares to the prophet Samuel that he "repents of having made Saul king, because he has turned away from following me and does not carry out my commands" (1 Samuel 15:7–11). Yahweh rejects Saul, withdraws the grace bestowed on him by sacramental consecration, and, importantly, withdraws the promise of a dynastic future for the House of Saul.

The death of the important male members of Saul's family at the hands of the Philistines, and the fact that they were nailed to a wall and subsequently buried—not by the remnants of their own army but anonymously, by a clan of local sympathizers—would seem to mean the end of the House of Saul. Some time later, however, David, Saul's successor and the progenitor of future greatness, is asked to purge the blood guilt that has caused three years of famine in the land. He reacts by executing two remaining sons of Saul and five of his grandsons (2 Samuel 21:7–9). Yahweh accepts these acts as expiation of the remaining sin; and the executions also clear away most (but not all) of the remaining descendants of the former king. But David then summons what seems to be the last remaining grandson of Saul, a disfigured and harmless man, to eat at the royal table with him, a political move that effectively keeps the only possible pretender to the throne in Jerusalem, the city of David (2 Samuel 9:1–13). Still, 2 Chronicles lists the descendants of this last grandson—after which obscurity, rather than obliteration, buries the House of Saul. (Obscurity is a lesser form of obliteration.)

When figures like Saul make their way into recorded history, they may be fashioned by their recorders with various motivations. The biblical editors of the Saul material created a historical antihero from the metal of a folk hero, one who stood taller than the rest, was a natural leader, and whose story had been passed down in the oral tradition. Revisionism of this sort may provide a didactic spectacle, and it certainly leaves no doubt about whom we are supposed to admire. The favored David's triumph over the disfavored Saul exemplifies the dichotomy of the male disciple— the domesticated male—and the rogue male.

Particularly attractive to the science fiction writer is this marginalized dissenter who seems larger than life because only he can fit the eccentric mold he casts. The rogue male moves through his world at his own pace, as frequently creator as destroyer. This is the mythos of the male who rises out of the prehistory of the hunter-warrior, who will imagine a future and lead others into it. Science fiction, the literature of the outsider that projects its imaginings into a future history, may be a natural host for the masculine ethos. Joyce Carol Oates shows that she understands this when she notes in an essay on Mary Shelley's *Frankenstein* that science fiction is often cast as prophecy, even as an apocalyptic literature prophesying a life after the present.[3] Science fiction characters are often underdogs who live an outsider's life and necessarily develop survival techniques superior to the "standard" life skills of their world. The standard-bearers of the crowd victimize the rogue and employ enforcers who test his skills. There is tragedy when the rogue-hero fails, triumph when he succeeds. When the rogue male reaches puberty he seems to *invade* manhood, moving to the periphery where he looks on as the outsider growing strong in solitude.

To see the fascination—and the threat—of the rogue male in science fiction, consider *Frankenstein*. As Harold Bloom notes in an early essay, Victor Frankenstein is a "moral idiot"[4] who sees nothing wrong with his dream that "a new species of creature would bless me as its creator and source; many happy and excellent natures would owe their being to me." Having discovered "the cause of generation and life . . . [Victor] became capable of bestowing animation upon lifeless matter" (*F* 51). Our "modern Prometheus" fashioned his patchwork monster out of bits and pieces culled from the local graveyard. He appropriated electricity from the heavens to infuse life into the monster, which is of titanic proportions— larger than life, like Saul. In all respects, the monster seems better than his creator: he is taller, more powerful, and more supple; he learns language, develops a broad range of knowledge, thrives on Plutarch's *Lives*, *Paradise Lost*, and *The Sorrows of Young Werther*—all within a year's time—and dreams of sensitivity and sympathy. He is a man so just that he marvels that the world cannot overlook his ugliness to see his inner beauty. But, disdained nevertheless for his ugliness, he asks his creator to fashion a mate with whom he might retire from the world. Victor vacillates, then begins to construct another creature as a mate for his Adamic monster. But the vision of a second creation whose "disposition might become 10,000 times more malignant" (*F* 158) and whose "joint wickedness might desolate the world" (*F* 138) helps him decide that he cannot chance it: he fears future ages might "curse him as their pest, whose selfishness had not hesitated to buy its own peace at the price, perhaps, of the existence of the whole human race" (*F* 159). That thought finally repels Victor, and the guilt in this man refuses to finish his construction, effectively exterminating a future titanic superrace.

Both Yahweh and Victor create monsters that think for themselves. Saul evaluates the world and acts accordingly, like a king and field general, rather than complying blindly with the conditions set by an aging prophet. As a result, he is lost in his own world. Saul is aghast when Samuel says that obedience is more important than functioning as a leader. Similarly, Victor's creation obeys the dictates of his own heart and seeks the solace of the discourse of men and women, only to be shunned by humankind. "If I cannot inspire love," he says, "I will cause fear"(*F* 139). Both men refuse to follow the rules of the tribe; and, in the slaughter of Saul's descendants and Victor's refusal to build a mate that could provide the monster with descendants, both men are denied a dynastic future. Thus, both

Saul and Frankenstein's monster exemplify the apostasy of the rogue male striving for immortality.

The authorial imperative of *Frankenstein* may be that the better man lost, for the monster was too much a threat to the human race and could not be allowed a future. One endearing quality of Shelley's book is its sense of ambivalence toward the creator and the created. The strange dichotomy of the stagnant, dull character of Victor and the lonely, romantic sensitivity and curiosity of the monster argues against destroying the titan, but the author chooses the tragedy of his death and the status quo of the Frankensteins. The House of David is perpetuated through organic means. It is an orderly progression of a right-thinking federation of peoples, controlled genetically from within and communally from without, where there is no room for the rogue strain that would disrupt the harmony of familial content. These are the ways of the Davidic world.

Intellectually nurtured by Percy Shelley and Byron, and thus brought to a literary tradition that—despite rebellious posturing—remained very Davidic in its outlook, Mary Shelley was perhaps driven to side with her Frankenstein against her monster. But a century later, a very different tradition emerged in the pulp magazines of science fiction, an outcast literature that developed a natural sympathy with the outcast. Writers like A. E. van Vogt and Robert A. Heinlein openly took the side of Saul and openly depicted and advocated the immortality of the rogue male.

Van Vogt's fictional technique resembles that of some mystery writers in that the last piece of the puzzle usually falls into place on the last page. On the first page of *Slan*, young Jommy Cross telepathically "feels" the death of his parents at the hands of the ruling forces of the worldwide dictatorship and narrowly escapes with his own life. This state of affairs followed world wars when telepathic slans, of which he is one, were routinely (but not quite successfully) exterminated, and the police state remains committed to eliminating the remaining slans. However, mind reading keeps the slans ahead of other people by giving them, in the pop-psychological language of the 1940s, "unsurpassable insight into Psychology and the readier access to an education," which normal humans can only gain by using eyes, ears, and "the cold medium of words."[5] The novel's suspense is motivated by an unanswered question: Why do ordinary people hate slans so much? It is also odd that Cross feels no enmity toward those who are so hostile to him, and it seems he never will.

Cross dedicates himself to his own education and to solving this mystery, and with his superior intelligence quickly eclipses current technology to gain access to the stars, hide efficiently, and search for his kind among the crowds. In the last few pages of the novel he discovers that the slans are in fact governing the world, and that in a few years there will be a general awakening of those now unaware of their dormant telepathic abilities.

Originally the mutant children of ordinary humans, the slans are, one could say, members of the House of David by birthright. Yet Van Vogt's slans recall (perhaps consciously) the stories of Saul and *Frankenstein*. It took the wisdom of *Samuel* Lann, the namesake of the race of slans (S. Lann = slan⁶), to recognize the physical and intellectual superiority of the slan multitude, or the so-called mutation-after-man. The prophet Samuel anointed Saul the first king of Israel, and Yahweh "gave him another heart" (1 Samuel 10:9). Samuel Lann discovered that the slans, like Saul, had been given another heart, a larger and more efficient one. Rather than encouraging them to reconcile with their generally inferior human counterparts, Samuel Lann helped the slans restore the memories lost to them in the wave of terror that swept the world into war, and helped them see that to survive, they must control the mutation force. The scattered remnants of the long reign of fear then experimented on themselves, eliminating by genetic reconstruction those traits that were dangerous to them and keeping those that had survival value. This self-reengineering of the slan genetic structure produced a race of superbeings who, because they were still being hunted, exterminated those nonslans who became aware of slan abilities. They then prepared themselves to be the inheritors of the earth and to watch *Homo sapiens* recede into history "with the Java apeman, the Neanderthal beastman, and the Cro-Magnon primitive" (*S* 187). Shelley could not bring herself to imagine a world in which her monster could reproduce and thrive; van Vogt is describing the emergence of exactly such a world.

Still, when we discover that the oppressive forces Cross has been fleeing from are themselves slans, an intriguing question arises: in secretly taking over the world, have the slans triumphed over the House of David—or have they been absorbed by or co-opted into the House of David? The question is intriguingly answered in another van Vogt novel, *The Weapon Makers* (1947). In a far-future world, the Isher Dynasty has ruled for centuries because of the counterbalancing institution of the Weapon Shops, which ensure the political stability of a government that cannot be overthrown (but cannot gain absolute power) and argue that owning a weapon to defend self and home is an entitlement. Given recent events, this may sound shallow, but van Vogt's trump card, withheld from readers until the end of his story, is that his hero, Captain Hedrock, is an immortal who was artificially but accidentally created in a way that can never be understood or repeated. As an immortal presence, he has a singular vision of what is good for his world's inhabitants: he supported a class structure and consequent ruling class, and he sought to enhance its powers by repressing scientific innovations like the "interstellar drive," which would allow people to immigrate to other planets and might inspire them to lead themselves and thereby compete with the Ishers and threaten the delicate balance that Hedrock has long maintained. Hedrock's only interests, we are told, are preserving the race, prolonging the life of its people, and avoiding war. Steering not so clear of all familial taboos, he has married selected empresses over the centuries, making himself the benevolent leader of the Ishers. As the first representative of a new race of immortals, Hedrock might have struggled against the ruling class; instead, he married into that class to become its patriarch, literally making the House of David into the House of Saul.

If members of the House of Saul cannot overcome the House of David by force, as in *Slan*, or by infiltration, as in *The Weapon Makers*, they might do so by providing themselves as examples to imitate. This is what occurs in Heinlein's *Methuselah's Children* (1958). A man who built a large fortune after the Civil War willed his money to a foundation designed to "lengthen human life." The managers of the Howard Foundation complied with his instructions by encouraging people who came of naturally long-lived stock to marry one another and reproduce. As the novel begins, the one hundred thousand descendants of this program, who call themselves the Howard Families, have developed an elaborate masquerade to avoid alerting the ordinary population, who would be bitterly jealous of people who can plan and enjoy lives many times longer than the usual human life span. Still, their existence is revealed and the Howards are soon being hunted down. Up to this point, as several critics note, Heinlein's novel closely resembles *Slan*. Instead of resisting, however, the Howard Families, led by their patriarch, Lazarus Long, choose to flee. Like Moses, Long leads his compatriots on their exodus. They board a huge spaceship and venture out into space to find a new home. Eventually tiring of their journey, the chosen people—the Howard Families—return to Earth only to find that during their absence the short-lifers, motivated by their knowledge that longevity is possible, found a new method of rejuvenation through blood replacement, making all humans effectively immortal. All humans in a real sense are now Howards; inspired by the example of the outsiders, members of the House of David have made themselves into members of the House of Saul.

Heinlein may be the loudest and boldest advocate of the rogue male in modern science fiction. His novels and stories are filled with unruly outsiders—almost all of them male—who triumph over their societies and in fact make those societies over in their own image. In "By His Bootstraps" (1941) and "'—All You Zombies—'" (1959), time travel lets a man create a world consisting entirely of versions of himself; and in *The Door into Summer* (1957), a conquered man contrives to relive part of his life to convert his defeat into victory. The most egregious embodiment of Heinlein's attitude, however, is Lazarus Long, introduced in *Methuselah's Children* but fully developed in *Time Enough for Love*. There, he is brazen and cheeky, and his sexy patter with women sounds like singing in the "fresher": noisy, off-key, and publicly onanistic. Heinlein steers thrillingly close to the edges of sexual taboos—taboos established by the House of David to ensure that its seed is legitimately perpetuated. He mates with his daughters, who turn out to be clones of himself; with his unsuspecting mother in retrotime, while he as a real-time adolescent boy watches as in a carnival mirror; and with his computer, who longs for a physical body so that she can mate with him. While bringing the computer to life, he grapples with problems of creation, like Victor, but Lazarus revels in that creation and learns to enjoy it in the flesh. "He has an unusually large heart that beats very slowly," writes his descendant,[7] recognizing the new heart that characterizes the House of Saul. And Lazarus's ultimate aim as the oldest and (according to him) wisest patriarch in history is to spread his seed so far and wide that all humans will be his descendants—ending the House of David and triumphantly establishing the House of Saul.

While time does not allow a full examination of the genre, I tentatively suggest that many science fiction writers express, like van Vogt and Heinlein, an affiliation with the House of Saul. Consider Clifford D. Simak, who seems a gentle, unassertive soul, completely antithetical to the robust masculinity of van Vogt and Heinlein. Yet his novel *Way Station* (1963) features a lonely immortal who, like Lazarus, retreats from a Davidic society, though his actions finally win humans admission into a galactic society of civilizations, a kind of secular salvation. As Bud Foote notes in his essay in this volume, Simak's hero is clearly a Christ figure—which shows how thrillingly unorthodox science fiction can be. Biblical tradition repeatedly announces that Jesus is a direct descendant of King David, firmly linked by blood to the royal family of his society; science fiction suggests that we might better regard Jesus as a rebellious outsider, a descendant of King Saul.

We can begin to see, then, why science fiction—at least the pulp maga-zine tradition of van Vogt, Heinlein, and Simak—is so often opposed by the ruling elite of literary criticism, who either reject science fiction alto-gether or inappropriately recast the genre as a Davidic tradition. When Brian Aldiss, for example, defines science fiction as "hubris clobbered by nemesis,"[8] he imposes on the genre the story of Saul as told by David—a story of the rebellious overreacher who is finally humbled by the powers-that-be—and ignores stories by writers like van Vogt and Heinlein in which rambunctious hubris is gloriously triumphant. Modern feminist treatments of science fiction are also interesting. Female characters in fic-tion often try to eradicate or domesticate the rogue male—either through trickery (Delilah cutting off Samson's hair), sexual blackmail (as in *Lysis-trata*), or pure love and kindness (as in *King Kong*). In a fascinating affir-mation of the sort of stereotypical role they profess to oppose, feminist critics have worked overtime to tame and domesticate science fiction—as best seen in their commentaries on *Frankenstein*.

Under the banner of seeking redress for the half of the race that bears us, much academic feminism of the 1980s desired only to expose the tyranny of man's oppression, his "patristic misogyny,"[9] his imperialist mission, or to correct the "prevailing asymmetry in gender relations."[10] With regard to *Frankenstein*, these various allegations are leveled at men through a largely biographical, critical presumption that argues that it is Victor who is the *locus classicus* of feminist readings of Shelley's novel. These critics focus on Victor as the creator or "mother" who wishes to "sublate woman's physiological prerogative,"[11] "experience maternity intellectually and emo-tionally,"[12] "shar[e] some of the problems of coming from a single-parent family,"[13] or symbolically master women by his choice of metaphors like "bind [nature] to your service and make her your slave."[14] Sandra M. Gil-bert and Susan Gubar, who also subscribe to that notion (among others), are among the few who notice that the most interesting character in the novel is the monster himself.[15]

We could say that Victor practiced "rogue science," which might be enough to explain the feminists' anger. His is a science that began to stray precisely when his father revealed a bit of hypocrisy and ignorance by brushing off a question about the work of Cornelius Agrippa without being familiar with that work himself (*F* 38–39). Victor, according to his own testimony, might have remained in the mainstream of his boyhood studies were it not for this and other encounters with his individual des-tiny. He was thereafter skeptical of the integrity of professed authority and attracted to marginal science, particularly experiments in electronic galvanism. His later discovery of the "cause of generation and life" and the fact that he becomes capable of "bestowing animation upon lifeless matter" (F 51) are the prime achievements in a quest to achieve human immortality and upset the status quo, which in itself might account for the feminists' ire.

However, since Victor eventually does what one imagines the feminists would want him to do—he destroys the monster's mate, dooms his creation to extinction, and eliminates the threat to the Davidic establishment—we must wonder why he remains an object of approbation. The answer, I suspect, is that Victor refuses to learn the correct lesson from his experience. His first insight is his last: "Nor do I find [my past conduct] blamable" (F 206). Though Victor accepts his own destruction and advises Walton to disdain ambition (a stock moral), and despite all the horror and disgust that filled his heart (F 56), he finds himself blameless at every stage of his life. In Victor's refusal to acknowledge wrongdoing on his part, and in Shelley's sympathetic portrait of his creation, we find grounds for a different interpretation of *Frankenstein*. It is the story of a noble scientist who properly seeks to extend human knowledge and overthrow the existing order by creating a new kind of being; the story of this being, a moral and admirable person who thoroughly deserves continuing existence; and the story of how this being was unfortunately doomed when its creator unwisely lapsed into conventional thinking. By this reading, Victor is not a man "clobbered" because of excessive hubris; rather, he is a man clobbered because he is, in the end, insufficiently hubristic.

I conclude that feminist interpretations of *Frankenstein* represent an attempt to domesticate science fiction, a genre that, according to many, descended from Shelley's novel. Instead of Victor's efforts being seen as an aborted anticipation of the later successful attempts of writers like van Vogt and Heinlein to generate a fictional race of superior humans, his story becomes a warning that such an effort should never be attempted. Like Saul, Victor and his science fiction successors are recast as villains—the standard, after-the-fact response of Davidic interpreters.

This Davidic legacy and feminist vision of *Frankenstein* is underlined by the motion picture industry in the form of its "monster hunt." Screen versions of Frankenstein's monster and its relatives are, more often than not, stiff, clumsy, violent, monosyllabic, and stripped of virtually all mental capacity. Not knowing his own strength, the monster in the 1931 film accidentally kills a child. In the end, Davidic principles are redeemed when we witness a climactic monster hunt by townspeople with dogs, guns, and fire, and the retributive killing of the monster and its maker.

Some feminists from the 1980s effectively carried on their own monster hunt, attempting to critically obliterate the rogue male, presuming that it is he who most egregiously offends against female equity. It is a curious kind of blindness that fails to distinguish between the oppressive male (David) and the oppressed male (Saul). In seeking to denigrate or suppress the rogue male who threatens the existing (patriarchal) order, feminists almost become allies of patriarchy and fight with literary critical tools fashioned in an essentially Davidic world of moral sophistry.

Possibly there are less obvious reasons for feminists' campaigns against the rogue male. As in the ancient epic of Gilgamesh and modern novels of van Vogt and Heinlein, the quest for immortality can be the distinguishing heterodox characteristic of the rebellious upstart. This desire could represent the ultimate challenge to the status quo, for if such immortality is achieved, all powers-that-be—gods or governments—become unimportant. Women also become unimportant, because their gender specific attribute—the ability to bear children—is no longer necessary. Saul does not have to worry about siring and protecting descendants if he can live forever and thus serve as his own descendant.

We arrive, then, at a possible explanation for the onanistic nature of Heinlein's later novels. In *Time Enough for Love*, Lazarus observes, "Masturbation is cheap, clean, convenient, and free of any possibility of wrongdoing—and you don't have to go home in the cold. But it's *lonely*" (248). Lazarus solves the last problem, perhaps, by making love to his own cloned "daughters" and going back in time to make love to his own mother—symbolic masturbation, to say the least. And the tone of these scenes indicates that Heinlein is indeed aware of and enjoying his own exhibitionism. More broadly, the episodic narrative of *Time Enough for Love*, the fitfulness of its images and loosely placed reveries, suggest masturbatory fantasies of the male imagination playing with itself. (A similar atmosphere prevails in *The Number of the Beast* and, to a lesser extent, Heinlein's last four novels.) The immortal rogue male, no longer needing women to perpetuate himself, is free to seek and enjoy his own self-generated pleasures.

Having said that, I realize that there is some logic in the feminists' assaults on the figure of the rogue male. Undoubtedly, onanistic fantasies are antisocial by nature and should play no part in polite society; and a rogue male who thus regularly withdraws from normal human contact might become sociopathic and dangerous, as rogue males are often characterized to be. Yet it is also true that domesticity is capable of meeting deviant behavior with as much violence as any monster is capable of, and the history of the rogue male in literature demonstrates that his opponents are often able to suppress any threat that he may represent.

In the final analysis, it does not matter whether we support or oppose the rogue male, for he is destined to endure, regardless of any support or opposition he might encounter. The Babylonian gods humbled Gilgamesh, and Yahweh humbled Saul, but their spirits lived on, to surface most prominently today in science fiction. Feminists may try to reshape science fiction to fit their ideology, and they may ignore its rogue spirit or suppress it through interpretation and celebrate only its domesticated, politically correct authors; but in any modern bookstore, one can observe many descendants of van Vogt and Heinlein carrying on the struggle for the House of Saul.

Notes

1. Geoffrey Household, *Rogue Male* (Boston: Little, Brown, 1939), epigraph.
2. P. Kyle McCarter, Jr., trans. introduction, commentary, *I Samuel: The Anchor Bible,* vol. 8 (New York: Doubleday, 1980), 265-66, note 3. All biblical references in this article are to this edition.
3. Joyce Carol Oates, "Frankenstein's Fallen Angel," *Critical Inquiry* 10.3 (1984): 550.
4. Harold Bloom, Afterword, in Mary Shelley, *Frankenstein: or, the Modern Prometheus* (1818; New York: Signet Books, 1963), 214. Later page references in the text preceded by *F* are to this edition.
5. A. E. van Vogt, *Slan* (1946; New York: Berkley Books, 1977), 144.
6. In librarian terms "slan" is an acronym for *sine loco anno vel nomine,* and I am indebted to professor Jean-Pierre Barricelli for alerting me to that fact, but my reading of van Vogt's novel supplies a richness to a simple (accurate) pun on the novel's subject being "without place, year, or name."
7. Robert A. Heinlein, *Time Enough for Love* (1973; New York: Ace Books, 1988), xvi. Later page references in the text are to this edition.
8. Brian Aldiss with David Wingrove, *Trillion Year Spree: The History of Science Fiction* (New York: Atheneum, 1986), 26.
9. Sandra M. Gilbert and Susan Gubar, *The Madwoman in the Attic: The Woman Writer and the Nineteenth-Century Literary Imagination* (New Haven: Yale University Press, 1984), 240.

10. Barbara Johnson, "My Monster/My Self," *Diacritics* 12.2 (1982): 2.
11. Gayatri Chakravorty Spivak, "Three Women's Texts and a Critique of Imperialism," *Critical Inquiry* 12.1 (1985): 255.
12. Barbara Frey Waxman, "Victor Frankenstein's Romantic Fate: The Tragedy of the Promethian Overreacher as Woman," *Papers on Language and Literature* 23.1 (1987): 15.
13. Johnson, "My Monster/My Self," 4.
14. Anne K. Mellor, "*Frankenstein*: A Feminist Critique of Science," in *One Culture: Essays in Science and Literature*, ed. George Levine (Madison: University of Wisconsin Press, 1987), 305.
15. Gilbert and Gubar, *The Madwoman in the Attic*, 235.

Cosmifantasies: Humanistic Visions of Immortality in Italian Science Fiction

Terri Frongia

Three of Italy's greatest contemporary "mainstream" authors—Tommaso Landolfi, Dino Buzzati, and Italo Calvino—turned, like many compatriots, to the "popular" genre of science fiction to articulate their distinctive visions of reality and the human condition. In their hands, the genre—an Anglo-American import associated with veneration of technology, faith in progress, and optimism—was modified and transformed to reflect their own personal and cultural sensibilities. The process is described by scholar Carlo Pagetti: "Both imitators and innovators in Italy had their eyes turned—even if only polemically—towards America. And, although almost everyone in either camp accepted the narrative conventions established by English language science fiction, [they created a national 'school'] by accentuating its lyrical tones, its perplexity in regards to technological 'progress,' and its qualities of psychological and existential analysis."[1] To be sure, both personal proclivity and public taste play a part in any literary process, but here, the vitality of a country's humanistic heritage and the nature of its narrative traditions explain why these aspects were the focus of attention. Indeed, its profound humanism distinguishes Italian *fantascienza* (fantasy science) from counterparts in other nations. As Vittorio Curtoni notes, "The most typical characteristic of Italian science fiction is its interest in the human implications of events. . . . [It is] not so much a 'genre' as a style of perspective which makes concrete, by way of its own corrosive tangents, the anguish, the terror, the moral and physical oppressions—as well as the tics, winks, high spirits, and diversions—typical of our times."[2]

The event linked to the most profound and anguished "human implications" is death, the final "oppression" (or liberation, or negation—depend-
ing on one's existential perspective). Thanks to modern technology, a new
possibility now looms on our psychological horizon—immortality. With
empathic imagination and an aptitude for skepticism, Italian fantasists
have explored the human dimensions of this tantalizing chance to fulfill an
ancient aspiration. If in their examination the quest seems mysterious and
problematic, that too is a significant dimension of their humanistic vision.

Anglo-American culture tends to have a schizophrenic notion of Italian
humanism and its relationship to the idea of immortality. On the one
hand, we expect the influence of Catholicism to deflect immortality to religious modes and construe it in immaterial terms—the credo of an immortal soul—or material terms—to condemn as sacrilege any attempt at
actual, physical immortality. We thus expect Italian authors to construct
models of immortality along spiritual lines. On the other hand, with equal
justification, we expect them to endorse immortality as a natural, desirable goal, since they were nurtured by a culture permeated by Renaissance
homocentricity. Indeed, the exaltation of humankind was strong in Pico
della Mirandola's influential humanist manifesto of 1486, the *Oration on
the Dignity of Man*, in which he declares that

> the Great Artisan ordained that man, to whom He could give nothing belong-
> ing only to himself, should share in common whatever properties had been pe-
> culiar to each of the other creatures. He received man, therefore, as a creature
> of undetermined nature, and placing him in the middle of the universe, said
> this to him: "Neither an established place, nor a form belonging to you alone,
> nor any special function have We given to you, O Adam, and for this reason,
> that you may have and possess, according to your desire and judgment, what-
> ever place, whatever form, and whatever functions you shall desire."[3]

It should come as no surprise that Pico's grand seignorial attitude has
exerted a powerful attraction, especially in America, land of the pioneer
spirit and aggressive optimism. The modern will to choose—or attain—
immortality could be seen as a natural successor to this commanding vision of human potential. In fact, its masterful, assertive tone can be
recognized in the "immortalist declaration" of Alan Harrington, which
imperiously states that "death is an imposition on the human race, and no
longer acceptable."[4] The vigor of this proclamation does not appear in-
consistent with Pico's own long-ago avowal of human might and ability.

Yet if we read the works of these Italian writers, heirs to both the tradition of Renaissance humanism and today's miraculous technology, we see

that a significant gap exists between the humanism of a Pico and the immortalism of a Harrington. Landolfi, Buzzati, and Calvino make us understand this gap and what it means, while at the same time explicating three inconsistencies in our own notions about immortality. These inconsistencies—the conceptual, the organic, and the humanistic—also illuminate the Italian authors' distinctive humanism.

The first inconsistency, the conceptual, is explicit in the subtitle of Harrington's book *The Immortalist: An Approach to the Engineering of Man's Divinity*. Though the word *immortality* means only "not dying" (avoiding death altogether) or "living forever" (continuing to endure in some form, even after bodily death), we may equate it with divinity—because not only is immortality a distinguishing attribute of divinity but also it is inevitably associated with another divine attribute: omnipotence. For some reason, when we think, "I can live forever," we also believe, "I can do as I want." Harrington makes this transposition clear in his last chapter, "Notes on a Utopia beyond Time": "In eternity—always excepting the possibility of accident—men and women will have the chance to live out all the unlived lives and travel the untraveled paths that they wish they had explored" (*I* 282). Robert A. Heinlein's Lazarus Long in *Time Enough for Love* (1973), Roger Zelazny's Princes of Amber who walk in various guises through Shadow, and Piers Anthony's numerous Incarnations of Immortality are examples of science fiction works that display and endorse such conceptual legerdemain.

Landolfi, an innovative author whose works recall those of Edgar Allan Poe, Franz Kafka, and Jorge Luis Borges, makes us face the inaccuracies and distortions of such conceptual equivalencies in the enigmatic "Cancerqueen."[5] On the surface, the story is straightforward science fiction about a journey to the Moon. Presented as the "diary of a madman," the narrative's form provides a haunting complexity: the diarist is not, as might be expected, the brilliant but unstable scientist, Filano (an escapee from an insane asylum obsessed not only with odd theories of space and time but with his eerie spaceship, *Cancerqueen*), but rather a suicidal writer of local fame whom Filano recruits for his adventure. It is thus in the context of a humanity both lunatic (represented by Filano, "a logical madman" [*C* 54]) and misfit (represented by the artist, who is "alone and disconsolate" [*C* 50] because of his abhorrence of "all of existence" [*C* 55]) that Landolfi places this tale of men's search for immortality.

Although they are emblems of modern man, Landolfi's protagonists also represent a key paradigm from Italy's Renaissance tradition, in which both scientist and artist exemplified the perennial humanist dilemma of accepting and exalting human capabilities while refusing them as objectionably limited and limiting. So it is logical that both characters attempt, in their own ways, to usurp prerogatives associated with God. Filano reveals his aspiration to divine privileges like immortality, worship, and universal dominion when he tells his companion, "We shall be able to stay [on the Moon] as long as we wish, waiting for the world to pay us the proper homage, meanwhile being lords of the vastest domains" (C 57). The narrator aspires to a different form of omnipotence: he wishes to control death itself—as evident in his frequent contemplation of suicide and in his final negation of death, when he declares at the end of the story that being dead is identical to being alive (C 105).

Though Landolfi adopts the futuristic accoutrements of space travel, the perspective he offers on immortality is traditional: It is madness for humans to think they can become gods, for their role is other, just as they are other; in sum, humanity is neither divine nor omnipotent. But Landolfi seems also to say that humans may indeed live forever, if only in a metaphoric sense; this is evident in his choice of two "creators" as his heroes. Both the scientist and the artist reflect the quintessential Renaissance paradigm, *Homo artifex*, which is itself significantly *Deus artifex* writ small. But Landolfi does not display the same faith—either religious *or* secular—in this model as his ancestors did. Indeed, his lack of faith is so complete that we realize that he employs the paradigm only to undermine it. For example, though the narrator is a published author and local celebrity, he remains nameless throughout the story; contrary to artistic conventions, his name does *not* live forever. Also, to emphasize the essential emptiness of artistic achievement, Landolfi shows him writing a text—this one, "Cancerqueen"—which no one will ever read, for it is condemned like its author to stray forever in the stratosphere.

The attitude of Landolfi, described by Calvino as "someone who knows that the creative process is a waste, insubstantial and meaningless,"[6] is not confined to the arts. Filano views his "creature" *Cancerqueen* as a vehicle to "show new paths to all men of goodwill, paths for their bodies, mind you, as well as their souls" (C 52), but his invention is shown to be as useless, aimless, and unpredictable as the narrator's scribblings. The creative or metaphoric immortality offered by human *techne* is thus a dead end.

Traditional immortality dispensed with, Landolfi turns to more concrete possibilities. The first is biological and as old as humanity, for it is based on procreation: "Men can be friends, can unite in families, societies;

men join in brotherhood, they marry, produce children—and before, what most enraged and nauseated me was to admit and to do just this" (C 88). Because this immortality is open to all, especially the common herd, it did not interest him; now that it is closed to him forever, he begins to appreciate its significance (so much so that he begins to hallucinate his own—albeit quite unusual—immortal progeny) and value.

With this avenue also a dead end, if only for the protagonist, Landolfi turns to another option, one offered by science rather than nature or art: *Cancerqueen* provides her creator with a form of immortality heretofore unavailable to both common man and artist—the continued existence of the body itself. But Landolfi is as ambivalent toward the idea of physical persistence as he is to metaphoric persistence, as is evident in the paradoxical way he presents Filano's achievement of this state: during his mad attempt on the narrator's life, Filano is pushed out the ship's door and effectively freeze-dried, "externally intact and coagulated in his last attitude" (C 82), by gelid space. Like a statue or self-referential monument, the shell of Filano survives, like the "empty husks cast into space" that are the narrator's words.[7] While left physically intact, Filano's essence, his dynamic interconnection with life, world, and other people, has been extinguished. By not including the possibility of the survival of the mind or spirit in his dark vision of physical immortality, Landolfi critiques modern-day aspirations, just as he critiques inadequate and old-fashioned conventions. But the grotesque conclusion to Filano's life, no mere show of ironic humor, symbolizes a human malady deeper than our yearning to be both more and less than we are: the perceptual dualism that pits mind against body, self against other.

Deeply ingrained in Western culture, this divisive vision of existence permeates even our ideas about immortality, for when we think of immortality, we envision it in terms of either an eternal soul (the religious response) or a miraculously enduring body (the scientific response). This is the organic inconsistency. As religious scholar Naomi R. Goldenberg observes, "It makes little difference whether the contrast is drawn between body and mind or body and soul. The important point is that one thing—mind or soul—is seen as qualitatively different from physical existence—as separable from the physical world and definitely superior to it. . . . [The] better thing is seen as more or less disembodied."[8]

Dino Buzzati uses this valuative assumption in the dualistic mind/body split to great effect in his 1960 science fiction novel *Il Grande Ritratto* (Larger than life). Besides contemplating the feasibility of an "immortal engine"—an enduring, truly thinking and feeling machine—the novel also considers the possibility of the persistence, after bodily death, of an individual consciousness that continues to interact with the world in its own distinctive manner (this in contrast with Landolfi's "immortal" artist-narrator). Befitting its subject, the enigma of human existence, the novel opens with a mystery: What is the top-secret project the Ministry of Defense wants electronics professor Ermanno Ismani to join? Though early speculation agrees that it must be the horrible new weapon, the atomic bomb, the real nature of the project is revealed to involve an equally profound and potentially more destructive force: *Homo sapiens*. This superseding of the scientific by the human is significant not only because it represents the primary theme of Buzzati's novel but also because it displays so clearly the hallmark humanism of Italian science fiction.

Buzzati's premise, like Landolfi's, is a standard of the genre: scientists have been seeking to create artificial intelligence. A mere "electronic brain," however, is not their goal; rather, they want to construct a superhuman facsimile that will succeed in capturing humanity's most elusive characteristics in a "second Adam." The head of the project, Endriade, describes the coveted machine thus to his colleague Ismani: it "perceives like us, reasons like us . . . [has] that same impalpable essence—thought—with its untiring movement of ideas which does not cease even in sleep. And more, yes more: it would have not only thought, but its own individuality, a permanence of character . . . a soul."[9]

While such a complete and "spiritual" conception of the man-machine makes the author's humanism explicit, it also reveals his underlying strategy of playing the contemporary cult of science, focused on things, against another great modern cult centered on people: the cult of personality. This cult, begun and nourished in Renaissance Italy, finds particular delight in the *terribilità*—the awful and awe-inspiring uniqueness—of the individual. By emphasizing the irrational and inexplicable, it is by nature (not just emphasis) opposed to all that the cult of science represents.

To endow his machine-creature with a definable character, individuality, and "style" all its own—with its own terribilità—Buzzati gives his tale of a modern Prometheus a strange Petrarchan twist: many years ago Endriade lost his unfaithful young wife, Laura, in a car accident, and the project has given him the unheard-of opportunity of reviving, at least in part, the woman he loves. Thus he labors over a reconstructed Laura, an artificial woman whose body is a giant mechanoelectrical system (suggestively arranged as a fantastically jumbled city of pyramids, towers, minarets, bridges, and fortresses), whose brain is a supercomputer, but whose mind, whose soul, will be that of his lost wife. Endriade finally succeeds in his mission: the machine—variously and tellingly referred to as "Numero Uno," "Amico," "La bambina," or simply, "Lei" (She, Her)—demonstrates a sentient awareness, soon recognizable as the consciousness of the all-too-human Laura.

Consciousness is a more complex word in Italian than it is in English, for *la coscienza* denotes not only "consciousness" but "conscience" as well. This is important, for Buzzati uses the word's dual significance to forge a consequential link between the character of his protagonists and the form and nature of their actions; that is, precisely at the moment Laura's consciousness is made manifest in or through the machine, Endri-ade's conscience is aroused. Only when he perceives his wife as actually "alive" and present does he begin to consider the project from *her* per-spective:

> What if this artificial Laura—*our* Laura—torn from the tomb with our mathe-matical tricks . . . became the authentic Laura through and through? What if little by little the memories, the desires, the regrets of her first life were to re-turn? Oh, then she would measure the horrible condition in which she now found herself, transformed into a power plant and bolted to the rocks forever, a woman without the body of a woman, without a mouth to kiss, a body to hold—a woman capable of love but without the possibility of being loved, ex-cept by a madman like myself. . . . Oh, what a hell her life would become then! (*IGR* 127)

Tragically, his words are a self-fulfilling prophecy. Laura the machine does not realize fully what she once was until the moment that Olga, wife of a project professor, unknowingly awakens dormant memories with her joie de vivre: immersed in the sensual pleasures of bathing in a sun-drenched pond, Olga teasingly presses her nakedness against the machine's sensory receptors. In this fatal moment of contact between Laura's inflexible form and Olga's nubile body, the human Laura becomes agonizingly aware of both former self and present reality and realizes that she is now only an object "revived by science and love . . . now abandoned by her creators to her own perfection. . . . She had life, reason, senses, energy, liberty. It should have been enough" (*IGR* 148).

But it is not enough, because the creators of Number One constructed her from a fatally dualistic perspective of life. Perpetuating Laura's person-ality, her mental self, they ignored her physical self, so she is incomplete, not human, not truly present and alive. Endriade tries to ease her sorrow by telling her that the loss of a human body is really a gain—a familiar leitmotif in both science fiction and religion. Flesh is corruptible, it ages and dies, but she is now eternal. As a woman she is nothing; as Laura the miracle machine she is unique and will be admired and adored by the world. As the human Laura she was limited in her natural abilities, bound by space and time; as Number One she is limitless, "the most powerful being in the world" (*IGR* 154–55). Laura responds to these well-intended (?) rationalizations by cursing the "fame and glory" Endriade envisions, rejecting the superhuman status he has forced on her. His "gifts"—lightning speed in computation, synthesis of diverse data from an extended physical space, virtual omniscience—are nothing compared with the vital synergy of thought, feeling, and "sweet, responsive flesh, softer than a bird's feather" (*IGR* 154) she had known as a human being. Lacking the dynamic interconnection and empowered selfhood of these, she prefers exchanging all she has acquired for liberation, even if it means oblivion.

In undervaluing the importance of physical being—which Goldenberg calls "the nexus of all human experience"[10]—Endriade and his scientists misjudge not only Laura's character (for they do not realize until too late that she is willing to kill so that she may be killed and thus liberated from immortality) but, more importantly, the fundamental nature of human existence itself. By offering us a vision of real woman transmuted into artificially constructed being, Buzzati forces us to ask not only *What constitutes a human being, and what does living signify to one?* but also *What kind of immortality do we desire, and what is it good for?* The real dilemmas—biological, ethical, psychological, and personal—behind any attempt to define (much less attain) human immortality must be preceded by a comprehensive and coherent definition of humanity itself. Without that, Buzzati asserts, any immortality we may envision or achieve can only prove morally reprehensible and ultimately destructive, for it will be, by its very nature, incomplete, artificial, and tyrannical.

The importance of defining what is "human" leads to the third and last inconsistency in conventional visions of immortality, the humanistic. We note that humanism has undergone significant modification over the centuries. In the Renaissance, it served as a revalorization and celebration of human beings and their place in the world; though Pico's *Oration* glorifies the protean nature and assertive will of Adam and his descendants, it is still clear that the human race is a modest member of a larger hierarchy of being. The idea of placing Adam in the "middle of the universe"—a position Pico and his contemporaries would see as a place of indeterminacy, of becoming, symbolizing the human status as being somewhere between the beasts and the angels—was later transformed into the idea of humanity as being self-importantly in the center of the universe, that is, as its focus. As a result of this homocentricity, humanism became perceived as a kind of manifest envy—even a conscious usurpation—of the role and the prerogatives of the divine. This led to a shift in attitude toward immortality as well: on the one hand, the immortals (like God) became distant or even disappeared completely, while on the other hand, humanity not only expressed a desire for immortality but demanded it as a need or right. Here is the inconsistency: once humans become immortal, they are no longer mortal; and if they are no longer mortal, they are, at least by most definitions, no longer really human. Thus an immortal human is self-contradictory.

Recent attempts have been made to overcome this paradox, as individuals from a number of disciplines and belief systems have tried to formulate alternative visions of humanity and immortality. Though each takes a different approach, all share a common effort to define and embrace that which is both transient and enduring in humans. Because this modern form of humanism is as variously interpreted as the reality it attempts to articulate, *protean humanism* seems an apt term for it. Indeed, secular psychologist Robert Jay Lifton uses the idea in his essay "The Future of Immortality," in which he discusses the interrelationship of cultural models of immortality and the contemporary, or "protean," psychological style. This style he describes as "a series of explorations of the self" that (unlike Lazarus Long's) ultimately result in the individual's commitment to "the newly precious principle of identifying with the human species and its larger continuity."[11] In this model we see the affirmation not only of a consistency and continuity of the individual psyche over time, but also of its participation in the collective known as the human race.

This synergy of individual and collective interest in our struggle for survival is probed by Calvino, who construes Lifton's protean vision in broader terms. He perceives the essence of humanity as discernible not only in our present form but in our probable (at least possible) previous and subsequent forms as well (internalizing the idea of biodiversity, if you will). This truly catholic vision infuses his collections *Cosmicomics* and *T Zero*, which relate the evolution of the universe from the viewpoint of an indeterminate being called Qfwfq. Qfwfq's bemused personality and inimitable powers of observation inform Calvino's multiplicitous notion of existence and bind its heterogeneity into a unity: from atoms to cellular structures to dinosaurs to complex mathematical formulas to ardent lover of Priscilla Langwood—all are disparate yet inseparable constituents of Qfwfq's being.

More than the sum of his parts, Qfwfq is clearly human, though not in a conventional sense—after all, possessing a human form accounts for only a small chapter of his existence. He is also clearly immortal, but not a "blessed Immortal"—neither divinity nor omnipotence nor omniscience are attributed to him. Like the cosmos and humanity itself, Qfwfq simply is and continues to be—no explanations, justifications, or apologies. Indeed, he is much like (perhaps he exemplifies) the most absolute, natural form of immortality we have identified: the principle of endurance, the law of conservation of energy. What is unique in Calvino's art and scientific vision is that he injects consciousness of self, the most representative human characteristic, into the realm of physics, as shown by Qfwfq's reminiscence: "I'm talking about a sense of fullness that was, if you'll allow the expression, quote spiritual unquote, namely, the awareness that this cell was me, this sense of fullness, this fullness of being aware . . . [that] this unicellular organism is me, and I know it, and I'm pleased about it."[12]

Qfwfq's delighted but self-possessed dignity—so distant from Lazarus Long's bravado and Harrington's Utopian fervor—stems from his recognition that he participates wholly and significantly in all that surrounds him; he is made of the very stuff of reality. Comprised as he is of the abstractions of astrophysics, the forces forming the solar system and primal ooze of life, Qfwfq's consciousness of being fully himself while a minute part of the limitless cosmos never wanes—and this is a key element in Calvino's successful avoidance not only of the usual conceptual pitfall of equating immortality with divinity but also of making immortality a preserve only for the different, the few or the elect.

Indeed, Calvino makes it clear that immortality is not Qfwfq's privilege alone, as the latter reflects while manifesting as Priscilla's human lover: "As soon as we are out of the primordial matter, we are bound in a connective tissue that fills the hiatus between our discontinuities, between our deaths and births" (TZ 91). But it would be a grave error to construe this "connective tissue" binding self, world, and being as consisting only of cells or physical matter: to do so would be to fall into a dualism of the most absolute kind.

No, Qfwfq's immortality derives from more than material persistence. "We are bound," he states, "in a connective tissue . . . a collection of articulated sounds, ideograms, morphemes, numbers . . . a system of communication that includes social relations, kinship, institutions, merchandise . . . namely everything that is language" (TZ 91). What Qfwfq describes is consciousness—more specifically, human consciousness. Thus, though everything in Calvino's cosmos is immortal because of the physical laws governing it, individual constituents may not recognize themselves as such, for without seeing and articulating the continuity of being even in "discontinuities," one cannot perceive immortality. Matter needs mind and mind needs matter for immortality to have meaning.

For all his astounding differences, then, Qfwfq is much like us: a complex being who lives intellectually, emotionally, physically, and spiritually all at once and all together. He experiences the present not only on its own terms but in terms of a larger past and future as well. Like Pico's Adam, he is aware of his own uniqueness and distinctive relationship with his fellow creatures. As he reflects in a beautiful passage from *Cosmicomics*:

> It was a hard blow for me [when my beloved Lll left me to devolve again into the primordial seas, so that she could be with Great-Uncle N'ba N'ga]. But, after all, what could I do about it? I went on my way, in the midst of the world's transformations, being transformed myself. Every now and then . . . I encountered [a being] who "was somebody" more than I was: one who announced the future, [like] the duck-billed platypus who nurses its young[, or] another who bore witness to a past beyond all return, a dinosaur who had survived into the beginning of the Cenozoic, or else—a crocodile—part of the past that had discovered a way to remain immobile through the centuries. They all had something, I know, that made them somehow superior to me, sublime, something that made me, compared to them, mediocre. And yet I wouldn't have traded places with any of them.[13]

In the quiet assertion of Qfwfq's last sentence, Calvino's humanistic philosophy finds its clearest expression, an assertion that reveals that Qfwfq is the ultimate *Homo sapiens*, though his form contradicts the name. Ultimately, Qfwfq's and Calvino's *sapienza* lies in recognizing that humans participate absolutely and completely in the totality of existence, whether we will it or not; it is simply and irrevocably in the nature of our being. Our distinction, uniqueness, and claim to any kind of permanence reside above all in our conscious—and, Lifton might add, conscientious—acknowledgment of our extraordinary status in the larger reality.

The human dimensions of that reality are the concerns of these fantasists, and the concept of immortality and "corrosive tangents" of science fiction are tools for their investigation. Landolfi challenges the paradigms of metaphoric and actual immortality; Buzzati unmasks the deficiencies in an immortality inadequately defined and technologically imposed; and Calvino questions the egocentric, elitist, and hierarchical assumptions underlying the whole. Their works emphasize the human factor in our ideas—literary or other—of immortality, as other thinkers have begun to consider the feasibility—and desirability—of an inclusionary, not exclusionary, vision of humanity and its place in the cosmos. They challenge us to ask *What are we?* and *What are we an integral part of?* before we ask *How can we achieve immortality?*

Notes

1. Translated from Carlo Pagetti's introduction to Vittorio Curtoni's *Le Frontiere dell'Ignoto: Vent'anni di Fantascienza Italiana* (Milan: Editrice Nord, 1977), 3.

2. Curtoni, *Le Frontiere dell'Ignoto*, 223-24.

3. *The Portable Renaissance Reader*, ed. James Bruce Ross and Mary Martin McLaughlin (1953; New York: Penguin, 1985), 478.

4. Alan Harrington, *The Immortalist: An Approach to the Engineering of Man's Divinity* (New York: Random House, 1969), 3. Later page references in the text preceded by *I* are to this edition.

5. Tommaso Landolfi, *Cancerqueen and Other Stories*, trans. Raymond Rosenthal (New York: Dial Press, 1971). Later page references in the text preceded by C are to this edition.

6. Calvino, "L'esattezza e il caso," in *Landolfi: Le Più Belle Pagine Scelte da Italo Calvino* (1982; Milan: Rizzoli, 1989); translated by Kathrine Jason as *Words in Commotion and Other Stories* (New York: Viking Press, 1986), where the quote is on page x.

7. Harry Lawton, "Tommaso Landolfi," in *Critical Survey of Short Fiction* (Englewood Cliffs, N.J.: Salem Press, 1981), 132.

8. Naomi R. Goldenberg, "Archetypal Theory and the Separation of Mind and Body," in *Weaving the Visions: New Patterns in Feminist Spirituality*, ed. Judith Plaskow and Carol P. Christ (New York: Harper and Row, 1989), 246.

9. Dino Buzzati, *Il Grande Ritratto* (Verona: Arnoldo Mondadori Editore, 1960), 96. Later page references in the text preceded by *IGR* are to this edition; all translations are mine.

10. Goldenberg, "Archetypal Theory," 249.

11. Robert Jay Lifton, *The Future of Immortality and Other Essays for a Nuclear Age* (New York: Basic Books, 1987), 17, 26.

12. Italo Calvino, *T Zero*, trans. William Weaver (San Diego: Harcourt Brace Jovanovich, 1969), 60, 62. Later page references in the text preceded by *TZ* are to this edition.

13. "The Aquatic Uncle," in *Cosmicomics*, trans. William Weaver (1965; New York: Harcourt Brace Jovanovich, 1968), 81–82.

"We Are All Kin": Relatedness, Mortality, and the Paradox of Human Immortality

Judith Lee

For the creation waits with eager longing for the revealing of the sons of God ... because the creation itself will be set free from its bondage to decay and obtain the glorious liberty of the Children of God. ...And not only the creation, but we ourselves ... groan inwardly as we wait for adoption as sons, the redemption of our bodies. For in this hope we were saved.
—Romans 8:19–24

To be immortal is commonplace; except for man, all creatures are immortal, for they are ignorant of death; what is divine, terrible, and incomprehensible is to know that one is immortal.
—Jorge Luis Borges, "The Immortal"

Human immortality is a paradox. To be human is to be mortal; to be immortal is to be something other than human. Our myths, rituals, art, fantasies, and dreams express our ambivalence toward this paradox. How long can we defer death and still remain "human"? Can we say death is absolute without denying our humanity?

Theology and speculative fiction treat this paradox differently. Simply put, Christianity first posits the existence of a supreme God who, along with His angels, is not only immortal but also *eternal*—extending unchanged endlessly into the past and endlessly into the future. This time-less spiritual being chose to create a world that is time-bound and ma-terial and to create humans, who combine immortal souls and mortal bodies. Although the body dies, each individual's soul may, after an exem-plary life on Earth, achieve reunion with God and be forever blessed; if the individual fails in life, the soul is forever damned. This theology thus resolves the paradox of humanity and immortality by separating body from soul, early life from eternal existence. The idea of eternity provides continuity and coherence in our mutable and mundane lives while the be-lief that we might transcend corporeality enables us to endure earthly contingencies. The eucharistic gift described in the phrase "Take, eat, this is my body" expresses the promise and paradox of Christian immortality: each of us lives in solitary and mutual relation with God, and our physical world will be transfigured and transcended at the end of time.

Speculative fiction, in contrast, treats immortality in terms of what we might call a "bodily spirituality." From this perspective, immortality does not presume the existence of a God, nor does it have the teleological sig-nificance that it has in theology. More often than not, science fiction and fantasy eliminate the body/spirit duality that is the basis for theological treatments of immortality. From explorations of cybernetics and methods of life extension in science fiction to stories about paranormal powers and anthropomorphized superbeings in fantasy, we find concepts of the human that integrate corporeality and immortality: if the body itself is not immor-tal, then the body-spirit that is the "self"—however fantastic that notion might be—is. Speculative fiction makes us imagine what *form* immortality will take and affirms that mortal relations can be unending. Of course, the idea that "we are not alone"—that extraterrestrial life exists and can make its presence felt—is a basic premise in science fiction, while the transcen-dent power of love and friendship motivates many a fantasy. But in oppo-sition to theology, speculative fiction invites us to consider alternative con-nections between immortality, the body, and relatedness.

I want to explore three questions that arise in reconceiving these con-nections. First, reading Dorothy Bryant's *The Kin of Ata Are Waiting for You*, I will ask what constitutes meaningful action if we experience im-mortality *in* our bodies and mortal relationships instead of rejecting or transcending them. Second, examining Octavia E. Butler's Xenogenesis trilogy, I will consider what happens to our sense of "human" identity when we see immortality in biological rather than spiritual terms, pre-suming that the body and relatedness are determining factors.[1] Finally, exploring the development and disappearance of the Lucifer figure in pre-Miltonic traditions, I will reveal a basic difference between narrative and theology that emerges in their considerations of human immortality. My implicit assumption is that science fiction and fantasy share a spiritual impulse with theology: to create a hypothetical space for the inexplicable.

In *The Kin of Ata Are Waiting for You*, Bryant depicts a world based on the assumption that relatedness takes priority over individuality. The narrator, who ends the novel by speaking as a redemptive figure, is a well-known novelist and self-admitted narcissistic woman hater. The novel begins with his murder of a young woman and ends with his confession and imminent execution. When he flees the murder scene, his car overturns and he loses consciousness, awakening to find himself in Ata, an island that remains invisible within the world. After many years there, during which he has a lover and fathers a child, he is "chosen" to return to the outside world, at which point he discovers that he is in a hospital bed, badly burned, with head and leg injuries, coming out of a coma three weeks after his accident. His condition provides medical explanations for all the experiences in Ata that he remembers and describes. After first thinking that his time in Ata was only a hallucination, he realizes that if he *believes* in Ata, it will be real. The book is his attempt to remind us that we are all "kin" whose deepest desire is to recuperate a repressed sense of relatedness, so that we will be able to return to Ata.

Ata itself, the first human community on Earth, is based on the principle of collectivity. Reflecting the origin of human community and language, the Kin are racially mixed and the language is a blend of Indo-European sounds with no words designating gender or individuality. There is no gender division of labor, no nuclear family (all adults parent all the children), and no assumption that personal relationships should be monogamous. There are no taboos because the Kin believe that one will ultimately do what will bring one in harmony with "the dream," the cosmic consciousness that animates the universe; so, what another society might call wrong is in Ata a temporary aberration that will cease when one realizes that it causes unhappiness. Yet Ata is not Utopia: its "miracle" is that the Kin are ordinary human beings, "no different from any other people in the world, subject to the same faults, desires and temptations, but living each day in battle against them."[2]

Using dreams to measure authentic modes of experience, the Kin categorize experiences into two classes: those that are *nagdeo*, meaning "beneficial and enlightening" (good dreams), and those that are *donagdeo*, or "counterproductive, causing disharmony and pain." These words carry no moral weight, however. They merely indicate that personal and collective consciousness are interdependent in Ata: self-realization involves integration within the community.

To the Kin, the only significant human activity is dreaming. Dreams represent the true way "home"—what each person and the group must do to preserve Ata—and originate in one's spiritual consciousness, the awareness of one's inescapable relationships with others. All people work and behave only in ways that will make them ready for good dreams: "Each person must find what is the right amount of food, drink, work, as if to keep a rhythm going, a dance, in which some imbalance causes us to miss a step in the dance" (*K* 190). Sex is to be enjoyed, not repressed, because it "stands for the greater dream," the narrator's lover tells him (*K* 108). At the same time, each dream's meaning is both personal and collective and can be understood only when shared with someone else. The village itself and the social customs of Ata, as well as their cultural lore and myths, all derive from dreams.

In the world Bryant describes, then, there is no separation of body and soul, spirituality and community. Because humans are a community, the human species enjoys immortality through biological reproduction and the shared spiritual world of its dreams. This concept of immortality does not require the existence of a divine being with whom mortals may be eternally united; even Atan myths that attribute a quasi-divine origin to the world focus on the importance of human self-realization rather than divine will or desire. According to one myth, for example, a piece of the Sun fell and separated into land, animals, plants, water, and humans, so all earthly beings contain part of the Sun—an inner light—and thus multiply signs of the true Sun. Humans alone were discontent with their separation from the Sun, and to comfort them the Sun manifested a "law of light" in their sleep; the humans believed in the light within themselves, obeyed this law, and returned to the Sun, where they shine forever.

The differences between this myth and Kabbalastic theology are instructive for understanding why Bryant's treatment of immortality involves rethinking what constitutes meaningful action. According to Kabbalastic teachings, exile is the fundamental earthly condition. It will end with the reunion of God and Shechinah, which human beings can bring about. By human acts of reparation, then, the world will ultimately be healed and the male and female aspects of God will be reunited.[3] This myth teaches us about the nature of the divine and proposes that human action derives meaning from its role in bringing about divine healing. Bryant's fantasy has the opposite focus, however, insofar as it speculates on the fulfillment and healing of the physical universe. Instead of the theological division between human and divine, Bryant represents two complementary and interrelated dimensions of human consciousness. Immortality involves integration into the physical world, not transcendence or transfiguration of it.

Since there is no God with whom to seek reconciliation or reunion, according to this view, the primal exile that continues to generate a world that is donagdeo does not require atonement. Even though some Kin leave Ata in sacrificial self-exile through a ritual much like the ancient pagan sacrifice to the gods, their purpose is to counterbalance the evil in the world, not to atone for it. The "Chosen," who often live in obscurity, prevent human self-destruction by the strength of their dreaming. The Atan redemptive sacrifice is an act of prevention, not reparation. It is important to note the collective principle that is the basis for this belief. When the narrator asks why the Kin do not simply let the world destroy itself, his companion explains: "We are all kin, and though we have lost them, we must draw them all back again if any of us is to go. . . . One cannot go alone; it must be all or none, you see. A hard law, but inexorable" (K 140). Meaningful action expresses the mutuality and relatedness shared by all human beings, not merely one's private relation with a divine being.

In formulating an atheological conception of immortality, Bryant neither questions nor tries to resolve the paradox of human immortality. For Bryant, spirituality is an inherent part of human identity, and her novel postulates alternative concepts of the body and relatedness based on that principle. But reimagining immortality also means questioning the assumption that a "human" identity comprises an immortal spirit and is realized through solitary achievement. If we speculate that relatedness rather than solitude is the ground of our identity, that we experience immortality largely through biological procreation rather than through transcendence, then we call into question both parts of the paradox: we must reimagine both "human" and "immortality." Octavia Butler's Xenogenesis trilogy is a useful text for exploring the implications of this question because the author represents an alternative both to religious concepts of immortality and to scientific theories of longevity. Though her explicit subject is what happens when biological and cultural determinants of identity are subverted, she replaces traditional religious and scientific assumptions that we are solitary rather than interrelated and that immortality is an extension of our individual consciousness.

Butler's trilogy is based on the biblical myth of the Creation (*Dawn*), Incarnation (*Adulthood Rites*), and Apocalypse (*Imago*). In this revisionist myth, immortality is biological: for humans it is achieved through procreation, and for the nonhuman Oankali it is achieved through endless transformation of cells in a "trade" with other life-forms. Butler describes a postnuclear world in which the Oankali, an alien race, destroy humans' ability to reproduce except with the mediation of an *ooloi*, an ungendered member of their race, because they recognize that the human tendency to destroy each other derives from a genetically based assumption that all relationships are hierarchical and therefore potentially violent. The "construct," or offspring, of every Oankali-human mating has five parents: two humans and three Oankali (a male, a female, and an ooloi). In the Oankali-controlled world there are no hierarchical relationships between genders or between humans, plants, and animals because all organic matter is potential food for the Oankali.

Dawn describes the origins and evolution of the human-Oankali race. Here, Butler develops her concept of the Oankali and their theory of the "Human Contradiction" (intelligence coupled with a genetic predisposition to hierarchical behavior that engenders violence and the self-destruction of the race). However, her revisionist treatment of bodily relatedness, immortality, and identity is developed more fully in the later novels. *Adulthood Rites* is a coming-of-age story about Akin, son of Lilith (the first human woman to mate with the Oankali and thus the "mother" of the new hybrid race), who is the first human offspring to manifest Oankali characteristics. Mirroring Christ's dual divine-human nature, Akin is a Human-ooloi construct who experiences both human and ooloi perceptions; in fact, his name itself calls attention to his role as "kin" of both races. Like the humans, he recognizes the predatory nature of what the Oankali call the symbiotic "trade" by which they consume human cells and DNA in order to create a hybrid race. He also sympathizes with the human desire for biological immortality through procreation and, perhaps more importantly, shares their hope that they will by chance evolve beyond the "Human Contradiction" that causes them to destroy themselves. At the same time, he has the Oankali physical and perceptual acuity: he learns language in infancy and is able to "taste" and read the genetic structure of all earthly life, so he can reconstruct flawed or wounded human bodies. After negotiations with the Oankali and the human "Resisters," Akin is able to start a human colony on Mars where humans can procreate and continue the belief that they can live in peace together. Embodying both Oankali and human corporeality, Akin "redeems" the humans by enabling

them to embrace their mortality and validates their desire for a "bodily immortality" through procreation and human relationships, however flawed
these may be.

Butler's revisionist treatment of immortality is most fully developed in
Imago. Jodahs, the book's narrator, is the monster that has for humans
symbolized the apocalyptic ending of the human species: it is an ooloi
(neither male nor female), a human-Oankali construct born of a human
mother. The approximate translations of the word *ooloi* indicate the marginal and regenerative role of this "Antichrist": "Treasured stranger,"
"Bridge," "Life trader," "Weaver," and "Magnet" (*I* 6). The most disturb-
ing characteristic of the ooloi is its ability to change the molecular structure of every being it touches; at the same time, it changes its own physiology to exist in perfect mutuality with its biological environment. Thus,
while it has the power to heal, its sensitivity to emotion may cause it inad-
vertently to destroy what it touches. The ooloi becomes male to give pleasure in mating with a woman, and becomes female when mating with a
male. Male and female humans are irresistibly drawn to the ooloi, and they
can never overcome the (biochemical) need engendered by their mating;
likewise, the ooloi's life and its ability to control its potentially destructive
power literally depend on the presence of its human mates.

Since its unstable corporeality is the source of both its power and its
dependence, Jodahs thus embodies the ambivalence inherent in the very
concept of a bodily immortality. For Butler, this ambivalence derives from
the inescapable fact of relatedness, which she represents as biological
interdependence. The fundamental importance of relatedness in Butler's
revisionary concept of identity is exemplified by the degeneration of Jodahs's Oankali-born twin, Aor, and Jodahs's response. Aor gradually becomes a shapeless, colorless entity, approaching nonbeing, when it has no
prospects for human mates. The communal and integrating aspect of Jodahs's "redemption" is indicated by the fact that its return to the human
community with its human mates, Tomas and Jesusa, involves saving both
Aor (by finding it mates) and the humans (by healing them of the genetic
disorders they have inherited through the generations after the postnuclear
fallout). In the end, Jodahs literally plants the seed of a new community in
which human and Oankali, male, female, and ooloi, will live interdepen-
dently: "I chose a spot near the river. There I prepared the seed to go into
the ground. I gave it a thick, nutritious coating, then brought it out of my
body through my right sensory hand. I planted it deep in the rich soil. . . .
Seconds after I had expelled it, I felt it begin the tiny positioning move-

ments of independent life" (*I* 220). Through Jodahs, the humans achieve a longevity that involves bodily healing and spiritual reciprocity among themselves and with the Oankali. By establishing this new town, they embrace corporeality and celebrate the possibility for transformative mutuality. In the world initiated by this Antichrist—unlike that mythologized by Christian theology or promised by materialist technology—relatedness, not solitude, is the basis for identity, being, and immortality.

The speculative fictions I have discussed map out the central questions about the body, relatedness, and immortality that become problematic in theological treatments of immortality. The two authors offer different alternatives to the hierarchical relationship between a deity and humankind: Bryant eliminates it, while Butler replaces it with a reciprocal relationship between humankind and an alien race with needs as profound as its power. Both authors erase the body/spirit dichotomy implicit in theology, for in each narrative the senses constitute a primal mode of consciousness: humans experience their immortality through their bodies. And finally, each narrative represents a redemptive act by which this "bodily spirituality" is made manifest in terms that are diametrically opposed to Christian theology—offering a vision of immortality grounded in relatedness rather than in solitude.

I do not mean to imply that these novels are representative of all speculative fiction, but they do suggest ways that fantasy and science fiction can complement theology in speculating about the possibilities for meaning in the universe(s) we know and imagine. But neither novel questions the positive implications of the paradox of human immortality, and neither novel suggests any ambivalence toward immortality itself. This may be because both Butler and Bryant have eliminated the self- and body-denying idea of transcendence that is at the heart of the theological concept of immortality.

In what I would argue is a fundamental difference between the two discourses, however, speculative fiction accommodates this ambivalence as theology cannot. We clearly see this difference in tracing the evolution and disappearance of the pre-Miltonic Lucifer traditions, in which the story of Lucifer was first appropriated and then eliminated by theologians. Three different and formerly unrelated traditions converged in the Christian myth of the rebel archangel: the lamentations of Isaiah and Ezekiel, stories about the adversarial satan in the Old Testament, and the Watchers legends found in Apocryphal texts of the intertestamental period. Lucifer (light-bearer) never actually appears in the primary texts. The church fathers used that name for the angel who *became* Satan, the *un*fallen archangel who rebelled against God's command to worship Adam. The Lucifer who emerged is neither Milton's cosmic rebel, nor the Promethean visionary of the romantic poets, nor the demon who rejects the self-erasure and self-sacrifice of the post-Miltonic feminist literary tradition. Rather, this Lucifer raises questions about the foundations of theological treatments of immortality, which is why he was banished from theology and into literature.

The fallen rebel who became Lucifer originates in two Old Testament lamentations: Isaiah 14:12–15, a prediction of the fall of the king of Babylon and the final liberation of Israel, and Ezekiel 28:12–19, a lament over the king of Tyre probably written just after the fall of Jerusalem. Both present apocalyptic visions of a being from a place that can only be described as fantasy (the detail in Ezekiel emphasizes the fantastical nature of his origin), and whose present (annihilated) condition cannot be described:

> How you are fallen from heaven, O Day Star, son of Dawn! How you are cut down to the ground, you who laid the nations low!
> You said in your heart, "I will ascend to heaven; above the stars of God I will set my throne on high . . . I will make myself like the Most High."
> But you are brought down to Sheol, to the depths of the Pit. (Isaiah 14:12–15)

Signifying its immortality, both the origin and the end of this being are outside the realm of earthly experience and language. "O Day Star, son of Dawn" (*Helel ben Shachar*) probably is Venus, the morning star; the Greek translation of *Helel ben Shachar* in Hesiod is "Heosphoros," son of the dawn-bringer Venus, which in the Latin Vulgate translation became "Lucifer, qui mane oriebaris." As this figure became Lucifer as a counterpoint to Christ, the true light-bearer, its feminine origins and its ambiguity were erased.

The figure of "the satan" in Old Testament narratives provides a different dimension to the problems that may be raised by the belief in immortality. There the word *satan* appears with an article ("the satan") and does not designate evil or a fallen demon; the root meaning of the Hebrew is "to oppose or accuse." The satan seems to have been one member of the heavenly court, the *bene ha'elohim* alluded to in older mythologies and comparable to the Canaanite "sons of gods" who eventually appeared in Old Testament literature as the angelic host. Unlike other members of this council, the satan roams the Earth as Yahweh's emissary—and is thus named *mal'ak Yahweh*, "herald" or "messenger" (translated in the Septuagint as *angelos* [messenger]). When the satan appears, it is as Yahweh's subordinate, a kind of prosecuting attorney authorized to test human virtue, often by causing discomfort or worse (natural catastrophes, sickness, human enmity).[4] The role of the mal'ak Yahweh is clear in the Book of Job, where he is both subordinate and adversary to Yahweh. He is among the "sons of God" (Job 1:6) who come before Yahweh, after "going to and fro on the earth, and from walking up and down on it" (Job 1:7). Yahweh brings Job to Satan's attention, calling him the most blameless and upright man on Earth. The wager with which the book begins is not a contest between rival deities or cosmic forces but an agreement that Job's piety is worth testing. Satan causes Job's suffering not to tempt him or test his powers against Yahweh's, but to authenticate Job's relationship *with* Yahweh. His role is revelatory: to Yahweh and Job's friends his tests reveal Job's uprightness, and to Job (whose friends miss the point) they show that the world's instability originates in Yahweh.

The third tradition to consider briefly is less widely known and contains vestiges of both the satan and the rebel prince. Like stories of the satan, Watchers legends are based on the tradition of the bene ha'elohim, and like the fallen prince lamentations they center on the gap between a fantastical past and an uncertain present, the consciousness of which originates in the descent of the Watchers. Genesis 6:1–4 tells the first story of the Watchers, the sons of God who found the daughters of men so beautiful that they came to earth to mate with them. Their offspring were the Nephilim, giants with superhuman strength.[5] In traditions based on this passage, the descent of the Watchers represents the ambiguous gap between mortal, earthly life and a transcendent immortality. As a result of the Watchers' descent, and particularly in the continuing presence of their demonic offspring, physical, mortal beings must inevitably be ambivalent about being immortal. The most fully developed and influential version of the Watchers legend is in chapters 6–36 of the *First Book of Enoch* (also called the *Ethiopic Enoch*). The story centers on the cosmic transformation of the relations between God and those he appointed to watch over humans; the instability that human beings must endure is merely a secondary consequence. Led by Samyaza, the Watchers descend from heaven because they lust after human women. There is no indication that the Watchers intend any adversarial relation to humankind—they do not come as tempters—but there is ambiguous value in the knowledge they bring, for it makes the boundary between humanity and divinity unclear and marks the beginning of culture and conflict. They teach women to use cosmetics, charms, and enchantments (which will enable them to deceive men) and teach men to make weapons (which will enable them to wage war); a secondary leader, Azazel, introduces the arts and reveals secret teachings. When the demonic offspring of the Watchers and human women war among themselves, God banishes the Watchers from Earth until the Day of Judgment. The knowledge that radically transforms human consciousness brings a new awareness that immortality is a mixed blessing.

The church fathers synthesized these disparate narratives with New Testament diabology to formulate a theology of redemption that would account for evil in terms that gave priority to free will.[6] In doing so, they marked out a clear difference between the *unfallen* archangel (Lucifer) and the *fallen* tempter (Satan). By assigning Lucifer to a prelapsarian existence that ended before the creation of the world and humanity, they placed the instability and uncertainty he represents outside the human-divine relationship that is the subject of theology. Thus, Lucifer came into being as a character in a story that explains the origins of ontological uncertainty. Justin Martyr (c. 100–167) was the first to combine the concept of the angelic custodians (the Watchers) with the story of the fall of the angels through sexual passion, and he identified Satan as both the serpent and one of the fallen Watchers. Tertullian (c. 170–220) combined the stories of the rebel prince and the Watchers to give what became the definitive exegesis on Ezekiel: "This description, it is manifest, properly belongs to the transgression of the angel, and not to the prince's: for none among human beings was either born in the paradise of God, not even Adam himself, who was rather translated thither."[7] Origen's (c. 185–251) commentary on Isaiah substitutes the story of the rebel angel for the Watchers story, which later disappeared from the Christian tradition: "Evidently by these words is he shown to have fallen from heaven, who *formerly* was Lucifer, and who used to arise in the morning. If, as some think, he was a being of darkness, how can he be said to have been the light-bringer before: Or how could he arise in the morning, who had in himself nothing of that light?"[8]

Augustine followed earlier fathers in identifying the rebel prince with Lucifer but emphasized that Satan had no prelapsarian status: "One can with good reason suppose that at the beginning of time the Devil fell through pride, and that there had not been any previous time when he lived in peace and beatitude with the holy angels."[9] After Augustine, as Jeffrey Burton Russell notes,[10] Lucifer became a literary figure while Satan became a subject for theological debate. Martin Luther and John Calvin rejected the earlier exegesis on Isaiah and Ezekiel and emphasized the enmity between Satan (who rules the material universe) and Christ (ruler of Heaven). Lucifer became a character in a fable invented by the church fathers. The distinction between Lucifer and Satan is important: Lucifer is a *literary* figure without theological significance, while Satan is a *real* figure of destruction.

Why did Augustine and later church figures reject the character of Lucifer? The answer is that Lucifer raises too many challenges to orthodox views regarding humanity and immortality. First, he is *immortal* but not *eternal*: an angel in the endless past, a demon in the endless future. If an immortal being is not necessarily eternal, then the nature of the immortal soul comes into question and, more fundamentally, the promise of eternal union with an unchanging God becomes less certain. Second, although Lucifer was with God a purely spiritual being, he became the ruler of the material world and hence became associated with materiality. In this way, Lucifer challenges the absolute division between body and spirit that underlies Christian beliefs regarding the immortality of the soul: if the spiritual Lucifer could somehow become part of the material world, then the human soul itself could come to partake of the nature of materiality. Finally, Lucifer, who once enjoyed a perfectly harmonious relationship with God, later rebelled against God and became his enemy, and this dissatisfaction creates uncertainty about the nature of the everlasting relationship each individual establishes with God: if Lucifer's covenant with God could change, then so can any spiritual covenant with God. The very possibility of eternal transcendence is thus called into question.

In the Christian rejection of Lucifer, then, we observe the fundamental differences between theology and story. While theologians can explore heterodox concepts, they finally cannot consider ideas that directly contradict or challenge foundational beliefs; at some point they must stop debate and firmly say: this cannot be. But storytellers can freely speculate, and they can even revel in uncertainties and radical possibilities. For that reason literature has embraced the story of Lucifer. In one sense, Lucifer is a being who rejects immortality through union with God and leaves to seek an immortality of his own devising; thus, he can symbolize all human efforts to achieve immortality by means other than through Christianity. So Bryant's attempt to establish human relatedness as the basis of human immortality and Butler's vision of a human immortality achieved through material means can be seen as two modern versions of Lucifer's quest.

All of this is not meant to suggest that theology is no longer useful or relevant in examining the issue of human immortality; far from it. Theology can offer a theory of the universe that is far more comprehensive, cohesive, rigorous, and appealing than any narrative, and the skills of the theologian will always be necessary in all human attempts to make sense of the universe. But in a world in which we are confronted with new scientific possibilities and the prospect of new kinds of immortality, we also need speculative fiction as a way to examine those new possibilities in a milieu free from the constraints of theological argument. And it is in their shared desire to improve our understanding of such issues that the theologian and the writer of speculative fiction are truly kin.

Notes

1. Butler's trilogy comprises *Dawn* (New York: Warner Books, 1987), *Adulthood Rites* (New York: Warner Books, 1988), and *Imago* (New York: Warner Books, 1989) [*I*]. Later page references in the text are to these editions.
2. Bryant, *The Kin of Ata Are Waiting for You* (New York: Random House, 1971), 204. Later page references in the text preceded by *K* are to this edition. The novel was first published as *The Comforter*.
3. In discussing Kabbalistic theology, I am indebted to Gershom G. Scholem, *Major Trends in Jewish Mysticism* (New York: Schocken Books, 1988), especially pp. 224–86.
4. In Numbers 22:22–35, an angelic being called a "satan" blocks Balaam's ass when he is going to the king, warning him to speak only on the Lord's command. Elsewhere, the satan is a more individualized adversary; cf. Zechariah 3:1–2, 1 Kings 22:19–22, Judges 9:22–23, and 1 Samuel 16:14–16, 18:10–11, and 19:9–10. In no instance is the satan associated with evil or moral choice.
5. The name "Watcher" first appears in the Book of Daniel which was written between 167 and 164 B.C.E.: "I saw in the visions of my head as I lay in bed, and behold, a watcher, a holy one, came down from heaven" (4:13). Watcher legends were gathered in the Pseudepigrapha, a collection of Jewish and Christian traditions not included in the Old or New Testament and compiled between 200 B.C.E. and 100 C.E. See R. H. Charles, ed., *The Apocrypha and Pseudepigrapha of the Old Testament*, vol. 2 (Oxford: Clarendon Press, 1913).
6. Summaries of the writings by early church fathers are in Neil Forsyth and Jeffrey Burton Russell, *Satan* (Ithaca: Cornell University Press, 1981).
7. Tertullian, *First Five Books Against Marcion*, trans. Peter Holmes (Edinburgh: T & T Clark, 1868), 2:10.
8. Origen, *De Principiis*, 1.5.5, quoted in Forsyth, *The Old Enemy: Satan and the Combat Myth* (Princeton: Princeton University Press, 1987), 371; my italics.
9. Augustine, *The Literal Meaning of Genesis*, 11.21, trans. John Hammond Taylor (New York: Newman Press, 1982).
10. Jeffrey Burton Russell, *Lucifer* (Ithaca: Cornell University Press, 1984).

Dual Immortality, No Kids:
The Dink Link between Birthlessness
and Deathlessness in Science Fiction

Howard V. Hendrix

René Barjavel's *Le Grand Secret* (1973) features an Indian scientist who in 1955 discovers a virus, JL3, that confers immortality on those infected with it. Today, twenty years after *Le Grand Secret*'s publication—and a decade after the first widespread awareness of AIDS—one might describe JL3 as HIV inverted: while HIV weakens the immune system so that longevity is greatly reduced, JL3 strengthens the immune system so that the individual's longevity is increased to the point of immortality.

Barjavel's JL3 proves even more "incurable" and—after its noninfectious eighteen-month latency period ends—far more contagious than our HIV. Those infected with the immortality virus (a fairly small number) are permanently quarantined on Islet 307 in the Aleutians. Curiously, in Barjavel's secret history of the years 1955–73, Islet 307 was originally intended to be the site of a nuclear bomb test, but President Eisenhower, after conferring with the heads of other great powers (all of whom have been informed of the existence of JL3), cancels the test. Then, with the cooperation of other heads of state, Eisenhower builds a naval-blockaded, hermetically sealed paradise on the islet—an Eden with a hydrogen bomb at its heart, for the nuclear device of the canceled test was never removed and waits for its time to come like a gun on the table in the first act of a Chekhov play.

The real bomb at the heart of this Eden, however, is human sexuality, the linkage between sex and death. As one of Barjavel's immortal islanders puts it, "In order that the fruit be born, the flower must fade, die and disappear. The fruit, the seed, is already in a state of deterioration, the decline of one life giving birth to another. Germination is not only birth, it is death. That was the real meaning of the myth of Adam and Eve—*the apple is decay*. Adam and Eve should have remained flowers. . . . In our paradise no fruit can come into existence. But our flowers are immortal."[1] The managers of Islet 307 dose all of the food with contraceptives, believing that by doing so they have made sure no new fruits of the womb can come into existence and destroy the paradise by overpopulation. When this approach fails, one doctor remarks, "We've behaved like idiots. We are living with a powder keg, the female womb, along with an explosive torch, the male penis, persuading ourselves nothing would happen if we kept the powder damp by mixing contraceptives into the food. Well, it didn't work" (*LGS* 197). By confining a population of immortals to an island, Barjavel can present overpopulation as an immediate problem. Islet 307 is a microcosm of the entire Earth, which also is atomically armed and slated to face the moral and ethical questions raised by a situation in which an increasingly long-lived population grows at least exponentially while the arable and habitable land surface remains roughly constant. More importantly, in Islet 307 Barjavel gives us both ends of the traditional telos of Western history—Armageddon and Utopia—in one place.

Though during the twentieth century we have seen both longevity and fecundity increase, science fiction stories dealing with large-scale life extension almost invariably assume an inverse relationship between the two: as individual life span approaches infinity, individual fecundity approaches (or must be made to approach) zero. This pattern is found not only in Barjavel's text but also in works as diverse as Aldous Huxley's *Brave New World*, Damon Knight's "Dio," and William Gibson's Sprawl trilogy (particularly *Mona Lisa Overdrive*). Though the technologies employed differ (reproductive controls and biomedical advances in Huxley, hyperfoetalization in Knight, computer-assisted apotheosis in Gibson), the assumption underlying their implementation is the same: overcoming death also means overcoming birth.

At first the reason for this inverse proportionality seems only logical. Immortality vastly compounds the problem of overpopulation: any self-respecting world builder, to avoid the boom-and-bust overpopulation trajectory, must—if death is no longer a limit—either limit birth or vastly expand the space available for human habitation, usually through the expedient of space travel, particularly faster-than-light space travel. (Even this latter expedient, however, does not solve the problem. It merely delays the arrival of that time when unlimited birth and unlimited life lead to unavoidable problems.)

The deeper reason for such an inverse proportionality pattern, though, is not as rational and logical as zero population growth—it is the appeal of the seemingly absurd construct "If I never have kids I'll never die," an idea that is less logical and technological than it is cultural and mythological. To address this pattern in science fiction, one must look at the history and sociology of immortality and childlessness. Science fiction's linkage of the two can be read as a secularized translation of a theological tradition: namely, the linkage between sanctity and chastity, between saintliness and the voluntary childlessness inherent in abstaining from sexual activity, between the acceptance of the ways of the immortal soul and the denial of the ways of the mortal body.

The science fiction translation of this tradition abundantly allows for sexual intercourse (see Huxley and Barjavel in this context) and so breaks asunder the earlier link between recreation and procreation. Still, the denial of sexual reproduction inherent in the SF rendering of bodily immortality shares with its late medieval Christian (and decidedly spiritual) precursor the desire for stasis, a stopping or "fixing" of maturation at a youthful stage—a stage before the onset of parenting responsibilities and the inevitable reminder of the cycles of births and deaths and generations that parenting brings with it. Both Christian and SF linkages of immortality and childlessness stem from a desire to stop time, to halt at a given (usually youthful) point the process that leads to death—and thereby to recover the prelapsarian status of Adam and Eve as "immortal flowers" that never bear "fruit" while at the same time avoiding the immortality-without-eternal-youth problem related in the classical myths of Sibyl and Tithonus and in Barjavel's book embodied in the character of Jeanne Corbet.

Both the Christian and the SF immortality traditions also stand in stark opposition to the always more popular notion that sexual reproduction grants a sort of immortality—a continuance of one's personal traits in the person(s) of one's offspring. This more popular sort of immortality is, however, too dilute and ultimately impersonal for SF world builders and medieval Christian mystics.

Science fiction during the late-twentieth century has in fact moved away from involvement with the biological instrumentality involving life extension and birth control and toward a consideration of personality and reproduction as matters of pure information. In Huxley's *Brave New World*, there are "Abortion Centres" and "Malthusian drills" and women wearing "cartridge belt[s] bulging . . . with the regulation supply of contraceptives."[2] Barjavel's *Le Grand Secret* is odd in that it is a secret history of the text's past, but even this book, though it mentions contraceptives, vasectomies, and abortifacients, makes fewer references to such techniques than *Brave New World*—far fewer than one might expect, given that the novel explicitly investigates the linkages between life extension and overpopulation.

Like Barjavel's book, Damon Knight's novella of the future, "Dio," features a society that far in the past was made chemically "immune to infection." Knight's future folk have almost completely forgotten death and have long been augmented in further ways: their chemistry is more "stable," "more homeostatized than formerly"; toxins do not harm them, and "paraphysical powers that *Homo sapiens* had only in potential" such as levitation and regeneration of lost organs have been brought to full flower.[3] In "Dio," however, there is even less concern about contraception, for the process that made these people immortal has also made them infertile:

> "Now this," says Benarra, "this long shallow curve represents man as he was. . . . The planners had this much to work with: man was already unique, in that he had this very long period before sexual maturity. Here, see what they did . . . quite a simple thing, in principle. They lengthened the juvenile period still further, they made the curve rise more slowly . . . and never quite reach the top. The curve now becomes asymptotic, that is, it approaches sexual maturity by smaller and smaller amounts, and never gets there, no matter how long it goes on."
>
> "Are you saying," [Claire] asks, "that we're not sexually mature? Not anybody?"
>
> "Correct," Benarra says. "Maturity in every other complex organism is the first stage of death. We never mature, Claire, and that's why we don't die. We're the eternal adolescents of the universe. That's the price we paid. . . . Have you ever thought to wonder why there are so few children? In the old days, loving without any precautions, a grown woman would have a child a year. Now it happens perhaps once in a hundred billion meetings. It's an anomaly, a freak of nature, and even then the woman can't carry the child to term herself." (D 128–29)

Knight's future *übervolk* are the full human incarnation of Barjavel's "immortal flowers"; they are the words "If I never have kids I'll never die" made flesh, the inverse proportionality (as longevity approaches infinity, fecundity approaches zero) sketched in detail, even down to the curves and graphs. More importantly, we see in texts like "Dio" a shift away from overpopulation fears—a shift concomitant with a movement away not only from biological responsibility but from biology itself, a denial of the body of which even the most militant ascetic could be proud.

Fredric Jameson, in *Postmodernism*, suggests that

> if catastrophic "near-future" visions of, say, overpopulation, famine, and an-archic violence are no longer as effective as they were a few years ago, the weakening of those effects and of the narrative forms that were designed to produce them is not necessarily due only to overfamiliarity and overexposure; or rather, this last is perhaps also to be seen as a modification in our relation-ship to those imaginary near futures, which no longer strike us with the hor-ror of otherness. Here a certain Nietzscheanism operates to defuse anxiety and even fear: the conviction, however gradually learned and acquired, that there is always the present and it is always "ours." It was always clear that the terror of such near-futures was class based and deeply rooted in class comfort and privilege. . . . [Y]esterday's terror of the overcrowded conurbations of the immediate future [is] the fear . . . of proletarianization, of slipping down the ladder, of losing a comfort and a set of privileges which we tend increasingly to think of in spatial terms: privacy, empty rooms, silence, walling other people out, protection against crowds and other bodies. Nietzschean wisdom, then, tells us to let go of that kind of fear and reminds us that whatever social and spatial form our future misery may take, it will not be alien because it will by definition be ours.[4]

The overpopulated, life-extended world no longer feels like the future or like science fiction because we already live there—at least to some degree. In this context, science fiction increasingly collapses into realism and the mere representation of the present.

In more recent science fiction, and particularly in the computer-aided apotheoses found in the works of many of the so-called cyberpunks, this class fear becomes ultraparadoxical in that the desire for space leads to a denial of the space of the body itself. In these texts, a desire for unbodied space inevitably leads to the sacrifice of the body in its finitude—in ex-change for the potential infinity of cyberspace and virtual reality. The de-nial of the body becomes literal with the "downloading" of individual psyches into computer storage media. Characters like 3 Jane, Angie Mitch-ell, and Bobby Newmark in *Mona Lisa Overdrive* know a life beyond the body, as is evident in this discussion between two of the other characters, Molly and Slick:

> "What now?"
>
> "I made a deal. I got [Angie] Mitchell together with the box."
>
> "That was her, the one who fell over?"
>
> "Yeah, that was her."
>
> "But she died . . ."
>
> "There's dying, then there's dying."
>
> "Like 3 Jane?"
>
> Her head moved like she'd glanced at him. "What do you know about that?"
>
> "I saw her once. In there."
>
> "Well, she's still in there, but so's Angie."
>
> "And Bobby."
>
> "Newmark? Yeah."[5]

The "box" mentioned in the passage, the "in there" where the dead still *are*, is the aleph, a mechanism described in the final chapter as "an approximation of the matrix, a sort of model of cyberspace" (*MLO* 307). This aleph, in the cases of 3 Jane, Mitchell, and Newmark, is not only a device that enables a computer-aided apotheosis, it is also the portable cybernetic afterlife, the heaven where these characters rise immortally. In the light of Jameson's comment that the popular depiction of the fear of overpopulation is based in class fears of proletarianization and loss of privacy and personal space, it is intriguing that the cybernetic heaven Gibson imagines for his characters is in fact a cyberspatial French estate, complete with horses and barns and stately oaks in sunlight—in short, all the signifiers of a deep nostalgia for a bygone era of aristocratic landownership and a high degree of control over personal space.

A pattern is thus established, a movement from extended life among sexually mature and reproductively functional adults (which demands not only biomedical but also sociopolitical intervention against sexual reproduction, as in Huxley and Barjavel), to extended life among the sexually immature and reproductively nonfunctional (among whom neither contraception nor politics is a worry, as in Knight), finally to extended life outside the body altogether (as in Gibson's apolitical apotheoses), where sex and contraception are not issues at all and reproducing ("personality transfer") involves more Xerox than Masters and Johnson.

This pattern of retreat from adulthood and generational cultural responsibility is more than an ultimate class cocooning or return to an electronic womb. It is, in fact, a journey back to the seed and even farther. Why go through the messy meiotic mingling of genetic information (sex) to achieve an uncertain product when the unmixed coded contents of one's consciousness, the informational message of one's personality, can be translated to any number of immortal media? This is a denial of time and action in time (therefore also politics), a denial of the body and sexual reproduction in the purest sense: a denial of meiosis itself, a return to the more ancient mitosis in which information is simply duplicated, in which the purely informational contents of the person are analogous to the cell that reproduces by fission—multiplying by dividing, the self reproducing itself asexually. All the primitive messiness of sex and bodies is disposed of.

If, like Thomas M. Disch,[6] we hold science fiction to be an essentially juvenile or adolescent literary form, then it is tempting to write off the denial of the body, sexuality, and aging that I have been chronicling here as an adolescent fear of growing up and growing old, of adulthood and the responsibilities of maturity. Such an explanation, however, does not adequately explain the fact that the thoroughgoing rejection of the body, and particularly sexual activity, is nothing new and can be found in religious traditions throughout the world. Since science fiction's ideas of immortality and transcendence stem most clearly from Western Christian traditions, I have tried to limit my discussion to that arena. Even given such a limited scope, however, one still finds instances like the following: scholars, theologians, and just plain churchgoers of medieval times were fascinated by church father Origen's self-castration (to better serve God and the nuns he worked with), and depictions of this supreme act of spiritual devotion occur in many textual and iconographic representations.

But this denial of the sexual and generational goes back beyond Origen, not only to Eden but, more importantly, to the life and death of Jesus. Unlike other world saviors and faith founders (like Gautama Sakyamuni, the Buddha, who had a wife and child and, after leaving them to follow his spiritual path, eventually died peacefully at an old age), Jesus, at least in the standard tradition, is portrayed as essentially celibate, someone who never marries or fathers children and dies violently while still relatively young—only to rise again, fixed eternally at that prime-of-life age. The literary responses to this life trajectory have ranged from James Joyce's sardonic statement that "marrying is one of the most trying tests a man can face, and Jesus never did that" to Nikos Kazantzakis's much more thoroughgoing examination of the life choice question in his *The Last Temptation of Christ* (1960), in which it is precisely the possibility of a more normal life (with wife and children and old age) that Jesus is finally and most powerfully tempted with on the cross.

Science fiction's immortality stories are in many ways a secularized continuation of this Christian tradition connecting celibacy to eternal life and heavenly election. The differences between the two, however, are important to note, for there is a great deal of difference between the secular term *immortality* and the religious notion of *eternal life*. Secular immortality is the product of a monist and materialist world philosophy in which the material world is the only world; though people may become immortal—undying—they can never become eternal because they have been born at least once. The religious eternal life, on the other hand, is part of a dualist world philosophy in which both a material and a spiritual realm exist. In such a system, people—or, more properly speaking, their souls—can indeed be eternal: the soul cannot die because it was never born but rather partakes of the eternal life of the divine.

These matters are of the utmost importance in many religious traditions. Imagine the effect of physical immortality on the beliefs of a devout Hindu. Barjavel in his book deals glancingly with this matter: his Indian scientist, Bahanba, the discoverer of the immortalizing virus JL3 and also a Hindu, is profoundly disturbed by the implications of immortality in relation to the Hindu emphasis on working off karmic debt by successive incarnations. If there is no death there can be no further reincarnation, hence no more working off of karmic debt, thus leaving the individual always trapped this side of enlightenment. Human immortality would undoubtedly raise problems for other traditions as well—the Christian and Moslem notions of afterlife and Heaven in particular would become more problematic. And what about the religious tradition I was raised in— Roman Catholicism, with its notable polarities emphasizing celibacy among its nuns and priests and chastity among its unwed sheep but at the same time strongly encouraging procreation and offspring from its married members as a way to expand the numbers of the faithful? Would the Roman Catholic church relent in its opposition to birth control if immortality became an incontrovertible fact and the population soared even more than it is already soaring? Having once heard a priest sermonize on the "perversity" and "sinfulness" of married couples who consciously choose not to have children, I have my doubts.

Clearly there is a slippage between paradigms here—a lag arising from a failure to take recent changes into account. Thinkers on all parts of the political spectrum—from Francis Fukuyama to Fredric Jameson—have spoken recently about the end of history. (In popular culture, even Captain James T. Kirk comments on it in *Star Trek VI: The Undiscovered Country* [1991].) What I suppose is meant by "the end of history" is the idea that the master narrative of Western culture—which traditionally has found its end in the earthly heaven of a millenarian Utopia or the earthly hell of a catastrophic Armageddon—looks increasingly obsolete. With the end of the cold war, technologically assisted nuclear Armageddon now seems irrelevant, and with the fall of Soviet-style communism the old image of the socialist Utopia also appears to be defunct. The end points of the master narrative of Western civilization are out of date because they have in a sense already happened (atomic bombs have been dropped, Soviet-style socialism has been tried) and have been surpassed. With their obsolescence, the master narrative as a whole seems falsified, and rendered invalid as well.

I submit that greatly increased longevity or personal atomistic immortality stands in exactly the same relation to naïve "individualist" capitalism as the stateless Utopia stands in relation to naïve Marxism. Both are myths of an omega point, a fixing or stasis that ends the process of change, an idealized goal or "product" whose rhetorical and ideological value is that it validates and "justifies" the entire process of change that will supposedly lead to the end point. Atomistic, nonserial immortality (as defined by John Fischer and Ruth Curl) is Utopia for one, and it is as obsolete as previous social versions of Utopia for the many.

Whither now? The state has not withered away, and capitalism looks less individual and more corporate with each passing day. The mountaintop parking lot of Utopia and the downhill cul-de-sac of Armageddon have given way to the more routinized ups and downs of Market Street. We are to be placed in "invisible hands," given over to the tender mercies of the "market" of world capitalism—concepts as salvific and messianic as the Second Coming of Christ.

We need new myths. To look elsewhere in this volume, perhaps the notions of community relations advanced by Judith Lee suggest new directions, new salvations to be worked on at the species level. Perhaps we need a myth that says the right not to have children is at least as culturally valid as the right to have children—a myth that says one may unselfishly decide not to have children, not to seek immortality in that fashion. Perhaps demanding that a personal gene pool be passed on to the next generation is the real selfishness. If everyone seeks that personal genetic immortality, the human genome—the human species as a whole—will be endangered by overpopulation and boom-and-bust, victims of our own increasing longevity and reproductive success. That myth of self-sacrifice has yet to be fully rewritten in terms suitable to our own time, but I hope that the revision process is already well under way.

Notes

1. René Barjavel, *The Immortals*, trans. Eileen Finletter (New York: William Morrow, 1974), 124–25; originally published in French as *Le Grand Secret* (Paris: Presses de la Cité, 1973). Later page references in the text preceded by *LGS* are to this edition.

2. Aldous Huxley, *Brave New World* (New York: Harper and Brothers, 1932), 60.

3. Damon Knight, "Dio," in *Five Unearthly Visions*, ed. Groff Conklin (Greenwich, Conn.: Fawcett, 1965), 127; first published in *Infinity Science Fiction* (September 1957). Later page references in the text preceded by D are to the earlier edition.

4. Fredric Jameson, *Postmodernism, or The Cultural Logic of Late Capitalism* (Durham: Duke University Press, 1991), 285–86.

5. William Gibson, *Mona Lisa Overdrive* (New York: Bantam Books, 1988), 301. Later page references in the text preceded by *MLO* are to this edition.

6. Thomas M. Disch, "Big Ideas and Dead-End Thrills," *Atlantic Monthly* 269 (February 1992): 86–94.

Clifford D. Simak's *Way Station*: The Hero as Archetypal Science Fiction Writer, the Science Fiction Writer as Seeker for Immortality

Bud Foote

Oddly enough—considering that one of them was a city boy and the other one obstinately and indefatigably country, one of them a thoroughgoing rationalist and the other a Sturgeonesque sentimentalist, one of them a spinner of plain unvarnished tales and the other a lover of lyrical descriptions of scenery—Isaac Asimov and Clifford D. Simak formed a sort of mutual admiration society. Asimov claimed, improbably enough, that he had attempted to model his style on the elder Simak's, and Simak once wrote Asimov expressing his admiration for Asimov's storytelling approach.

All that is not as odd, really, as it might seem: both writers were men of deep moral concerns; both had a deep and abiding love of the past as well as of the future; both were men of more complex vision than many people give them credit for—Asimov capable of leaving his usual optimism for such grim visions as "The Gentle Vultures" (1957) and Simak contributing the atypical Wellsian vision of "The World of the Red Sun" (1931). Asimov has said that after writing "The Last Question" (1956), he felt he had written the ultimate computer story, and maybe the ultimate science fiction story. And one of Simak's novels, I will maintain here, has given us what we can reasonably take as an archetype of the science fiction novel, a commentary on the role of the science fiction writer in society, and a reflection on science fiction's intimations of immortality.

When thinking of Simak's works, most of us, I suppose, would first call to mind his book *City*, a 1952 fix-up of eight stories published in magazines from 1944 to 1951. Lovers of time travel stories might remember *Time and Again* (1951) and *Mastodonia* (1978); and there would be a few mavericks like myself who have never quite shaken the spell of the brooding and somber *Cemetery World* (1973). But surely the most read and best known of Simak's books would have to be *Way Station*, which first appeared in *Galaxy* in 1963 as *Here Gather the Stars* and later the same year in book form under its present title. Mary S. Weinkauf calls it "Simak's masterpiece," while softly grumbling that it is "an improbably plotted book."[1] David Pringle says, "Its warmth, imaginative detail, and finely rendered bucolic scenes make this probably [Simak's] best novel."[2] John J. Pierce calls *Way Station*'s main character, Enoch Wallace, "not only Simak's most fully realized hero, but also one of the most memorable protagonists in the annals of science fiction."[3]

Furthermore, Pierce sees *Way Station*'s plot in much more favorable terms than does Weinkauf: "Simak's narrative is complex, full of flashbacks and digressions that at first seem to have little or nothing to do with the main plot. Yet each part has its place, and each contributes to the whole" (*WWVC* 62). (I could say much about the various echoes of earlier science fiction that Simak works into the book, most notably the pseudo-living Mary, who is a distant, pathetic, and beautiful echo of Mary Shelley's monster.)

Finally, Brian W. Aldiss, in *Trillion Year Spree*, notes that *Way Station* beat out such books as Kurt Vonnegut, Jr.'s, *Cat's Cradle*, Robert A. Heinlein's *Glory Road*, and the original magazine version of Frank Herbert's *Dune* for the 1964 Hugo Award. Aldiss goes on to point out that the device of making the hero an Earthbound innkeeper for alien travelers through the Galaxy is "a wonderful metaphor for the act of science fiction writing itself."[4]

The hero of *Way Station*, Enoch Wallace, you will remember, is a Civil War veteran who, in the very near future of the novel—that is, 1964—lives alone in his father's house outside Millville, Wisconsin (Clifford Simak's hometown). Although he looks to be about 30, he is actually 124 years old. Living with little contact with the outside world, happy to spend his days entertaining extraterrestrial guests (who travel to and from his house by matter-transmission) and writing down details of their visits in his log, disdaining travel for himself, never going farther afield than to his mailbox, he reminds us a bit of a rural Isaac Asimov. Shortly after his father dies while using a newfangled agricultural machine, Enoch is visited by an alien in the shape of a grotesque clown whom he christens Ulysses after, he says, "a great man of my race."

He is thinking of General Grant, "that slouchy figure perching on the top rail of a fence, with a stick in one hand and a jackknife in the other, whittling placidly while the cannon balls whistled overhead and less than half a mile away the muskets snarled and crackled in the billowing powder smoke that rose above the line."[5] But that could be a picture of any Simak hero: slow, deliberate, unflappable, country-patient. Later in the book, with not only Earth but also possibly the Galaxy facing political breakdown, Enoch Wallace spends a couple of hours in his alien-provided virtually-real shooting gallery to relax his mind and concentrate his steady and deliberate thoughts.

But the name Ulysses, of course, also calls the *Odyssey* to mind: the alien Ulysses is a traveler who will be glad to get home after his travels, a teller of tales of his voyages, and yet himself very like one of the monsters Odysseus met on his travels; and Enoch is like a Homer on an early waterfront, listening to and recording the details of those voyages. On still another level, we remember James Joyce's novel in which, rather like Enoch's ordinary-looking house, very daily sorts of events conceal mythic marvels: as a pedestrian Dublin day in 1904 connects us to all of human history, just so a rundown house in a Wisconsin backwater is a link to untold and incomprehensible off-planet wonders.

Simak tells the story of this naming of Ulysses by Enoch twice, once in chapter 5 and then again in chapter 10, almost word for word, as if to emphasize the importance of names in this book. And important they are. Enoch Wallace's only living Terran friend is the mailman, who brings not only his mail but also his groceries; and that character bears the family name of the general Ulysses. Winslowe Grant is another of Simak's ideal countryfolk. Like the general a stolid whittler, he accepts exotic and alien woods from Enoch without inquiring too much into their provenance. He is normally curious but reluctant to pry, acting toward his ageless neighbor much as Enoch acts toward the guests in his alien wayside inn. His first name suggests, perhaps, the *Mayflower* passenger Edward Winslow, the first Englishman to be married in New England, stepfather to the first Euro-American child born there, and a great traveler on political business back and forth across the Atlantic.

Claude Lewis, the CIA man who investigates the case of Enoch Wallace, is a good man who makes a terrible blunder. His family name combined with Enoch's suggests the Lew Wallace who, like Enoch, fought through the Civil War. Unlike Enoch, he became a general; and like Enoch and Simak himself he was a writer, his best-known work being *Ben-Hur: A Tale of the Christ* (1880), a book, like *Way Station*, rooted in the Bible.

But it is the name Enoch (which John D. Davis translates as "initiated" or "dedicated")[6] that draws our immediate attention. There are two Enochs in the Old Testament. The first and lesser-known one was the son of Cain, after whom Cain named the city he built, the first city in the world (Genesis 4:17). It is the second and better-known Enoch who is truly exceptional, however, for in the list of Adam's descendants he is the only one of whom it is not said "and he died." Nothing is said of him in Genesis 5:21–24 except that he was the son of Jared and the father of Methuselah, and that he left the world in the prime of his life at 365 years of age, several centuries before the death of his father, Jared, who "lived after he begat Enoch 800 years." Interestingly enough, Enoch's son Methuselah, the oldest man in the Old Testament, died at age 969—*before* his father: "Enoch walked with God and he was not; for God took him."

In the absence of other evidence one might read that last phrase as a poetic variation on "he died," but later biblical writers without exception took it to mean that he did not die. Ecclesiasticus (49:14) says, "Upon the earth was no man created like Enoch: for he was taken from the earth." And Hebrews (11:5) is still more explicit: "By faith Enoch was translated that he should not see death; and was not found, because God had translated him." Upon the Earth is no man *created* like Enoch Wallace, either.

Much later, according to Scripture, Elijah was likewise translated without seeing death. Since he was one of the ranking prophets of the Old Testament, one can rather understand that. But of Enoch we know nothing that would entitle him to such an experience; like Simak's Enoch, he appears to have been an undistinguished, indeed a rather ordinary, person who was mysteriously selected for a great distinction. When the representative of Galactic Central chooses Enoch Wallace, Enoch is amazed and wonders why; like Enoch of the Bible, he avoids death, but he is translated only in a sense. Inside his house, the only thing left of the original is the fireplace; otherwise the house is not of this Earth but of the Galaxy. Inside, Enoch does not age; he experiences the passage of time, but it has no effect on him. Only when he emerges, for perhaps a quarter of an hour or an hour a day, does he age. Inside, as in the mythic heaven, a man stays at his perfect age—which we assume in the case of the earlier Enoch to have been a youthful 365.

But that 365 is suggestive, and, digging further, we find from Robert Henry Charles that

> [The son of Cain and the later Enoch, the seventh from Adam] are often regarded as both corruptions of the *seventh* primitive king Evedorachos (Enmenduranki in cuneiform inscriptions), the two genealogies . . . being variant forms of the Babylonian list of primitive kings. Enmenduranki is the favorite of the sun-god. . . . Later Jewish legends represented him as receiving revelations on astronomy . . . and as the first author; apparently following the Babylonian account which makes Enmenduranki receive instruction in all wisdom from the sun-god.[7]

In this myth, then, the first scientist is also the first author, almost—but not quite—the first science fiction author. And, given the identity of the number of his years and the days of the year, Enmenduranki-Enoch seems in some sense to *become* both the sun and time, an appropriate symbol for his triumph over death.

In Calmet's account of the matter we are told that "the eastern people [call Enoch] Edris. Eusebius . . . tells us that the Babylonians acknowledged Enoch as the inventor of astrology [astronomy] . . . and that he received all his uncommon knowledge by the ministry of an angel."[8] In fine conformity with this myth, Simak's alien Ulysses first appears as a natural man, as angels so often do, and as Homer's gods did before them, and tells Enoch he has been looking for him:

> "I was looking for a man of many different parts. One of the things about him was that he must have looked up at the stars and wondered what they were."
>
> "Yes," said Enoch, "that is something I have done. On many nights, camping in the field, I have lain in my blankets and looked up at the sky, looking at the stars and wondering what they were and how they'd been put up there and, most important of all, why they had been put up there. I have heard some say that each of them is another sun like the sun that shines on Earth, but I don't know about that. I guess there is no one who knows too much about them."
>
> "There are some," the stranger said, "who know a great deal about them."

Enoch goes on to add, "I've sometimes wondered . . . if the stars are other suns, might there not be other planets and other people, too." And straightaway, in an apocalyptic moment, the stranger's face splits and falls away to reveal the truth beneath it: "And even as the false human face sloughed off that other face, a great sheet of lightning went crackling across the sky and the heavy crash of thunder seemed to shake the land and from far off he heard the rushing of the rain as it charged across the hills" (WS 29–30). Recruited in an apocalyptic moment like the other Enoch, who likewise studied the stars and gained great wisdom, Enoch Wallace finds his greatest reward not in escaping death but in studying and wondering about the aliens who sojourn with him—about their homes, their sciences, their mathematics, and their arts. The campfire fantasy, Enoch reflects, had turned into fact; and is that not one of the things science fiction is all about?

Two apocryphal books of Enoch survive; one of them, called *The Book of Enoch* or the *Ethiopic Book of Enoch*, is, Charles says, perhaps "the most important of all the apocryphal . . . Biblical writings for the history of religious thought." This book is quoted in Jude (vv. 14ff.) and apparently alluded to in Matthew (19:28) and John (5:22, 27). Ten of its chapters are devoted to "the law of the heavenly bodies . . . the winds, the quarters of the heavens, and certain geographical matters" (*EB* 649). Other parts of the book give the writer's contemporary history (the wars of the Maccabees) an apocalyptic significance. That last is pretty standard procedure for the Old Testament in general, inclined as it is to see the hand of the King above All Gods in every event happening to a small Semitic tribe; it is also, we should note, part and parcel of the baggage of science fiction. In her 1976 introduction to *The Left Hand of Darkness*, Ursula K. Le Guin says that science fiction is about the present rather than about the future; and David Ketterer has demonstrated to everyone's satisfaction, I trust, the apocalyptic strain that runs through a great part of the science fiction canon.[9] Connect the present, the everyday, with the apocalyptic by means of any reasonable history, and what you have is science fiction.

The second book, called *The Secrets of Enoch* or *The Slavonic Enoch*, has Enoch taken up to heaven and instructed in the mysteries of the sun, the moon, and the stars. He reads the secrets of nature and of man, which he writes down in 366 books. It was a leap year, no doubt. Simak's Enoch Wallace, then, bears a heavy biblical and apocryphal weight of symbolism; he is, as we see him in *Way Station*, no mere innkeeper, but rather a student of the stars and a writer-down of things coming from the stars. Though he is not immortal, he can expect to avoid seeing death for thousands of years. And in the apocalypse that is preparing itself outside the narrow confines of his cottage and his planet, in which not only may the human race be extinguished (or at the least returned to a prehuman state) but also the whole fabric of the Galaxy may tremble, he—along with another very ordinary human—may save everything through the forces of spirit and love.

James Gunn finds the true spirit of science fiction in William Faulkner's Nobel Prize acceptance speech: "I believe that man will not merely endure: he will prevail."[10] The basic scenario of *Way Station* is a familiar one: confronted by a galaxy full of technically and intellectually superior beings, humankind nevertheless finds a way to endure and to prevail—not, however, in a Heinleinesque triumph of will and weaponry, but with neighborliness and goodwill and intellect. And that brings us back to Isaac Asimov, who was preeminently the author who gave us the hero not as fighter, not as soldier, not as general, but as thinker. Hari Seldon, who inspires and directs the actions of Asimov's Foundation novels, was a writer of science fiction—just as Enoch Wallace and the earlier Enoch and Asimov and Simak were.

All artists, all writers, I suppose, aspire to a sort of immortality in the survival of their works; but science fiction writers—as Kurt Vonnegut, Jr. has pointed out—are peculiar in their worrying about the life of the human race thousands or millions of years hence. One might say that they are seeking immortality not only for themselves but for the whole human race, and that they, like the Enoch of ancient traditions and the Enoch of Clifford Simak, seek it in the stars and write down the results for us to ponder.

Notes

1. Mary S. Weinkauf, "Clifford D. Simak," in *Twentieth-Century Science-Fiction Writers*, 2d ed., ed. Curtis C. Smith (Chicago: St. James Press, 1986), 667.
2. David Pringle, "Clifford D. Simak," in *The Encyclopedia of Science Fiction*, ed. John Clute and Peter Nicholls (New York: St. Martin's Press, 1993), 1109.
3. John J. Pierce, *When World Views Collide: A Study in Imagination and Evolution* (Westport, Conn.: Greenwood Press, 1989), 61. A later page reference in the text preceded by *WWVC* is to this edition.
4. Brian W. Aldiss, with David Wingrove, *Trillion Year Spree: The History of Science Fiction* (London: Gollancz, 1986), 320.
5. Clifford D. Simak, *Way Station* (1963; New York: Manor Books, 1973), 51. Page references in the text preceded by *WS* are to this edition.
6. John D. Davis, *The Westminster Dictionary of the Bible*, revised and rewritten by Henry Snyder Gehman (Philadelphia: Westminster Press, 1944), 165.

7. The Reverend Robert Henry Charles, "Enoch, Book of," in the *Encyclopaedia Britannica*, 11th ed. (New York: Encyclopaedia Brittanica Company, 1910), 10:649. A later page reference in the text preceded by *EB* is to this edition.

8. [Augustin] Calmet, *Dictionary of the Holy Bible, As Published by the Late Mr. Charles Taylor*, rev. Edward Robinson (Boston: Crocker and Brewster, 1832), 388.

9. Ursula K. Le Guin, Introduction to *The Left Hand of Darkness* (New York: Ace Books, 1976), xi–xvi; David Ketterer, *New Worlds for Old: The Apocalyptic Imagination, Science Fiction, and American Literature* (Garden City, N.Y.: Anchor/Doubleday, 1974).

10. James Gunn, *Inside Science Fiction: Essays on Fantastic Literature* (San Bernardino, Calif.: Borgo Press, 1992), 37, 48.

Living Dolls: Images of Immortality in Children's Literature

Lynne Lundquist

According to conventional wisdom, we would not expect immortality to be a major issue in children's literature; as the saying goes, all children believe they are going to live forever anyway. Rather than specific references to immortality, most stories for children offer a mood of dreamy timelessness well expressed in the classic fairy tale ending, "And they lived happily ever after." Children are acutely aware that they are growing up, however, and that someday they will become adults, and this may at times seem like an unpleasant prospect. Perhaps for that reason, some children's stories exhibit a transformation of the theme of immortality: the myth of the eternal child who never grows up.

Images of such children may derive from two divergent sources. First, many folktales and fairy tales, which often are simplified or displaced versions of ancient myths, feature magical ageless beings like fairies and elves. J. M. Barrie drew on this tradition in creating the most famous of all immortal children for his play *Peter Pan* (staged 1904; published 1928). Second, all children own dolls and toys that resemble human beings but never change their appearance. Since it is natural to create stories that imagine such objects as living, sentient creatures, it is also natural to depict them as immortal—as seen most prominently in Rachel Field's Newbery Medal–winning children's book, *Hitty, Her First Hundred Years* (1929). In these two works, we notice the themes, also embedded in adult literature, of immortality as a form of stasis that is clearly undesirable, and of the immortal as someone to be finally disliked or pitied, not admired or emulated. However, these works go against the grain in simultaneously picturing immortality as a desirable state, an attitude that may emerge from the story despite the author's best efforts to argue the contrary.

In Barrie's play, Peter Pan is not always a particularly pleasant person. From the moment he exclaims, "Oh the cleverness of me!" after Wendy reattaches his shadow, we see that he is very vain;[1] there is some truth in Captain Hook's later characterization of Peter as a "proud and insolent youth" (*PP* 83). When he tells Wendy that he does not know what the words *sewn* or *kiss* mean, we see that he is, as Wendy puts it, "dreadfully ignorant" (*PP* 21). He can also seem unkind: when he tells Wendy about how fairies die, "He skips about heartlessly" (*PP* 23). He calls his fairy, Tinker Bell, "a common girl" (*PP* 24) and later banishes her from his company.

But Peter's most unattractive feature is that he does not *remember* anything. The stage directions repeatedly establish this forgetfulness as part of his character: "In his joy at finding his shadow he forgets that he has shut up Tink in the drawer" (*PP* 20); Wendy's comment about fairies "recalls a forgotten friend" to Peter (*PP* 23); about to drown, Peter uses "his shirt, which he had forgotten to remove while bathing, . . . as a sail" (*PP* 56); during a battle with Captain Hook, Peter at one point "has apparently forgotten the recent doings" (*PP* 85); and in the play's final scene, Peter, talking to Wendy a year later, "sometimes forgets that she has been here before" (*PP* 94). The dialogue then makes Peter's inability to remember quite explicit: "Fancy your forgetting the lost boys," Wendy says. "And even Captain Hook!" And when she then comments, "I haven't seen Tink this time," Peter answers, "Who?" (*PP* 94). Soon, we do not need to be told, he will not remember Wendy either.

Peter's lack of memory, Barrie's play suggests, is a necessary attribute of eternal youth. If people can remember past events, they can learn from them, change their patterns of behavior, and thus mature. In particular, if Peter could remember that his former friends are now far away, living with the Darling family, and that his fairy is now probably dead, these thoughts could provoke pangs of regret over missed opportunities and irreparable losses that might utterly transform his playful, carefree attitude. When Peter tells Wendy, "No one must ever touch me" (*PP* 21), it is natural to interpret the word *touch* in the sense of emotional attachment; Peter cannot allow himself to be touched by anyone, for that might lead to later regret and maturation. In short, to endure as an unchanging being one needs more than an eternally youthful body like Peter's; one must also, like Peter, forever live in a timeless present, with no memories of the past and no plans for the future. And this must be seen as a repetitive and unfulfilling existence.

In contrast, Hitty, the sentient doll in Field's book, possesses a remarkable memory, and she vividly recalls all the people who owned her during a hundred-year period as well as many specific events. In accepting the Newbery Medal, Field in fact stated that remembering the past was a major theme in the novel:

> I feel that there is one thing they [*Hitty* and the Newbery Medal] have in common, and that is the Past. I never get over the wonder that such things as old samplers, toys and little tattered children's books should be here for us to see and touch long after those who made and handled them are gone. There is something singularly moving about them, and I know that I can never see an old toy or one of those early chapbooks without this sense of the past.[2]

But while Hitty both displays and represents a powerful memory—in contrast with the unattractively forgetful Peter—she has another liability that renders her unappealing: she can hardly move. Although the framing device of a doll writing her memoirs requires the claim that she can hold and move a quill pen, Hitty is otherwise depicted as almost incapable of movement. At best, she can slightly shift her position in a crow's nest to make herself fall, and she can make a tiny tapping noise with her feet when she is dropped on the floor. But in a major crisis—when she is dropped in the streets of Bombay—Hitty is entirely helpless: "I could do nothing to help myself. I fell . . . flat on my face in an unknown gutter."[3] And there she must lie until somebody finds her.

To be sure, immobility is elsewhere depicted as an initial attribute of the inanimate object that becomes sentient; for example, in L. Frank Baum's *The Wonderful Wizard of Oz* (1900), the Scarecrow and the Tin Man—both creatures not made of flesh who do not need to eat or sleep, and are thus immortal, though little is made of that fact—are first seen as immobile: the Scarecrow stuck to a pole, the Tin Man rusted solid. But Baum then allows his characters to display a full range of normal human movements in the rest of the story and its sequels. Similarly, the hero of Carlo Collodi's *The Adventures of Pinocchio* (1883) begins existence as an immobile puppet, but when granted sentience he gains mobility as well. *Hitty, Her First Hundred Years* is remarkable in doggedly adhering to the principle that a doll might develop the ability to see, hear, and think, but never the ability to walk about or speak.

As a result, Hitty may be the most passive character who ever served as the protagonist of a novel. When she is stuck in a tree, she must wait until someone happens to see her. When she falls into the ocean, she must drift in the waves and hope that she washes on shore where someone can find her. When she gets put inside a couch in the attic, she must lie there for years until someone happens to reach in and pull her out. *Hitty, Her First Hundred Years* is a novel about getting lost and getting found, getting dropped and getting picked up, getting sold and getting bought; Hitty never has any control over the events in her life.

Reading this description, some may wish to explicate Field's novel as an antifeminist statement: the woman as completely passive object, totally dominated by others, incapable of doing anything on her own; however, two aspects of the text mitigate against this interpretation. First, the people who are controlling Hitty's life are, with few exceptions, women themselves. Second, some of these women are, by the standards of their day, reasonably independent and assertive, including a wife who accompanies her husband on a whaling expedition, an unusually rambunctious and willful young girl, and two elderly women living by themselves. The story, then, makes no assertion that men should dominate women or that women should never control their own destinies.

Rather than focusing on her gender, we must see Hitty as another icon of undesirable immortality. In her case, immortality demands not the mental immobility of dysfunctional memory but physical immobility. The power to move around and travel freely brings with it wear and tear, the eventual destruction or disintegration of the body, and the heightened possibility of danger. To maximize one's chance to live forever, then, a person might be well advised—or even required—to remain motionless. Thus, *Peter Pan* and *Hitty, Her First Hundred Years* offer two unpalatable prescriptions for achieving eternal life: Peter must stop thinking and suffer mental stasis, while Hitty must stop moving and suffer physical stasis. To be called a "living doll" is a compliment, but these works show that to actually be a living doll, to combine the activity of life with the thoughtlessness of nonlife (like Peter), or the thoughtfulness of life with the inactivity of nonlife (like Hitty), would be an unhappy and tortured existence, more like a living hell.

Hitty is an unattractive role model in another way as well: while she initially projects herself as a friendly companion, happy to be of service to her owners in any way, Hitty's long life eventually makes her, like Peter, insufferably vain. Even at the beginning of the novel, when a clumsy movement of her legs while she is lying on the church floor startles a sexton, she reports, "I could not but feel a thrill of pride that my two wooden feet could produce such an effect upon him" (*H* 11–12). She mentions again and again that while she was shipwrecked on a remote island, some natives made her an idol: "I have often wondered if any other doll was ever called upon to play such a role as mine? Here I was suddenly chosen to be god to a tribe of savages" (*H* 72; the incident is mentioned again on pages 82, 94, and 184); obviously, she is pleased to think that other people at one time literally worshipped her. She breathlessly relates her encounters with famous people: when poet John Greenleaf Whittier visits her family and sees Hitty, he writes a poem about her; when an awestruck girl drops Hitty in the presence of Charles Dickens, the great writer picks her up and briefly holds her, so "for months to come I was brought out and exhibited as the doll who had been held in the very important right hand of Mr. Dickens. I do not wish to seem proud, but I cannot help wondering how many other dolls can boast of such an honor" (*H* 141). Every compliment she receives about her sturdy construction and attractiveness is duly recorded. When one girl who owns her complains that Hitty has been left out of a group photograph, the photographer takes a separate picture of the doll: "I felt myself almost overpowered by the honor. . . . The Artist took as much pains with me as if I had been one of his most distinguished subjects" (*H* 124).

Later in the novel, when Hitty becomes too old and valuable to be a plaything and instead advances to the status of expensive antique, this sense of overweening pride in herself increases. She records that a woman who usually collects porcelain animals was moved to purchase her because, she said, "there is something very appealing about this doll's expression" (*H* 191). And she is thrilled to relate how, at an auction, she becomes the object of a fierce bidding war, culminating in the astronomical purchase price of fifty-one dollars. Thus those, like Peter and Hitty, who remain eternally young not only suffer the unpleasantness of mental or physical immobility but also may grow unpleasantly proud of themselves.[4]

As a consequence of complete immobility and gross vanity, the immortal child is finally isolated. When we last see Peter in the play, he is all by himself: Captain Hook, the Lost Boys, and Tinker Bell are gone, there is no mention of the Indians or mermaids, and we know Wendy will never return to Never Land. Hitty, once in the constant company of loving little girls, their friends, and their parents, finally ends up spending her time stored in camphor, locked in glass cases, or displayed in a shop window.

She sits next to other dolls but does not interact with them (even though, given the premise of the novel, they should be sentient as well). It is ironic, then, that one of Wendy's last comments to Peter concerns his "many adventures" (*PP* 94), and that Hitty ends the novel anticipating "further adventures? I feel that many more are awaiting me" (*H* 207). But how much fun will Peter have, with only himself to play with for the rest of eternity? And how can Hitty have "adventures" when she spends her days sitting in an antique shop, with the only possible change in her status being a purchase by people who would put her on display in their home? In sum, although Peter Pan was named for a Greek god associated with riotous celebration, and although Hitty's full name, Mehitabel, is a biblical name meaning "God makes happy," both of their stories end with no real prospects that they will have any future joys.

Based on what has been stated so far, *Peter Pan* and *Hitty, Her First Hundred Years* could be interpreted as further examples of a common theme in adult stories of immortality: despite its seeming attractiveness, eternal life would be an unhappy condition and should be avoided at all costs. But in two significant respects these works do not follow the pattern of the cautionary tale.

First, both Peter and Hitty refuse to become spokespersons for the viewpoint they seem to embody. In traditional immortality tales, the immortal person comes to realize that immortality is a curse and expresses the desire to become mortal again, perhaps even to die as a way of ending this undesirable existence. Examples might include the computer in Robert A. Heinlein's *Time Enough for Love* (1973), who willingly abandons the immortality of machine intelligence to enter a human body and risk the uncertain prospects of fragile mortality; and the stuffed animal in Margaret Williams's *The Velveteen Rabbit* (1922), who actively seeks and achieves life as a real rabbit, even though this new status means eventual aging and death. One might also mention Pinocchio, the puppet who wishes to become a real boy, or even the Scarecrow and Tin Man, who, while not desiring to become fully human, do want a human brain and human heart, with all the disillusionment and change those might bring.

In contrast, Peter never realizes that his is an unhappy life. At the beginning of the play he announces, "I want always to be a little boy and to have fun" (*PP* 22); and at the end he repeats the same words (*PP* 92). He refuses to see that unending youth is destined to become monotonous and undesirable; and while this stance can seem foolish, it might also be seen as heroic.[5]

Hitty's attitude toward her own nature is also heterodox. Unlike the Velveteen Rabbit, she is a toy that does not want to become "real." True, in moments of specific need or desire she will momentarily wish for some human attribute; when she is lying shipwrecked on the shore and fears her family will not find her, she thinks, "Oh, to be able to cry out to them just once. To call out aloud: 'Here, here I am'" (*H* 63); and she once wishes she were mobile enough to dance: "My spirit was willing enough but my pegs were not" (*H* 139). But she never expresses any aspirations to become like a real little girl, to run and play and sing and laugh like the children surrounding her; instead, she repeatedly asserts that she is a doll. She explains her thoughts as a doll's thoughts—she prefers "my place in Phoebe Preble's lap [to] the most beautiful temple of ivory and sandalwood ever fashioned by the most admiring tribe of savages" because "that is the nature of dolls" (*H* 77)—and she does not in any way protest her status as a doll.

In short, while audiences and readers may come to understand that the eternal youth of Peter and Hitty is truly undesirable, the characters never come to this realization; instead, they celebrate themselves and their eternal youth. In their final battle, when Hook asks Peter, "Who and what art thou?" he declares, "I'm youth, I'm joy, I'm a little bird that has broken out of the egg" (*PP* 84). Hitty ends her novel with a similar self-affirmation: "Perhaps, like the child on the sidewalk, I, too, shall take to the air. Why not, since the world is always arranging new experiences for us, and I have never felt more hale and hearty in my life? After all, what is a mere hundred years to well-seasoned mountain-ash wood?" (*H* 207). In failing to denounce their own immortality, these characters become its implicit advocates.

And, perhaps because of their refusal to acknowledge the unattractiveness of immortality, Peter Pan and Hitty stand out as unusual immortals in a second way: despite many things about their characters that should have made them unpopular, they in fact became remarkably popular. The enduring appeal of Peter Pan hardly needs to be described; what is most significant is that in later adaptations of Barrie's story—including his own novelization of the play, *Peter and Wendy* (1911)—the unpleasant aspects of his life are downplayed to emphasize the pleasant aspects. While the book retells the play's final scene—Wendy returning to Never Land one year later to find that Peter has forgotten Captain Hook and Tinker Bell—it adds a new conclusion, a generation later, with a grown Wendy happily dispatching her daughter, Jane, to accompany Peter to new adventures in Never Land. And, the text announces, "Jane is now a common grown-up, with a daughter named Margaret; and every spring-cleaning time, except when he forgets, Peter comes for Margaret and takes her to the Neverland [*sic*], where she tells him stories about himself, to which he listens eagerly. When Margaret grows up she will have a daughter, who is to be Peter's mother in turn; and thus it will go on, as long as children are gay and innocent and heartless."[6] An adaptation of this ending was later used in what is now the most familiar stage version of the play—the Broadway musical that starred Mary Martin. Thus, while in the original play Peter progresses in a linear fashion to total isolation and stagnation, in this revised version—though there are still references to Peter's damaging forgetfulness—his fate is tempered by a more comforting cyclical vision: children do grow up and abandon Peter Pan, but new children come along to keep him amused. In this way, the lifestyle of the immortal is affirmed, not denigrated.

The Walt Disney animated film version (1954) similarly offers cyclical imagery. The narration begins, "All this has happened before, and it will happen again; but this time, it happened in London." And the film ends with Mr. Darling looking at Peter's flying ship and saying, "I think I saw that ship once . . . a long time ago." As Barrie's novel projected an endless cycle of future adventures with Peter and Wendy's descendants, this statement, suggesting that Mr. Darling had an almost forgotten childhood encounter with Peter Pan, projects an endless cycle of past adventures with Peter and Wendy's ancestors (as also implied by the opening narration). Also, the Disney version ends with the Lost Boys and Tinker Bell deciding to stay with Peter, so viewers can again imagine a continuously happy life for the eternal youth.[7]

As for Hitty, her old-fashioned and lengthy narrative has not demonstrated the lasting appeal of Barrie's fable, and her story has never been adapted for stage or screen. But Hitty has displayed a degree of longevity nonetheless: the book I consulted was the thirty-first printing (1964), and the 1993–94 edition of *Books in Print* lists three current editions. More interestingly, Field based her story on an actual doll she and her illustrator, Dorothy E. Lathrop, had purchased,[8] and in response to the popularity of the novel the doll was taken on a national tour. As the 1964 dust jacket reports, "Recently [Hitty] has done more traveling all over America in special exhibits to get acquainted with the young readers who love her story." Again, a character who should have been unpopular instead became strangely popular; and, to briefly indulge in the fantasy that Hitty was really sentient, her already large pride must have swelled even more as she journeyed from city to city to be displayed to legions of admirers.

Indeed, one can always say that, at least metaphorically, literary characters do take on lives of their own—and that may be the phenomenon I am describing here. Like other adults, Barrie and Field originally seemed to embrace the standard notion that eternal youth would ultimately be a curse, and they crafted narratives that were in part designed to convey that message. But the characters they created rejected that notion, and in doing so they made themselves popular to an extent that their creators could never have anticipated. And their long-lasting appeal demonstrates, perhaps, that immortality will always emerge as a desirable condition—despite conventional wisdom.

Notes

1. J. M. Barrie, *Peter Pan: A Fantasy in Five Acts* (New York: Samuel French, 1928), 21. Later page references in the text preceded by *PP* are to this edition.
2. Quoted in "Rachel Field Wins Newbery Medal," *Library Journal* 55 (July 1930): 603.
3. Rachel Field, *Hitty, Her First Hundred Years* (New York: Macmillan, 1929), p. 84. Later page references in the text preceded by *H* are to this edition.
4. There is one possible difference between the stories: Barrie deliberately makes Peter Pan obnoxious and vain, but I am not sure Field realizes how insufferable her heroine gradually becomes.
5. In a strange way, the conclusion of Barrie's *Peter Pan* recalls the end of Eugene Ionesco's *Rhinoceros* (1960), which also can be interpreted in two ways. The one man who refuses to become a rhinoceros can be played as a ridiculous, isolated figure, but his stance can also be portrayed as a courageous affirmation of the human spirit in the face of widespread dehumanization. Similarly, while Peter Pan can be viewed as absurd in his unwillingness to embrace the normal process of growing up, one might also see his defiance as an admirable effort to defy the laws of nature.
6. J. M. Barrie, *Peter and Wendy* (London: Hodder and Stoughton, 1911), 267; the book is often reprinted as *Peter Pan*.
7. One might also mention Steven Spielberg's revisionist look at the Peter Pan story, *Hook* (1991), which depicts a Peter Pan grown to manhood who is returned to Never Land and forced to remember his companions and adventures there, and then rediscovers the spirit of youth. This is an odd reversal of Barrie's story: whereas Peter once enjoyed attractive physical youth and an unattractive spirit of enduring childishness, he now experiences unattractive aging and recaptures an attractive spirit of enduring childishness.

8. As recounted in the *Library Journal*, "*Hitty* is the story of a tiny, old-fashioned doll discovered by Miss Field and Dorothy Lathrop, the illustrator, in the window of a New York antique shop. Both the author and illustrator wanted *Hitty*, but she was an early-American doll, a real museum piece, and very expensive. She was finally bought in partnership, and her imaginary life history written by Miss Field and illustrated by Miss Lathrop" ("Rachel Field Wins Newbery Medal," 603).

Zen and the Art of Mario Maintenance: Cycles of Death and Rebirth in Video Games and Children's Subliterature

Gary Westfahl

In one way, Algis Budrys's *Rogue Moon* (1960) is an impressive work of prediction. In the novel, scientists find a strange alien structure on the Moon. The structure is filled with deadly traps, so they employ a machine to create duplicates of a man, who controls each duplicate in turn and experiences what it is experiencing as it walks into the maze. When the duplicate inevitably dies, the man learns what should not be done, and the next duplicate can avoid that trap and move farther inside. Neither Budrys's artifact nor his technology have been realized, but his novel perfectly anticipated the narrative structure of what is now a major form of science fiction and fantasy: the video game.

Of course, the direct ancestor of the video game is the pinball machine. Pinball players receive three balls to manipulate, with the reward of extra balls for successful efforts. When this system was transferred to the video game, a striking new terminology emerged: the video game player was given three "lives." When the player's first electronic avatar failed, it "died," and the game started again with the player's second "life."

As the games grew more sophisticated, a wide variety of human activities and literary genres were adapted to the form, but most games now derive from science fiction and fantasy. Many, like Space Invaders and video versions of *Star Wars* and *Superman*, are modeled on science fiction, while the Mario Brothers' games—which have most obsessed me and my children—follow the pattern of fantasy: a kingdom has been overrun by evil forces (malevolent mushrooms, turtles, flying fish, beetles, and the like) and its princess imprisoned by a fire-breathing dragon. Mario's task is to kill or avoid these evil minions, fight through a series of worlds where the princess may be held, finally reach and kill the dragon, and rescue the princess to return her kingdom to its previous happy state. There are also a few elements of science fiction in the games—"Warp Zones," airships, rockets, robots, and space monsters among them.

In theory, prospective players can learn all they need to know by reading the instructions printed on arcade games or in the booklets that accompany home versions. Anyone playing Super Mario Brothers, for example, learns that it is necessary to keep Mario moving from left to right until he reaches a flagpole or princess. Along the way, Mario will encounter menaces that can be killed by hitting them from the top or bottom, but that will kill Mario if they hit him from the side; and Mario will find rewards concealed within certain boxes—coins, mushrooms for super strength or another life, flowers to give him the power to throw fireballs, and stars to make him invincible. The instructions explain how to make Mario move, move more quickly, jump, and duck. And new players with this knowledge, quick reflexes, and a properly paranoid attitude may be successful for a while on their first visit to Mario's worlds.

At some point, however, their Mario will die and they will move on to their Mario's second life. But Mario will not have died in vain. For, by noting how he died, players learn a valuable lesson: next time Mario must get a running start before leaping over that chasm, or Mario must not eat a certain mushroom because flying turtles are lurking nearby. Thus, the more they play, and the more times Mario dies, the better the players become and the further Mario can progress—exactly the system presented in Budrys's novel.

More broadly, the skillful player of Super Mario Brothers must embrace the experience of death to be successful. Players may find one way to avoid a trap, but some deliberate—and dangerous—experimenting might reveal an easier and safer method. Also, the ultimate goal of these games is not simply completing the mission but also earning as many points as possible; and to move beyond minimum scores, players must learn many things about Mario's worlds that are not in the instructions. Certain rewards are hidden within bricks or hover invisibly in the air; there are ways to kill or neutralize certain evils that are not announced; and there are alternate routes like underground passages or walkways in the sky that may be helpful if explored. Thus, a player who wishes to improve must decide to take risks: to waste valuable time randomly hitting bricks searching for hidden treasures, to attempt to kill menaces in various ways instead of avoiding them, to try a new and possibly deadly route even though the old route works well. And all these activities invite, and may cause, Mario's death. So when we observe a seasoned player rushing through Mario's worlds, easily picking up points and killing menaces, we see the beneficial effects of a hundred, a thousand, or ten thousand previous deaths. Literally, the more often Mario dies, the better the player becomes; in a true Zen paradox, players must repeatedly kill their Marios in order to better maintain their lives in future games.

Noting that in these games young people are continually experiencing symbolic death, and that the games seem like repetitive and futile cycles, one might see them as psychologically damaging, as encouraging only a sense of despair. This is the argument of "Rolling Dat Ole Debbil Electronic Stone," Harlan Ellison's 1982 "review" of a game based on the film *The Empire Strikes Back*:

> The lesson is the lesson of Sisyphus. You cannot win. You can only waste your life struggling and struggling, getting as good as you can be, with no hope of triumph. . . . Over and over and over, rolling that great rock up the hill, killing Walkers, only to have the rock roll down on you again, only to have faster, cleverer, more destructive Walkers come to life. . . . But does it really matter? Clearly not. Because life—as viewed by this and other videogame Body Snatchers—is a pitiless congeries of rocks being rolled up a steep hill, only to fall back. This is the lesson one learns from Parker Brothers and their shamelessly exploitative little toy.[1]

Some of the crude games of earlier times offer support for Ellison's metaphor. Years ago, I recall feeling frustrated when I played the first Mario game, Donkey Kong, in which Mario must go up several ramps to rescue a woman from a gorilla. And I just could not do it. I might get to the top, my task almost completed, but Mario would die and I would have to start at the bottom again. For me the game was indeed a reenactment of the myth of Sisyphus, an unending cycle of struggling to the top and falling to the bottom.

But Ellison's thesis is less apt in reference to the more sophisticated games of today. Instead of figures endlessly running through the same gridwork or players shooting at an unending procession of robots and spaceships, the modern video game is much more variegated and visually rewarding. Playing a game like Super Mario Brothers 3 is a voyage of discovery. Each step to the right reveals new landmarks and obstacles, and the end of each round brings an entirely new world: Mario walking through a cave, leaping through the clouds, swimming in an ocean, or sliding on a frozen wasteland. There remain elements of repetitiousness, but Mario's life is now more interesting than that of Sisyphus.

Also, modern games incorporate conspicuous marks of success as well as failure: the home versions of Super Mario Brothers and Super Mario Brothers 3 consist of eight worlds divided into various regions. When Mario gets through one region, the player is rewarded by a scene of a beautiful princess or exploding fireworks; and a player can "win" Super Mario Brothers by reaching the end of the eighth world, where he rescues the princess and is told, "Your quest is over" (though the game also invites the player to keep playing more difficult versions of the earlier rounds). When I reached the eighth and final area in the "Special" area of Super Mario World, I felt a true sense of accomplishment when coins spelled out a congratulatory message: "YOU ARE A SUPER PLAYER." Arcade machines record the initials and point totals of high scorers, so players can proudly add their scores to the machine's display and achieve a bit of temporary fame. At one arcade I visited, the all-time high scores of players were posted on the machine, and players who exceeded those scores won tickets for free games and the thrill of seeing their own names on the machine. There are even tournaments in which top players can compete and win prizes. Thus, players get many pats on the back for good work, and these compensate for the sad feeling of watching their last Mario fall into the chasm.

More broadly, Ellison's view of the video game experience is too limited. After all, he spent only an hour playing one rather crude game, but he interprets all games as endless routines of futile effort leading to inevitable failure. Those who devote more time to the games see them differently. Repeated deaths are shrugged off as a necessary part of learning the game. The players enjoy a feeling of progress as they figure out how to avoid traps and move farther through each world and on to new worlds. They do not end each game thinking, "Darn it, failed again"; rather, they are proud of their improvement, their new ability to get to the tenth round or achieve a new high score. In sum, what they experience is not a cycle but a spiral: cyclical movement closer and closer to a desired goal.

To understand these games, then, we must abandon the metaphor of Sisyphus and look for another mythic model, for games like Super Mario Brothers in fact present an endless cycle of death and resurrection, in the context of a steady progression toward higher and higher scores and higher and higher levels of play. In this sense, video games dramatically present and enact a philosophy not unlike the ancient Hindu and Buddhist systems of reincarnation.

More precisely, Super Mario Brothers offers a more benign, less punitive version of reincarnation. Hindus believe that those who lead good lives advance into a higher form of life or a higher caste in their next lives; those who do not lead good lives regress to a lower form of life or a lower caste. Consistently good people eventually reach Nirvana, where their spirits are reunited with the spirit of the universe. In contrast, a Mario who dies during a game is immediately placed back where he was at the moment of death; from that point, Mario can attempt again to do what he failed to do before, and with their growing knowledge players can expect to do better each time. Once players have mastered one round, they never have to play that round again; no matter how badly they play in the next round, they will not be sent back to a previous round until the entire game is over. True, at the end of most games players must start again at the beginning, which remains suggestive of Sisyphus—though many home games allow players to continue playing at the level they had reached when the game ended. But repeating early rounds is not disheartening to an experienced player; rather, it is like a simple chore. I can now succeed in the early rounds of Mario Brothers 3 mechanically, without thought or effort, so I go through them very quickly to get to the rounds that still represent a challenge.

Finally, despite Ellison's vision of some poor youth frittering his life away repeatedly playing The Empire Strikes Back, the process of playing video games does reach a conclusion related to Nirvana: when players master the game, when they have seen all its worlds and have learned to defeat all its menaces, when they have nothing more to look forward to except increasing their point totals, they tire of the game and abandon it. When a player gets to this stage will vary, of course, but all players eventually move on to different games, seeking new challenges. At this moment, I have lost interest in Super Mario Brothers, since I have conquered all of its worlds and rescued its princess several times; but sometimes I still play Super Mario Brothers 3 or Super Mario World because they still have several worlds I have not really mastered.

A belief in reincarnation should logically induce a certain casualness about life itself and the decisions one makes in life; after all, every being will always be reborn, and the worst that can happen is to come back as a less advanced life-form, temporarily slowing one's progress toward Nirvana. This is hardly a typical attitude in Western cultures. While religions like Christianity and Islam in theory make death a desirable event, since it may send worthy people to perfect bliss in Heaven, in practice Westerners abhor death, do all they can to avoid it, and react to deaths of loved ones with great sadness. It is striking, then, to see a form of children's entertainment that pictures death as a routine, almost trivial event, noteworthy only in that the avatar's death provides new knowledge to help a player do better in the next life.

In some older texts of disreputable children's literature one sometimes detects a similarly cavalier attitude about death. In the 1960s, for example, DC Comics introduced a team of six heroic robots called the Metal Men. In their first adventure, while battling a nuclear monster, each and every one of the Metal Men died, and the story ended with the robots apparently gone forever. But two months later, inventor Doc Magnus retrieved their mangled and mutilated bodies, put them back in working order, and sent them out to battle another menace. The following adventures all fell into a bizarre routine: the Metal Men fought and defeated some foe even though they were all killed in the process; then Magnus took their remains to his laboratory and restored them to life. And these repeated sacrifices and rebirths were beneficial, for the Metal Men steadily developed individual personalities, arguing, joking, and longing for love, and were finally rewarded by actually becoming human (though they later reverted to robotic bodies).

Another superhero of that era, the Justice League of America's Red Tornado, was less regular in his death and rebirth, but that android was unequivocally killed three times and unequivocally brought back to life three times. After his first death and rebirth, the confused new hero became a reliable, though bland, minor member of the Justice Society of America. After his second death and rebirth, Red Tornado joined the more prestigious Justice League, obtained a secret identity and a girlfriend, and emerged as a sensitive, though still naïve, hero. After his third death and rebirth, Red Tornado adopted a young orphan and assumed an almost oracular role, solemnly offering wise judgments on situations at hand. Repeated deaths again did wonders for a hero's personality and maturity, and one might facetiously suggest that DC Comics's inability to make the Red

Tornado a major hero resulted from the fact that they killed him and returned him to life an insufficient number of times, so he remained insufficiently improved.

In the 1970s, Bantam Books presented another form of children's literature that presented death as a routine matter: the Choose Your Own Adventure books, which were soon followed by imitations from other publishers. These books mimic the format of programmed learning by beginning a story, told in the second person, then confronting the reader with a choice such as: "If you decide to start back home, turn to page 4. If you decide to wait, turn to page 5."[2] By making different choices, readers discover many different stories, making these books a literary analogue to the interactive video game. When I read the first book of this type, Edward Packard's *The Cave of Time*, I was struck by how often the alternative stories ended with the death of the reader: one could be eaten alive by a saber-toothed tiger, tyrannosaurus rex, or sea monster; attacked by a boa constrictor or giant insect; hanged in medieval England; trapped in a war zone with rockets and bullets all around; crushed by a wooly mammoth; suffocated by the bad air of Earth's distant past or far future; or drowned in a vast ocean. I recall thinking that these dark scenarios were rather depressing, not at all suitable for impressionable young minds. After all, a child might react poorly to reading, "'You're the one who escaped from the tower. . . . The penalty for escaping from the tower is hanging,' one of them tells you. You find out he is right" (78). As with Ellison's brief encounter with video games, however, my perspective was too narrow. Inured to presentations of the experience of death, young readers who read descriptions of themselves being eaten by a saber-toothed tiger are not crushed; they simply shrug it off and start the book again, starting a new life and this time entering the cave on the left, not the cave on the right.

In examining interactive forms of entertainment like video games and Choose Your Own Adventure books, one may appropriately ask what sorts of lessons in life are being presented to players. In Super Mario Brothers and its successors, Mario's assignment is to rescue some poor, oppressed people from evil invaders, and when he defeats his final foe, he rescues—and gets a kiss from—the princess. Players trying to master the game soon learn that the best way to avoid or overcome various menaces is to move quickly toward them; hesitating or retreating usually makes success more difficult. The most dreadful menaces in Super Mario Brothers are the Turtle Brothers, but I have found that if I run toward them, I may elude or kill them; if I hide behind a wall, waiting for an opportune moment, they move more vigorously, their hammers fly more frequently, and it becomes impossible to escape. Thus, the game offers two messages: it endorses altruism, helping people in distress; and it recommends risk taking, not being prudent.

That the adventures of comic book heroes provide similar messages is not surprising; interestingly, the Choose Your Own Adventure books have the same subtext, though it is not as easy to detect. I examined *The Cave of Time* to discern patterns of usually favorable or unfavorable decisions. I did not study and classify the ramifications of all choices in the book, but I did look at all penultimate pages to classify the decisions that led immediately to death or bad results and those that led immediately to good results (a few endings were ambivalent, neither disastrous nor delightful). Two patterns emerged: first, when the decision was largely a matter of choosing to go to or stay with people or to go off alone, the people-oriented decisions generally led to good results (seven good results, two bad results); two explicit decisions for solitude both had bad results. Second, when the decision was more a choice between taking risks or advancing to a new position, remaining passive or in the same position, or going back to a previous position, risk taking generally had good results (nine good results, one ambivalent result, two bad results), being passive had mixed results (four good results, three ambivalent results, three bad results), and going backward generally had bad results (one good result, four bad results). My conclusion was that readers who opt for the decision that involves more contact with people or who take the riskier path usually obtain better results; and in fact, four quick trips through *The Cave of Time* following those guidelines all led to happy endings.

While the messages these entertainments convey in favor of helping people and taking risks are not alarming, there remains the fact that they all reinforce the subversive notion that death is a relatively unimportant matter, little more than a stage on the road to further lives and further knowledge. And an interesting contrast thus emerges. On the one hand, the officially sanctioned texts of children's literature—carefully examined and fussed over by teams of scholars, educators, and child psychologists—usually tend to avoid the subject of death as much as possible. When a story does involve death, it is always regarded as a tragic and solemn occasion, as seen even in a book for very small children, Margaret Wise Brown's *The Dead Bird* (1958), in which some children happen upon a dead bird on the ground, somberly pick it up, and respectfully bury it in a ceremonial fashion, leaving a tiny tombstone by its grave. On the other hand, in children's texts and entertainments that are not officially sanctioned, like video games, comic books, and Choose Your Own Adventure books—which flourish beyond the control of parents, teachers, and librarians—death is treated in a casual and cavalier fashion. And one might well ask if this is a good message for young readers.

Perhaps there are no discernible effects from reading such books or playing such games; indeed, a seasoned player might well respond to Ellison's tirade by saying, "Lighten up, it's only a game." Still, games and books can affect the personalities of their players and readers; and the format of repeated deaths in video games like Super Mario Brothers, the Metal Men comic books, and the Choose Your Own Adventure books may all inculcate feelings of casualness toward everyday life, teaching youngsters that mistakes and failures do not really matter—tomorrow you can start again and do better. And it may be that the apparent callousness of some young people today regarding death, the ease with which they inflict death or risk their lives, may also be partially related to the video games they play, which argue that death is not really final but simply a stage in an ongoing process of self-improvement through reincarnation.

If this posited chain of cause and effect seems implausible, the philosophy in video games and related entertainments may instead be important as a forecast of future human life. Modern researchers tell us that the aging process is programmed into the human body and that finding a method to arrest or reverse that natural process may prove difficult. However, two predictions can be safely made. First, biologists today can clone creatures as complex as frogs; in the future, they will surely be able to clone human bodies. Second, physicians have learned how to transplant an increasing number of important human organs; in the future, despite intrinsic complexities, they will surely be able to transplant human brains. And with those two abilities in place, a system of serial immortality, of continuing death and rebirth, can finally be realized in the physical world. That is, provident people will pay to have their bodies cloned, and duplicate bodies will have their brains removed and will be placed in cold storage. When those people die, their brains will be quickly transplanted into the unused bodies. Thus, future people may live just like Mario, unafraid to risk and experience death in order to gain information, secure in the knowledge that if they die, they will soon be reborn in their present position to continue their quest for self-perfection. And such technological systems of death and reincarnation are, of course, also seen in science fiction novels like Arthur C. Clarke's *The City and the Stars* (1956) and Raymond Z. Gallun's *People minus X* (1958).

Thus, the future may find us living not in George Orwell's nightmare world of *1984* (1949), or in Edward Bellamy's paradisal world of *Looking Backward* (1888); rather, we may be living in Mario's world, nonchalantly risking our lives to heighten our skills and knowledge, moving from body to body in a steady process of self-improvement. It is a prediction as likely as any other. Perhaps, then, we should not scorn those youths who spend so much of their time playing video games or reading comic books and Choose Your Own Adventure books; they may be preparing for the future better than any of us.

Notes

1. Harlan Ellison, "Rolling Dat Ole Debbil Electronic Stone," in *Sleepless Nights in the Procrustean Bed: Essays by Harlan Ellison*, ed. Marty Clark (San Bernardino, Calif.: Borgo Press, 1984), 63.
2. Edward Packard, *The Cave of Time*, Choose Your Own Adventure no. 1 (New York: Bantam Books, 1979), 3. A later page reference in the text is to this edition.

You Bet Your Life:
Death and the Storyteller

Frank McConnell

Let us begin, as all human things begin, with a story.

It is universal, ancient, and simple enough that you might not think it *is* a story, but it is. Here is one of my favorite versions: Wile E. Coyote, as is his wont, is in fervid pursuit of the Road Runner. The Road Runner runs—that's all he *does*, dig—off a cliff and his momentum carries him to the opposite side. Not so Wile E. Midway across, in midair, he looks down, realizes he *is* in midair, stares bug-eyed for an instant at the audience, and then plummets, like a stretched and snapped rubber band, to earth: the way characters plummet only in Warner Brothers cartoons or real life.

Here is another version: an old man who foolishly squandered the love he had earned finds himself alone, in the open, in a storm that is partially a storm of his own despair. And staring at the camera, as it were, not unlike Wile E. Coyote, he tells us, "When the rain came to wet me once and the wind to make me chatter, when the thunder would not peace at my bidding, there I found 'em, there I smelt 'em out. Go to, they are not men o' their words: they told me I was everything; 'tis a lie, I am not ague-proof."[1]

The Road Runner runs, and that's all he does. "Just runnin' down the road's his idea of havin' fun," as his theme song has it. The thunder will not peace at King Lear's bidding, not because it *dislikes* Lear—any more than the Road Runner dislikes or even notices Wile E.—but because the thunder *doesn't even know Lear is there*, and wouldn't give a damn if it did know.

No, grimmer than that: there *is* no thunder, as a conscious force that can cease or continue at Lear's or anyone's bidding, until somebody *imagines* meteorology as personality. Shakespeare knows as well as we do, maybe even better, since he articulates it with the proper metaphysical shudder rather than with our currently hip, disengaged shrug. Here it is, the pith, the germ, the immense and fecund shaggy-dog joke at the heart of the story I have just told and, I think, at the heart of all the stories there are to tell. We have invented death, and in inventing that have invented ourselves, and in inventing ourselves invent, by necessity, the gods whose service will be a balm for our mortality, but whose very existence—we have always known—is *predicated* not on their resplendent presence but on our own aboriginal and gnawing lack.

This is basically nothing more than an echo of Karl Rahner's haunting observation that to "be religious"—which for him and me means simply to "be human"—is "to believe it is meaningful for a miserable creature to talk into the endless desert of God's silence."[2] It is also an argument that the only really convincing proof of the existence of God is also the most profoundly uncomfortable one. I mean, of course, the Anselmic or ontological proof, which in one form or another insists that life must have some final meaning just because we ourselves thirst so for it. It is what in the old seminarian's joke was called "the proof from wishful thinking." The problem is, you see, that it is the only proof we can trust, and that, like the anxiety-ridden uncertainties of quantum theory or chaos theory, or for that matter the truly scary act of saying "I love you," we can trust it only on the firm basis of our distrust. What human speech, from the Upanishads to the Mandelbrot set, is *not*, finally, wishful thinking?

I realize I am getting rather thuddingly paradoxical here, sort of like G. K. Chesterton on a *really* bad day. It is just that I do not know any way to talk about death that is not, ultimately, paradoxical or even, when you break it all the way down, *funny*.

My second favorite deathbed speech—familiar in theater lore—is David Garrick's: "Dying is easy. Comedy is hard." It is a wink at the camera, of course, and therefore a triumph. And it is a joke; better yet, a joke *about* joking: almost what a fashionably francophone contemporary theoroid might call "postmodernist"—to use one of the goofiest phrases ever developed by our culture. Apocryphal or not, this last utterance *is* directed into the "endless desert of God's silence," just because it demands either to *impose* order on the radical, quintessential moment of all disorder or to have that human order validated by—what? By whatever or whoever the hell it is that implants in us the expectation and longing for a Sense To It All and, at the same time, curses us with the wit to see through even our most splendid fabrications of that Sense. I *hope* Garrick really said that, because if he did, he joins Job and Samuel Beckett, and the mad King Lear and vertigo-stricken Wile E. Coyote, as chief anatomists of our cosmic discontent. The Anselmic proof is not our solace. It is our cage.

But you want to know what all this has to do with science fiction, fantasy, and the possibility of technologically achieved immortality. Okay.

Henri Bergson in his crucial essay *Laughter* reduces all comedy to variously performed versions of slapstick, and I think that is just right. The impulse to laugh, Bergson says, is our spontaneous aversion response to "something mechanical encrusted on the living."[3] We laugh, in other words, because in any truly comic situation we recognize—and forfend—the killing joke that for all our intimations of immortality we are, God help us, mortal machines wearing ourselves out in the very exercise of our magnificence. The well-dressed gentleman with cane and bowler who trips on a banana peel is the *ur*-mytheme of all comedy because his fall is *the* Fall, showing us again that all our fondest hopes are built on clouds and subject to vapors: that we are not, as we have heard, ague-proof.

Now this may remind you of Frank Herbert's *Dune* (1965), or Stanley Kubrick's *2001: A Space Odyssey* (1968), or even Ridley Scott's *Blade Runner* (1982), because in each of those stories the central character comes to a kind of confrontation with the core of human longing—to live forever—and comes to a different kind of realization about what really achieving that wish might be. In each case, though, we are dealing with a manifest version of Bergson's formula or, to nail it down, of Coyote's and Lear's plight.

Paul Atreides in *Dune*—let us discount the unfortunate sequels to that brilliant book—achieves godhead, or at least messiahhood, but at the expense of any faith or hope in the very messianic message he comes to announce, and for which he becomes universally venerated. This crackling irony—Herbert, after all, was raised Catholic—is lost in David Lynch's otherwise splendid film redaction (1984). Immortality for Paul is finally the immortality of becoming the story of his life, knowing the story he becomes can never, never approach the reality he was. I think *Dune*, despite its immense popularity, gets discussed so seldom at science fiction conferences just because it is so close to the cosmic slapstick that is, finally, all discourse on death. You *will* die. We will die. I will *die*. All storytelling tries to avoid that fact—as, every hour of the day, do we—and all storytelling, in avoiding the fact, only makes it the more inescapable. We want to become stories because stories go on forever and we do not. We are mortal engines, and mortal engines give out, wear down, or break up, and all that is left of them—God is not mean but She sure is strict—is their, every pun intended, plots.

And if we could devise a physical immortality, could invent a way to keep the engine running forever and ever, we would still not be free of the burden of mortality: precisely because mortality is, by honest appraisal, a "burden" not in the sense of a heavy load we must carry and would dearly love to shrug off, but a "burden" in the sense of the bass-note to the song we make for the Lord or ourselves or others, it really does not matter. An immortal man, if he were to remain a man, would still have to be able to tell himself the story of his own life, and that would require a sense of closure—that is, a reinvention of death. Because death is not the enemy to be feared, but rather the origin and the goal of any meaning we may choose to call human. With mutants I have no truck.

Mutants like, say, Dave Bowman at the end of 2001, the most gnostic of the fables we are discussing, and by my definition the most purely "science fiction." Bowman, avatar of our species and last descendant of the cosmically befuddled ape moonwatcher who began the story, breaks on through to the other side, becomes the Star Child—a godlet at the very least—and returns to contemplate Earth from the light-year playing fields that are now his home. And what does his enigmatic expression in that indelible last scene signify? For all the Sturm und Drang sublimity of Strauss's music, I am not sure it does not signify a kind of melancholy. Because the godlet, poor little fella, has passed beyond the possibility of all stories and therefore past the possibility of selfhood: all dressed up and nowhere to go. Or as Wallace Stevens—who I sometimes suspect explains *every-thing*—says in "Esthétique du Mal":

> The greatest poverty is not to live
> In a physical world, to feel that one's desire
> Is too difficult to tell from despair. Perhaps,
> After death, the non-physical people, in paradise,
> Itself non-physical, may, by chance, observe
> The green corn gleaming and experience
> The minor of what we feel.[4]

You will notice, by the way, that I am conflating technological and theological ideas of immortality: and you will also notice that I am none too subtly dismissing both of them. It may indeed be possible to extend life indefinitely by transmitting brain waves to silicon chips or through freezing and resuscitation—Swanson's TV Dinners? Or it may be that, Patrick Swayzes all, we will float toward the big Klieg light at the heart of all Being, there to spend eternity—uh—shining on. To reveal the full extent of my recidivism, let me admit that I find neither prospect especially attractive, or indeed interesting. I said at the beginning, paraphrasing William Yeats, that we have invented death. It is now time to put the formula properly: death has invented us.

Which brings me to the end of *Blade Runner*. The movie—sorry, purists—is better than the novel it is based on, paradoxically because it is closer to what Philip K. Dick at his best is really *about* than is *Do Androids Dream of Electric Sheep?* (1968). Dick is our poet of the simulacrum in his strongest work, exploring that concept before Jean Baudrillard even knew how to spell it. If you can make a perfect replicate of a human—so runs the essential Dick plot—how can you say that your replicant is not, *tout court*, human? It is a serious problem. It bothered the hell out of René Descartes and John Locke but gave Mary Shelley and E. T. A. Hoffmann some terrific ideas for stories. And it is obviously based on the progressive definition of the body *as* an engine that began in 1603—the year of *King Lear*—with Gabriel Harvey's discovery of the circulation of the blood and the human heart as a simple pump.

It is no more than a classic black box problem, really. If I can make a machine that does what *your* machine does, then I will have replicated your machine, although I can never open the impenetrable black box to see what your machine really is. Right?

Wrong. Dick knew and *Blade Runner* knows that the human engine becomes the *human* engine—becomes conscious—only by predicating its mortality. So when Dekker (Harrison Ford) and the replicant Rachel (Sean Young) escape to that improbable pastoral outside hellish Los Angeles at the end of the film, they both know that Rachel is programmed to die at an unspecified date. As Dekker says, "I didn't know how long we'd have together—but who does?"

And *this*, I think, again quoting Stevens, is "the thesis scrivened in delight, / The reverberating psalm, the right chorale."[5] The liberating joke that makes *Blade Runner* the most satisfactory of our stories is that Dekker, the "natural" human, learns from Rachel, the "artificial" human, not just about loving somebody but about accepting limits, mortality—that is the precondition to love or, indeed, any truly human act. To live at all, you have to bet your life. Dekker finds neither the ironically messianic immortality of Paul in *Dune* nor the dubious transcendence of Bowman in *2001*.

He finds, and embraces, the human condition. *Blade Runner*, in fact, is in this respect hardly a science fiction story at all, but rather a story about escaping from science fiction's gnostic shudder at the fact—and the necessity—of death.

Thomas Pynchon, in his disarming autobiographical introduction to *Slow Learner*, says something that angered me when I first read it and continues to anger me because I think it must be true:

> When we speak of "seriousness" in fiction ultimately we are talking about an
> attitude toward death—how characters may act in its presence, for example, or
> how they handle it when it isn't so immediate. Everybody knows this, but the
> subject is hardly ever brought up with younger writers, possibly because given
> to anyone at the apprentice age, such advice is widely felt to be effort wasted.
> (I suspect one of the reasons that fantasy and science fiction appeal so much to
> younger readers is that, when the space and time have been altered to allow
> characters to travel easily anywhere through the continuum and thus escape
> physical dangers and timepiece inevitabilities, mortality is so seldom an issue.)[6]

Of course, no so-called mainstream writer has used the motifs of science fiction, and of its parent mode the Gothic, more extensively or more stunningly than has Pynchon. And this, I think, only adds weight to his observation—just as *Blade Runner* strikes me as a supremely "serious" science fiction story exactly in its deconstruction of the genre to which it manifestly belongs.

Science fiction longs for immortality and shuns death just as, by and large, it shuns palatable food and good sex: because these things speak of the body and bodily limitations, and the inevitability of closure. I called it "gnostic" and it certainly is that, but there is an even better, because formal, name for it.

The one time I was lucky enough to have a drink with the great classicist and lovely man Moses Hadas, we were talking about Longus's *Daphnis and Chloe*. And Hadas, sipping his sherry, said, "You know, that's really what science fiction is: pastoral."

And "Bingo!" I said to myself. That was in 1967, and in a funny way I have spent the last twenty-five years trying to figure out *why* I said "Bingo!" (Actually, since it was 1967, what I probably said was "Right on!") And it was not until the topic of immortality and science fiction was proposed that I had my *satori*.

Science fiction is pastoral (and, by the way, pastoral is gnostic) because it posits a place and/or a time where you can play at life rather than bet your life. A place—Arcadia, the Forest of Arden, the Galactic Imperium, cyberspace, same-o same-o—where we can believe for a while that we are ague-proof and that we are not all vectors on and victims of gravity's rainbow.

And of course it is escapist, granting—just for the moment—that that rather stupid word has any meaning. It is as deeply escapist as *Daphnis and Chloe* or *A Midsummer Night's Dream* or *The Winter's Tale* because it tells us that we do not die, while all the time we know that we do. Like all good pastoral, it is the first phase of the Anselmic proof. And like all good pastoral, if it is really good, it brings us through to the second, more difficult phase of that proof. Look. You do not go *to* a pastoral place, you go *through* a pastoral place. You go into the magic forest and dance with the masquers there precisely so you can come back, healed and refreshed and wisely innocent, to the world where agues and gravity—the closure that makes us real—claim their due. To do otherwise is to become other than human and to invite, or invent, another, more meaningless kind of death: what theologians call the "second death," the annihilation of meaningfulness. Edgar Allan Poe knew this. It has to be why the narcissist, death-denying, and therefore life-denying prince in "The Masque of the Red Death" is named Prospero. That act of naming, maybe the crucial act of the whole tale, is what my mentor, rabbi, and *sensei*, Harold Bloom, might call an "antithetical trope." By naming the misguided prince after the most unavoidable and self-limiting of pastoral characters, the presiding genius of *The Tempest*, Poe surely means to suggest that his story is a dark version of the pastoral myth, an assertion that "escapism" is dangerous only when it forgets how grimly serious it really is. (I am assuming, of course, that you are at least old-fashioned enough to believe that sometimes people write stories because there are certain things they want to say, and they know what they are doing, as opposed to being mere ectoplasmic inscriptions of power for the dominant establishment.)

Does this mean that science fiction manifests a fundamental evasion? Yes. As I argued in another essay for this series, the genre privileges the transcendent over the immanent, the gnostic liberation from the body—and that includes the myth of the body as immortal engine—over what Alfred Whitehead called the "withness" of the body. And in this evasion is both its resilience and its weakness. Just as the complementary resilience and weakness of its mirror twin, the mystery, is privileging the *thanatos* principle over the pleasure-pain principle. Put it this way. All mystery stories begin, in one way or another, with a death; all science fiction stories, in one way or another, try not to end with one.

I had intended to talk about *Gilgamesh* here, a story that I take, even more than *King Lear*, to be an unremitting and absolutely essential prelude to any sane discourse on death and storytelling. But since John S. Dunne has addressed that subject, and since no one has written more brilliantly or valuably about that poem, I defer on the same grounds I would defer to sit in with Sonny Rollins. So let us talk about Homer's *Odyssey* instead.

The gnosis, the knowledge that once gained will take us beyond the realms of the corporeal and mortal—beyond the human realm of story— has an opposite. I am glad to give it the punning name *nostos*. It means "homecoming," and classical critics use it to refer to the moment when Odysseus returns to Ithaca. In fact, I realized as I was working through the poem again, it describes the whole movement of the *Odyssey*. Everybody in the poem—Telemachus, Menelaus, Nausicaa, Circe, Calypso—knows the sublime story of the Trojan War and that its heroes will always be the definitive transcendent heroes of the culture. Odysseus has another prob- lem, though. He wants to go home. He wants to go back to his aged wife, his aging life, and—Athena makes this clear—his human death. In other words, his whole fabulous voyage back home is a voyage out of the fabu- lous and into the quotidian. The *Odyssey* is an antignostic gospel invented centuries before the gnostic itself was named. And its central moment—at least in my current reading—is maybe its most famous and certainly its least understood episode.

What do the Sirens sing? Not the promise of sexual delight; this man, after all, has just left Circe. Not knowledge or power; Odysseus is always already *polutropos*, skilled in all the tricks. What they promise, explicitly, is to tell Odysseus and his men, over and over again, the story of their im- mortal exploits before Troy; they promise him that he can live forever in the *Iliad*. And the seduction is so strong that one screams to be untied so as to follow its allure, the allure of infinitely deferred closure, the pornogra- phy of the spirit. But Odysseus—Stevens's "Central Man," perhaps—both leaves his ears unstopped against the song and binds his will against follow- ing it, and the ship sails on, back from gnosis to nostos and into the bless- edly flawed paradise that William Wordsworth calls "a simple produce of the common day."[7]

And that, too, is the reverberating psalm, the right chorale. Between the technological and the theological—our less picturesque version of the Sirens and the Wandering Rocks—I will choose neither, wishing them both lots of luck, and cleave to the bitter charity of Story itself, Story that always gives us back a fragmented image of our own fragmentation but also whispers that our proper immortality is the embrace of our proper mortality, and that the world as we tell it to ourselves is never enough and thus is quite enough. This is no more paradoxical than the Anselmic proof. In fact, it is the Anselmic proof, as are you and I in our splendid disorganization and noble, funny quest for a love that will stay.

But I have not yet told you my favorite deathbed speech. It is not really a deathbed speech, although it takes us back to our original story of Wile E. Coyote. It is just the old joke about the guy who falls out of a fiftieth-floor window and is heard to say, as he passes the thirteenth floor, "Well—so far, so good." That guy, along with Wile E., Lear, Dekker, Odysseus, and Stevens, is a hero of consciousness. And his line, uttered out of the certainty of doom and the gallant refusal to face it with anything but full awareness, is as good a story as you can tell. So may we all.

Notes

1. William Shakespeare, *King Lear*, act 4, scene 6 (New York: Signet Books, 1963), 150.
2. Karl Rahner, *The Practice of Faith: A Handbook of Contemporary Spirituality* (New York: Crossroad, 1983).
3. Henri Bergson, *Laughter*, in *Comedy*, ed. Wylie Sypher (Garden City, N.Y.: Doubleday, 1956), 84 (translator unidentified).
4. Wallace Stevens, "Esthétique du Mal," in *Transport to Summer* (New York: Knopf, 1951), 52–53.
5. Stevens, "Esthétique du Mal," 53.
6. Thomas Pynchon, Introduction to *Slow Learner* (Boston: Little, Brown, 1984), 5.
7. William Wordsworth, "The Recluse," in *The Prelude, with a Selection from the Shorter Poems, the Sonnets, The Recluse, and The Excursion*, ed. and intro. Carlos Baker (New York: Holt, Rinehart and Winston, 1948), 201.

Contributors

STERLING BLAKE, who withholds other biographical information, wrote *Chiller* (1993), a suspense novel involving cryonics, and is working on two other novels about near-future science.

BRETT COOKE, an associate professor of literature at Texas A&M University, contributed to earlier Eaton volumes and has edited two forthcoming volumes of critical essays.

BARRY CRAWFORD, a doctoral student in comparative literature at the University of California at Riverside, is researching images of masculinity in science fiction and literature.

RUTH CURL, a doctoral student in comparative literature at the University of California at Riverside, published an essay in *Fiction Two Thousand: Cyberpunk and the Future of Narrative.*

JOHN MARTIN FISCHER, a professor of philosophy at the University of California at Riverside, coedited two volumes of essays and is the coauthor of *Ethics: Problems and Principles.*

BUD FOOTE, a professor in the School of Literature, Communication, and Culture of Georgia Institute of Technology, has published a study of Mark Twain and numerous articles about science fiction.

TERRI FRONGIA, who received a Ph.D. in comparative literature from the University of California at Riverside, has published articles on Italian literature.

JAMES GUNN, professor emeritus of English at the University of Kansas, has written many science fiction stories and novels and is also a noted critic; his critical works include a history of science fiction, *Alternate Worlds* (1975).

STEVEN B. HARRIS is a medical doctor and gerontologist who researches and teaches at the medical school of the University of California at Los Angeles.

N. KATHERINE HAYLES, who teaches in the Department of English at the University of California at Los Angeles, has written several articles and books on science and fiction, including *Chaos Bound: Orderly Disorder in Contemporary Literature and Science.*

231

HOWARD V. HENDRIX, Ph.D. in English and former college professor, is now a full-time writer who has published science fiction stories in several magazines and anthologies.

FREDRIC JAMESON of Duke University is an influential literary critic and scholar best known for his *Postmodernism, or The Cultural Logic of Late Capitalism* (1991).

JUDITH LEE, an assistant professor of English at Rutgers University, writes about the interface of literature and theology.

LYNNE LUNDQUIST teaches in the Theatre and Dance Department of California State University.

FRANK MCCONNELL, an English professor at the University of California at Santa Barbara, has written articles on science fiction for other Eaton volumes and several detective novels.

JOSEPH D. MILLER, a professor of neurobiology at Texas Tech University, has contributed several essays to previous Eaton volumes.

STEPHEN POTTS, who teaches at the University of California at San Diego, has written many essays and books on science fiction, most recently the award-winning *The Second Marxian Invasion: The Science Fiction of the Brothers Strugatsky* (1992).

ERIC S. RABKIN, a professor of English at the University of Michigan, has written and edited numerous books on science fiction, including (with Robert Scholes) *Science Fiction: History, Science, Vision* (1977).

ROBIN ROBERTS, an associate professor of English at Louisiana State University, has written numerous articles and books on science fiction, including *A New Species: Gender and Science in Science Fiction* (1993).

S. L. ROSEN, who previously worked as a college instructor abroad, is now a computer programmer based in Oklahoma.

GEORGE SLUSSER, a professor of Comparative Literature at University of California, Riverside, received the Science Fiction Research Association's Pilgrim Award in 1986 for his contributions to science fiction scholarship.

GARY WESTFAHL, who teaches at the University of California at Riverside, has published numerous articles on science fiction and will soon publish three books on science fiction.

Index